D0853298

Advance Praise for

STOP MAKING SENSE

"Michael Fanuele has quantified the impossible. *Stop Making Sense* is a new manual for learning true leadership, a book about how to be the best version of yourself whether your arena is the boardroom, or the living room. INSPIRING others is all about selflessness, it's about acting your way into right thinking, it's about being the change in the world that you want to see by embracing compassion. If you are looking for contentment and unlocking your potential for success, however you define it, then Fanuele's set of simple principles that changed my life over the last quarter century will change yours in a matter of hours. If Simon Sinek and Brené Brown had a book baby together, you're looking at it right now."

—ANDREW ZIMMERN, chef, author, teacher, host and producer
of Travel Channel's *Bizarre Foods*

"Michael Fanuele shows us how our passion and emotion will take us farther than our logic ever can. I can't convince you to read this book, but I guarantee you'll be inspired by doing so."

—BETH COMSTOCK, author of *Imagine It Forward* and former vice chair, GE

"This is the book we need now: a blueprint for leading with heart, passion, and imagination. Fanuele is such a fun and generous storyteller you almost don't realize that he's murdering so many small and cynical voices."

—ANDREW ESSEX, Co-founder, Plan A; author of *The End of Advertising*;
former CEO, Droga5 and Tribeca Enterprises

"This funny, sweary, energetic, challenging book will push you into a whole new way to find that compelling inspiration we'd all secretly like 1000% more of."

—ADAM MORGAN, author of *Eating The Big Fish, A Beautiful Constraint,*
and founder, eatbigfish

"The best magic bends your brain, and that's exactly what Michael Fanuele does in *Stop Making Sense*. With wit and insight, he dismisses the myth that we have to wait for inspiration to strike. He reveals the secrets that can make any of us a muse, dazzling audiences and getting the very best out of our teams, families, and most important, ourselves."

—DAVID KWONG, magician, "The Enigmatist," author of *Spellbound,*
puzzle creator, and producer

STOP MAKING SENSE

STOP MAKING SENSE

THE ART OF INSPIRING ANYBODY

MICHAEL J. FANUELE

Post Hill
PRESS

A POST HILL PRESS BOOK

Stop Making Sense:
The Art of Inspiring Anybody
© 2019 by Michael J. Fanuele
All Rights Reserved

ISBN: 978-1-64293-229-4
ISBN (eBook): 978-1-64293-230-0

Cover art and interior charts and worksheets by JOAN Creative
Author photo by Ollie Fanuele
Interior design and composition by Greg Johnson, Textbook Perfect

No part of this book may be reproduced, stored in a retrieval system, or transmitted by any means without the written permission of the author and publisher.

Post Hill Press
New York • Nashville
posthillpress.com

Published in the United States of America

For my teachers, especially the one in the wondrous shape of Joanna.

Put your thoughts to sleep.
Do not let them cast a shadow
over the moon of your heart.
Let go of thinking.

—RUMI

Alice laughed. "There's no use trying," she said: "one can't believe impossible things."

"I daresay you haven't had much prac-tice," said the Queen. "When I was your age, I always did it for half-an-hour a day. Why, sometimes I've believed as many as six impossible things before breakfast."

—LEWIS CARROLL, *Through the Looking-Glass*

CONTENTS

———

On Hero-Making

*"The hero is
one who kindles
a great light in the world,
who sets up blazing torches
in the dark streets of life."*

—FELIX ADLER

1.

In the summer of 1977, in the winter of the Cold War, David Bowie was in West Berlin to record a new album. His band was working in a run-down studio less than half a mile from the Berlin Wall. It was an old ballroom where Nazis used to party.

One of the tracks on the album was supposed to be an instrumental. The band had the sound down: an experimental number with guitar feedback, a whirring synthesizer, and even a clanging ashtray.

Late one night, gazing out from the studio's window, David Bowie spied something mysterious in the shadow of that nearby wall: a man and a woman kissing, just steps away from soldiers patrolling with rifles. Love and guns, close enough to touch.

Possessed by that image, Bowie would write the lyrics to "Heroes" in a matter of hours, and that instrumental track would get its words.

As the band recorded the new song, the producer had a strange idea: with each verse, he would pull the microphone farther away from Bowie, forcing him to sing louder and louder so that, by the end of the song, Bowie had to shout just to be heard.

There was David Bowie, in an old Nazi partyplace, shouting at that wall about love and guns.[1]

2.

"It was one of the most emotional performances I've ever done. I was in tears. They'd backed up the stage to [the Berlin Wall] itself so that the wall was acting as our backdrop. We kind of heard that a few of the East Berliners might actually get a chance to hear the thing, but we didn't realize in what numbers they would. And there were thousands on the other side that had come close to the wall.... And we would hear them cheering and singing along from the other side. God, even now I get choked up. It was breaking my heart. I'd never done anything like that in my life, and I guess I never will again. When we did 'Heroes' it really felt anthemic, almost like a prayer."[2]

—DAVID BOWIE in 2003, recalling his 1987 performance at Platz der Republik in West Berlin, next to the wall that had divided the city for almost thirty years.

3.

"Good-bye, David Bowie. You are now among #Heroes. Thank you for helping to bring down the #wall."

—GERMAN FOREIGN OFFICE, Twitter, January 11, 2016,
  the day after David Bowie died.

Did a rock-and-roll song really help crumble the Berlin Wall? David Bowie's "Heroes" is not a patriotic anthem; no, it's a strange six-minute song that starts with a man wishing his lover could swim like a dolphin. *Like a dolphin.*[3] From there, the lyric goes on to share the scene of a clandestine kiss beside a wall, under a sky riddled with bullets. It's a beautiful, haunting image, but did this song really help change the course of history?

God, I hope so.

Beneath the geo-politics and macro-economics, beneath all the complicated factors that shift the real lives of people and yet seem so far out of their own control, is that thing called the human spirit. The human spirit—that force that has braved frontiers, on earth and in space, in technology and sport, that has birthed nations, industries, religions, and masterpieces, that has faced down tanks, tyrants, and the ugliest oppression—well, surely, *that* magnificent force can chip away at a few stones.

And we know—we know from our own highs and breakthroughs, from our own moments of mustering a strength we weren't sure we had—that nothing moves that human spirit like music does. It shifts our feelings, and then it changes our behavior. It starts with toe-tapping and shoulder-swaying and singing along, and it ends with you feeling understood or turned on or more powerful than you were mere moments before.

Music moves us, and it moves us.

Which is why the ancient Greek philosopher Plato believed that music, like a dangerous drug, should be regulated by the government. He loved its ability to bring order to the minds of children and rouse bravery in the hearts of warriors, but he worried that "innovation" in music might just incite society-spinning rebellion.[4] And he was right, of course. Look at the history of civil protest in America: there were slaves singing spirituals on southern plantations; there were hippies and radicals marching to the strums of folk songs; and there were gay rights activists in New York City discos where dancing itself was an act of exuberant political defiance. This music wasn't just the soundtrack of these movements; it was their *soul* food. Plato was right to be worried about the awesome power of ABBA.

So yes, I believe David Bowie's song did something big that day. It inspired. On an early June night, with springtime ripe in the air, that song stoked the ambition for freedom in the hearts of thousands of prisoners enslaved by an impoverished ideology. That night, they went back to their homes with a renewed conviction that their wall would certainly fall—and it would fall by their own hands. David Bowie—*who couldn't even see them*—was singing to their aching yearning for liberation, imploring it, "Yes, yes, be free! Be heroes!"

"It was almost like a prayer."

As Bowie's guitarist, Robert Fripp, remembers it, "[With that song] David was speaking to what was highest in all of us."[5] He was assuring those thousands—on both sides of the city—that walls and guns were no match for the awesome power of standing and kissing and dreaming, of being insistently human in a place hell-bent on stamping out that humanity.

I imagine it was the most beautiful sound in the world.

And David Bowie did all of that six days before President Ronald Reagan showed up at the very same spot telling Mr. Gorbachev the time had come to tear down that same wall. Reagan told Gorbachev to get the job done. He was working "top-down," as the management consultants say. But David Bowie knew who the real heroes could be— would be.

Of course, that wall was torn down almost exactly three years later, and I choose to believe that as those Berliners chipped, chiseled, and tossed aside those stones, so many of them still heard "Heroes" in their head from that night David Bowie sang it to them. Yes, Bowie's song moved stones.

And here's the twist of a gift David Bowie has given the rest of us with that song: the assurance that each of us can be a hero—*at least for one day*. It sounds so reasonable, right? Even those of us who feel surrendered to our humdrum lives could imagine a day—*just one day*—when we *Jerry Maguire* ourselves to do something remarkable. Even the most cynical amongst us can admit that, yes, we might each have *one day* on which we can stride the world like a giant and swim its oceans like a dolphin.

But then what?

What happens after the one day on which we flex our heroic muscles, the day *after* we quit our job, leap into love, stand up to bullies, put down the drugs, start a new business, or vow to crush our cancer? We already had our one day, didn't we?

Oh no, we just listen to the song again.

Each time we hear your song, Mr. Bowie, the counter gets reset, and we get *one more day* to be a hero, boundless opportunities to crush walls to rubble, and change the course of the world. Sure, we can be heroes, for one day—and that one day will always be the day ahead of us.

Bowie, Survivor, Aretha, Prince, Taylor Swift, U2, Chumbawumba, Eminem, and Beyoncé. Lincoln, FDR, Eleanor Roosevelt, Maria Mitchell, JFK, MLK, Obama, Oprah, Steve Jobs, Michael Jordan, Serena Williams, and Rosa Parks. Spielberg, Stallone, Jesus, Hamilton, Nike, John Irving, Toni Morrison, Coach Taylor, and Robin Williams. That girl crushing a video game. That other girl crushing a lacrosse game. That boy belting out a tune like a diva on a national television show. That obese guy at the gym who will not let that StairMaster beat him. Your greatest teacher, coach, friend, and lover. *Their* songs—the ones that are sung and the ones that are spoken; the ones we hear and the ones we witness—give us stone-moving strength.

They are Muses.

And we can be too.

At least for one day.

What Lies Ahead

This book has one goal: to help you be as inspiring as you need to be to achieve whatever extraordinary thing you can imagine. So ask yourself: what do you want to do?

Do you dream of quitting your job and pouring your passion into a business that feeds your soul's hunger for meaningful work? Do you want to rise up the ranks of your company and lead it to industry-rattling success? Do you want to close the deal, win the account, and save the day? Do you want to move markets by moving customers? Do you want to be the kind of manager that gets the very best out of her team?

Do you aspire to be the kind of parent that helps his kids navigate the tricky terrain of the modern world as they grow into being their very best selves? Of course, you do, but you also know parenting is such hard, tricky work. Or maybe you are that kid and your dreams are the biggest in the world: the fame and fortune and good-doing that can only come from sharing your one-of-a-kind gifts.

Do you want to win your weekend tennis match? Do you want to eat better, read more, or drink less? Do you want to rekindle a fading relationship?

Maybe you need to move an *actual* army or a congregation or a classroom or a team.

Heck, maybe you're aiming to change the whole damn world.

Each of us is a leader. Some of us have the official title, but each of us has the responsibility, the burden, and the privilege of leading people, of moving people. Yes, each of us is a leader.

And as you'll see, to lead, you'll need to be inspiring, to arouse emotions—both your own and others'—to the point of action. You simply can't will or wish or reason or muscle your way there. No, you'll need to tangle with the messy *feelings* of the very real people who stand between you and everything you desire. You'll have to turn on those feelings and let those people loose. You'll have to inspire.

Now, you might, like some old scientists, be thinking that "inspiration" is a gift from the gods, a natural skill, like perfect pitch or deft hand-eye coordination that some people are born with and others can never quite match. "I'm no Kennedy," you'd say.

And you'd be wrong. Inspiring is a learnable, practicable skill. Like singing or sports, not everybody will become great, but all of us can become good enough to get the job done. You see, the latest scientific understanding suggests we're all born with the building-block capacity to inspire; it's our ability to be emotional, to be passionate. If you can be excited, you can be inspiring. If you can feel Oprah, you can be Oprah. Well, *almost* Oprah.

As the great jazz musician Miles Davis put it, "Anybody can play. The note is only 20 percent. The attitude of the motherfucker who plays it is 80 percent."

Attitude. You got that, right?

There's a catch, of course. To be inspiring, you'll have to learn to do something else, something that won't come so easily to your reasonable self: You'll have to stop making so much sense. You'll have to be slightly delusional and very vulnerable. You'll have to speak strange words. You'll have to be emotional in environments that frown upon feelings. You'll have to shout and whisper and maybe occasionally use impolite language. You'll have to imagine that you are, in fact, a force of nature sent by the gods to change the very nature of the world. And you'll have to act like it. You'll have to make yourself a Muse.

But that's it.

It might even be fun.

Are you ready?

"You alone will have stars as no one else has them."

—ANTOINE DE SAINT-EXUPÉRY, *The Little Prince*

Exercise: Start With What

As we begin to explore the skills that'll help us inspire audiences and achieve our dreams, let's get concrete about what we actually want to accomplish. Use the worksheet on the next page to articulate a goal, something special you want to do—and go ahead and make it a great big good something. There's no advantage to modesty now. Maybe you want a promotion at work with a bank-busting raise or you'll launch your very own business, a fresh idea that'll change the world. Or maybe you'll slay some of the evils lurking around the globe— climate change, malnutrition, war, mental illness, and poverty. Maybe you'll make a masterpiece, a book or a movie, or achieve a personal best in a marathon. Maybe your aim is to help your struggling child find the right path for the rest of her life, or a dear friend find purpose again after a traumatizing loss.

Go on, pick something you want to accomplish. Write it on the next page in big bold capital letters and keep it in mind as you read. Keep it close.

And make a careful choice because you will, in fact, accomplish it.

MY AMBITION

THE ONE THING I REALLY WANT TO ACCOMPLISH IS...

_____

_____

_____

_____

_____

_____

_____

(PSSST... THIS IS NO TIME TO PLAY IT SMALL AND SAFE. THINK EXTRAORDINARY.)

PART 1

THE INSPIRATION ADVANTAGE

"Genius is not replicable.
Inspiration, though, is contagious."[1]

—DAVID FOSTER WALLACE,
"Roger Federer as Religious
Experience," 2006

CHAPTER 1

Mysterious Ways

"We can be in the middle of the worst gig in our lives, but when we go into that song, everything changes. The audience is on its feet, singing along with every word. It's like God suddenly walks through the room. It's the point where craft ends and spirit begins. How else do you explain it?"

—BONO, on "Where The Streets Have No Name,"
Los Angeles Times, 2004

May 17, 2005
East Rutherford, New Jersey

I hate Bono. I *fucking* hate Bono.

I hated him the night I was dragged to see U2 perform at the Meadowlands in East Rutherford, New Jersey. And my beef wasn't really with the band's music (although that was a bit too "mainstream" for my early-'90s alternative taste); no, my hatred was personal.

I thought Bono was a boorish loud-mouth, a throbbing ego in leather pants and stupid sunglasses. *God walking into a room!* Puh-leeze. This guy was a political dilettante who would hector policy-makers with his naïve goals and his silly notion that "music and marketing" could make a genuine difference in a world rife with complex challenges. Save the world, blah, blah. How dumb. How self-absorbed. How annoying.

I really hated Bono.

And yet I was trapped. My pal Jersey John wanted nothing more for his bachelor party than to see his favorite band with his favorite friends and so, as his best man, I had no choice but to oblige him. I was determined, however, to be miserable.

Arriving at the Meadowlands Arena that night, I had only one prayer: *Shut the hell up, Bono! Play some music and make it fast. We've got steak to eat.*

But then—well, then everything changed.

About one hour into the show, the concert became church, a rollicking rock-and-roll revival. At this pulpit on this night in East Rutherford was this most bizarre preacher. His eyes were obscured by his yellow-tinted lenses. His leather jacket hugged his black t-shirt. He led a young lady to lie on the altar where she, no doubt, felt his hot breath and heaving chest as he laid himself atop her. He actually stretched his body over her and sang a slow, sexy song. He couldn't live with her. He couldn't live without her. The congregation roared, a roar of faith and jealousy.

But then the bacchanal evolved. What had been a tableau of sex and sin became a story of redemption. The preacher looked to heaven and, as his sermon unfolded, banners unfurled, flags of every African nation descended from the sky as he invoked the spirit of the great martyrs, Martin Luther King and Nelson Mandela, and urged us all to join the "journey of equality" they had led in their own time. The preacher rallied the assembly with scenes from the struggle, from the "bridges of Selma to the foothills of Kilimanjaro," using the great leaps of history to imagine a near-future of perfect social justice. He commanded us to eradicate poverty, destroy AIDS, and stamp out bigotry wherever it exists.

And he did this all in a light-ring of love, literally, standing in the center of a massive neon heart as his church band began to strum the chords to the next rousing hymn, a song about streets without names and people without prejudice. [2]

This was *exactly* what I hated so much about Bono. This is the show I dreaded I'd see. For God's sake, in his litany of evils we ought to oppose, he might as well have included farts.

And yet...and yet I stood and raised my arms above my head, as if they were pulled by puppet strings. They swayed just once, with my palms up, fingers splayed and bending backwards, as open as could be, waiting to receive something, some sort of feeling or meaning just out of reach in the air above me. After that singular back-and-forth, my hands found their way down to my chest, my right hand over my left over my heaving heart. That's how I stood through the rest of the night: hands clasped, body still, and voice silent. I was mesmerized.

What the hell was happening?

I had decided it was time to save the world. In that moment. In that instant, my mind popcorned with possibilities, teeming with the many ways I might make the broken world a place of peace and love. I wanted to embrace the people around me. Heck, I wanted to quit my stupid day job at the multinational ad agency where I worked, fly halfway around the globe, and dig irrigation ditches in the most impoverished nooks of the whole known world. I wanted to suckle orphan babies at my breast. In my black jeans and Morrissey t-shirt, I was moved.

Now, a little personal context: I don't believe I was a bad person before that night. Sure, I worked in advertising as a brand strategist greasing the wheels of capitalism, helping banks and beer companies figure out how to sell you more of whatever they were selling, but I also gave some money to charity, occasionally volunteered my time for a worthy cause, and generally tried to be a conscientious citizen and thoughtful friend. But admittedly, I was no do-gooder.

And yet, while witnessing this spectacle, I *wanted* to be. I wanted to dance my way to Africa, where I would do God-knows-what to help the cause of goodness, but dammit, I would do it all with conviction. Distribute malaria-protecting mosquito nets. Teach poetry to children whose minds were as hungry as their bodies. Comfort the AIDS-stricken. Yes, yes, and yes. I would join this preacher's "life cult" (as Bono would one day describe his band), and I would be a bigger and better and more beautiful version of myself for doing so.[3]

Demons Possess Us But So, Too, Do Angels

I was converted. And I know I'm not alone. If you're one of the hundreds of millions of people who have seen U2 perform, you can testify to the quasi-religious power of the moment. You want to sing and move and write checks to Amnesty International. You feel a vital part of "one" human race. You see your brothers and sisters—the poor, the ill, the other-colored—as the angels they are. You commit to love the earth and the heavens and everything in between. It's an irresistible energy.

And, to my surprise, this wasn't a fleeting feeling of a newly-minted fan. This moment would actually change the way I worked. From this concert on, however, the goal of my marketing wouldn't just be to sell more of this and make more of that, but to use my skills to help the companies in my charge create a better world.

Like U2 use their talent with instruments to improve the human condition, I was determined to use my talent with marketing to do the same. I'd come to believe that electric guitars and television commercials could be immodest tools for building a better world.

Yes, I know this sounds preposterous but, since that day, the questions I ask at work have changed: *Can this bank do good? Can it democratize wealth or educate customers about the intricacies of the economy? Can this car company do more than just sell cars? Can it restore a sense of purpose to a divided nation? Can it point the way a new era of innovation? Heck, can this beer help twenty-somethings be slightly more interesting on a weekend night?* I wanted to make marketing that would do something decent, if not great. I eventually joined General Mills as its Chief Creative Officer with the sole ambition of helping a giant food company become a *good* food company—less sugar, less chemicals, more real food. I wanted to fix the tragic relationship America has with its food.

And yes, all because of Bono, the very same man I once couldn't stand.

While the work I've gone on to do has hardly dented the world with virtue, U2 deserve massive credit for the real deeds they've set in motion. They're not just a circus of soft feelings, but a powerful progress machine that has accomplished a great deal of good, raising awareness and money for myriad charitable organizations (by some estimates, near a billion dollars).[4] Through Bono's (RED) project, Apple alone has contributed more than $200 million to stem the spread of HIV. U2 has used their celebrity to lobby governments, to direct the world's attention to Africa, which is ravaged by disease, war, and poverty. Bono is the only rock star ever nominated for the Nobel Prize, an honor he received three times. Even President George W. Bush couldn't resist Bono's entreaties. The two partnered to bring record levels of foreign aid to Africa. "Bono floored me," Bush said, "with his knowledge, his energy, and his faith."[5] That's Bono: flooring world leaders and rousing their citizens. That's Bono: inspiring.

The Power is in Your Pants

So how does Bono do it? What is the magic of this supernatural shaman? What spirit does he wield that possesses populations and politicians?

Bono once shared his secret with an interviewer who asked how he gets himself stoked: I don't, he said, "You put on the leather pants, and the pants start telling you what to do."[6]

Maybe it *is* that simple. For sure, somehow, from the cauldron of his leather pants, swiveling hips, song, and almost-delusional righteous passion, Bono conjures a mighty force: inspiration.

I've come to believe inspiration is the most powerful force in the world. It possesses us. It changes our attitudes, our actions, and in so doing, our very lives.

And yet this awesome force remains a mystery. We know so little about how it really works, how it arouses our emotions and shifts our behavior. To many modern thinkers, inspiration is little more than what it had been to the ancient Greeks: an occasional gift from mercurial gods. Even Elizabeth Gilbert—*the* Elizabeth Gilbert who inspired us to eat, pray, and love—sees bolts of creativity coming from "the supernatural, the mystical, the inexplicable, the surreal, the divine, the transcendent, the otherworldly."[7] Oh, dear. No wonder it's been easy for scientists to dismiss inspiration as an artsy-fartsy phenomenon, and instead use their resources to study "persuasion" or "leadership." They prefer to measure hard, testable behaviors. Inspiration, as it had been for centuries, is seen as an uncontrollable, unpredictable "strike" of insight.

But what if inspiration *weren't* just some mystical, otherworldly force "beyond control" that we're lucky to occasionally encounter, meanwhile waiting for it to strike on its own stingy schedule? What if inspiration were a power any of us could summon? What if, instead of just hoping to be inspired, we could each learn to be inspiring? In fact, what if we *had to inspire* if we wanted to accomplish anything truly great?

Thanks to some cutting-edge experiments in neuroscience, we can begin to
cobble together a model for how inspiration "works" on our brains: strong emotions
activate our mirror neurons, the neurons
that help us learn by replicating—or "mirroring"—what we see. Like a baby sees her
mother's mouth move and begins to mouth

> *"You put on the leather pants, and the pants start telling you what to do."*

the same words, we witness Bono's righteous passion and feel that same passion ourselves. When we see the faith or determination or strength of a person, we feel strong ourselves. Essentially, emotions get "mirrored" by an audience. It's biological.

But that's the scientific explanation of inspiration. The more pressing question is how each of us can inspire as powerfully and consistently as Bono—or Bowie or Oprah or Lincoln or, better yet, our greatest teacher or best boss or favorite film. What are the tools we have and the tactics we can employ?

Now, based on my examples so far, you might think it has some-thing to do with music, with grand performances in big arenas, and there's no doubt those kinds of stages can easily become the sacred spaces where Muses descend. I'm aware, though, that most of you are not (yet) global rock stars. No, the inspiring you need to do rarely comes with a ready-built stage. You need to work your dazzling magic in far more mundane places: a conference room, perhaps, or an office or a classroom or a kitchen table and a car ride; often, it's that place in your head where whispers of doubt nag at your most exciting fantasies.

So how do we bring the inspiring power of a stadium spectacle to the humdrum hallways of our everyday lives? How do we communi-cate to make people move even if we can't carry a tune? Where Bowie and Bono sing, how do we *talk* like Muses?

There were certainly some clues at that U2 concert. In study-ing that band and some other great modern Muses we'll meet, I've identified **Six Skills of Inspiration**: six ways of communicating—*of being*—that can help any of us become more inspiring leaders. These skills can be practiced for you and by teams, organizations, brands, and even art—any "entity" that communicates.[8]

1. Ambition: Get Delusional

U2, like the greatest Muses, set Delusional Ambitions. They want to eliminate malaria, end poverty, eradicate racism, and stamp out gender inequality. These are not modest goals; in fact, they're preposterous. But as we'll see, it's the very audacity of these ambitions that inspires conviction. People are moved to do big things, to scale the highest summits and topple the most terrible enemies and so, as a leader, don't fear the grand and the slightly crazy. In fact, it's only when you set yourself and your team against almost-impossible goals that you turn yourselves into the most powerful people: underdogs, which are really just heroes spoiling for a good fight.

2. Action: Aim For Action, Not Attitude

U2 is a band of verbs. Pray. Dance. Sing. Donate. Buy. Write. Protest. Like Nike and Alcoholics Anonymous, their *first* priority is what they want people *to do*, not what they want people to believe. There's wisdom in this approach: if you aim to change behavior, beliefs will follow; the reverse, though seemingly sensible, is far too difficult. So don't waste your time trying to get your team to "buy into" your agenda or understand your vision; instead, be dead clear about what you want them *to do*. Identify your Inspir-Action, the specific directions that will set your audience on the path toward their Delusional Ambitions.

3. Atmosphere: Show Up To Stir Up

The ordinary is ordinary. It's the enemy of inspiration. Muses disorient an audience. They surprise, provoke, and break the rules—because, once the rules are broken, the possibilities are infinite. So defy the conventional expectations. Create some WTF Moments by using all the tools on-hand to shift an audience's expectations. U2, like many theatrical acts, does that with stadium-sized spectacle: stages cloaked in darkness then bathed in blinding light. But many inspiring leaders alter the atmosphere in equally powerful but more subtle ways: where they sit, how they dress, what they say. A teacher might sit on the floor and a coach could run laps with her team. Steve Jobs had his black mock turtleneck. Serena Williams dominates a tennis court in her full-body skin-tight catsuit. These are ways of showing up that create new opportunities by breaking old rules.

4. Attitude: Talk Like Music

In order to become a Muse, it helps to speak *lyrically*, with the kind of poetic phrases that become irresistible earworms. I'll offer some techniques for doing that, but worry not if writing words isn't your strong suit because, as we'll learn, the real secret of music lies in its ability to transmit emotion. Words themselves are powerful creatures and, the more lyrical they get, the more power they possess, but the *affect* attached to those words—*the feelings they carry*—is what makes people dance, what makes people move. Look no further than U2, whose lyrics are filled with as many clunkers as gems. Look as well at Muses like Knute Rockne or General Patton whose gruffness was more powerful than their word choice. Heck, look at Helen Keller or the woman working her tail off at the gym— Muses who Talk Like Music without uttering any single word.

5. Affection: Love, For Real

Inspiring leaders don't just ask their audiences to do difficult things; they express their confidence that the team can, in fact, accomplish those great things. *You can do it! I see you! I believe in you!* And when expressions like these are more than throwaway platitudes, when they represent a genuine faith rooted in an intimate understanding of a person's unique powers, they become the get-it-done energy of inspiration. So find the Only-You Awesomeness of your audience and share it with them. You will move people when you know them and support them with the kind of conviction that never doubts their unique ability to achieve the great tasks at hand. You will move them when you love them. And the same goes for yourself: find the Only-You Awesomeness within yourself—your superpower—and hold it dearly.

6. Authenticity: Be True You

A leader can't hope to move an audience if that audience sniffs a phony. As a band that grew up through The Troubles, hearing bombs explode on Dublin streets and losing friends to sectarian violence, U2 has a unique authenticity, one that bestows upon them a moral permission to preach about war and sectarian violence. Ironically, Bono is a creation, of course—a character, a rock-and-roll avatar constructed by a teenager called Paul Hewson. And yet he is so comfortable in his Bono skin, self-possessed and certain, sunglasses always on. Leaders can learn from that confident expression of character. Know yourself, for sure, and express yourself as a one-of-a-kind entity, a character with passions, quirks, and, yes, vulnerabilities and shortcomings all your own. In fact, we're at our most "authentic" when we muster the courage to share our Shadows, the very things about which we're most unsure or ashamed. These flaws inspire the broken parts in all of us.

So that's our Muse Potion: Delusion, Action, Disorientation, Music, Love, and You—and, as you consider each of these skills, I hope you see the perplexing insight that lies at the heart of all of them: in one way or another, they all require you to be *emotional* and *unreasonable*. They each ask you to express yourself in a way that's more feeling than logic. As we'll see, emotions are the fuel of inspiration, and reason is its speedbump.

You'll nod to the first part, for sure, agreeing that emotions are a potent whirlwind. You *know* they can move people. Passion, in particular, is powerful; it breeds conviction in those who feel it.

But it's the *second half* of that statement that will probably trouble you. *What do you mean, "reason is a speedbump"? What do you mean it gets in the way of inspiration? Are you really suggesting we become less logical?*

Yes.

As you'll see, analysis *kills* inspiration; in fact, "persuasion" and "inspiration" are actually *opposite and antagonistic* forces. The more we try to persuade—to explain, to convince, to argue—the less likely we are to arouse anybody to do anything. In fact, let me say that again because it is so darn critical:

> **The more we try to persuade—to explain, to convince, to argue—the less likely we are to arouse anybody to do anything.**

Emotions are the fuel of inspiration, and reason is its speedbump.

Bono knows this. Like a Muse, he speaks to the *hearts* in the heads of his audience, so they can feel his passion, not analyze his argument. All the great Muses know this, even if they'd never admit it.

Here's an analogy: In matters of exercise, the kind you do at a gym, "effort" and "comfort" are *enemies*. If you're feeling "comfortable" when you exercise, you probably aren't getting any stronger...*Go on, just a few more push-ups*...Now, does that mean you should exercise at *maximum* effort *all* the time? Of course not. You'd hurt yourself, kid. But in that *inverse relationship* between "effort" and "comfort," you'll have to find the right balance—the one that actually achieves your desired results. But make no mistake: as you add effort, you'll subtract comfort, and as you add more effort, you'll subtract more comfort. As you do, your body will change.

That's how it is with inspiration. Passion and Reason work *against* each other. Passion is the energy that wants you jumping out of your seat. Reason wants you to sit and think for a little longer. Adding one decreases the other. Reasoning with your audience sticks them in the concrete of thinky-thinky land.

Does this mean we need to commit to being completely irrational, unreasonable lunatics? Of course not. *You'd hurt yourself, kid.* By all means, use your reason and logic and the full force of your big brain in figuring out what's right and wrong, what you want to do and what you don't, in composing your *strategy*. But then, when it comes to moving people, to inspiring, I'm sorry, but Passion and Reason are indeed enemies. You'll have to find the right balance between adding one and subtracting the other.

And let me be clear: the truth that some terrible people, charlatans and snake-oil salesmen and bullies, "stir up" the emotions of mobs for very bad ends is *exactly* the reason that good people—people like you—need to learn to inspire. You can't fight feelings with facts alone. To beat the bad guys, you'll need the heavy artillery of inspiration.

This ability to sidestep logic, to quiet reason so that our passion can sing its siren song is the fundamental skill of becoming an inspiring leader. It's encapsulated by this simple formula:

The Inspiration Equation:
PASSION – REASON = INSPIRATION

That's right: to inspire, you'll not only need to share your passion for *what* you want to accomplish but, as you do so, you'll need to extract some reason from your communications. It's not enough to be emotional. You'll also have to make your communications less linear, less sensible, odder, more creative. There's a great Russian word that captures the idea: *ostranenie*; it's the process of "making something strange" and unfamiliar so that people see it in a fresh and exciting way.[9] Or, as one famous advertising executive recommends, you'll have to "put your ideas on acid."

And you can—but it won't always be comfortable. For one thing, communicating with emotional verve is a rebellion against a world that has taught us to tuck our strongest feelings tightly inside an armor of *being right.*

But the hardest obstacle to inspiration is actually one of our *own* making: our natural instinct to be clear and rational. *We* want to make sense. *We* want to make sense so desperately.

Well, we'll have to let that urge go. And when we do, it'll be worth it, for let's get one thing absolutely clear: inspiration isn't just some fluffy feel-good spirit that leaves us feeling great; oh no, it's a power, a competitive advantage in any realm. Muses don't just inspire. They kick ass. They win. And they do so with the full and fierce force of their messy feelings.

Chapter 1 Key Terms

Bono: (proper noun) Front man for U2; a throbbing ego in leather trousers, but ultimately, not a bad guy; a great example of a Muse: a person who inspires others to action by arousing their emotions with unreasonable passion.

Sample sentence: *Fear not if you hate Bono; the rest of the book will not be about him.*

Defining Terms:
Three Types of Inspiration

My high school debate coach taught our team that the most important thing to do when discussing any subject is to *start* by defining your terms. He'd likely think I've waited too long to sort this out, but here it goes:

Inspiration is a big word with many meanings. It's a kaleidoscopic phenomenon, a collection of dazzling colors that could be sorted into so many different varieties. We feel inspired when we see a majestic sun set over a rolling ocean. We feel inspired when we hear a song that pumps us up—or even one that makes us cry. We feel inspired by the life of Gandhi *and* that teenage kid whose name we'll never know that stood up to his friends bullying another kid at Burger King. We're inspired when we see somebody do something so brilliantly that we can't imagine it's real—be it Simone Biles on a gym mat or some strange guys juggling chainsaws on *America's Got Talent*. We're inspired when we see somebody focused, in the zone, doing their thing in their way, world be damned. We're inspired by artists and teachers and rebels and entrepreneurs, and occasionally, even politicians. We're inspired by science and nature and art and animals. We can be inspired by the Sistine Chapel and a quote on a bumper sticker.

And every single one of these moments of inspiration should be welcomed into our lives. They help us become more human because they help us feel—and feeling is what helps us connect with ourselves, with others, with the world.

But for our purposes, I'd like us to narrow the meaning of inspiration from some sort of catch-all notion that just means feeling something. Let's agree that inspiration is a feeling so intense that we are compelled *to do* something, to act, to change our behavior in some sort of meaningful way. Real inspiration has consequences.

And without wrestling all the magic out of the idea, let's identify three *forms* inspiration generally takes:

1. **Inspiration by Virtue.** When you ask people to name an inspiring person, they often choose figures whose life stands out as an example of virtue. Eleanor Roosevelt was brave. Mister Rogers was kind. Rudy was tenacious. My dad was loving. My mom was strong. These are people who "inspire" us because they live(d) their lives in a way that we find aspirational. We're "inspired" *to be like them.* They're classic role models. And certainly, there are moments, specific actions or episodes, in the lives of these people that dramatize their great virtue: *The day my dad threw his arms around me when my heart was broken.* Perhaps there are even moments we can identify when that virtue *first* appeared or grew even stronger: *The way my mom vowed to battle her breast cancer.* But mostly, these instances exemplify a virtue that has *always* been present in the person we admire. It's *who they are.*

This is the kind of inspiration we often find in movies and books, stories, true and untrue, about people who usually overcome ridiculous odds with grit and grace. Think about *Rocky.* Stories like these are distillations of virtue put in human, relatable form. We want to run when we see Forrest run.

We'll learn how to be inspiring by studying the awesome examples of these people, but I won't be teaching you how to inspire by being virtuous. I have neither the blueprint nor the moral authority to do so. You've got that covered.

2. **Inspiration by Genius.** We're also often inspired by what we witness. When we see somebody do something so brilliantly, like Serena Williams smashing a swinging volley with impossible ferocity or Jay-Z spitting words that rhyme their way to beautiful poetry faster than most of us can actually breathe, seeing that and then wanting to do it ourselves—that's *inspiration by genius.* Or we might see an extraordinary singular act of courage, a Tiananmen Square-style display of bravery or the gritty determination of a person grinding it out at the gym.

When we see episodes like these and simply go, "wow," and feel the stir of wanting to mimic what we see with our own bodies—that's being inspired, for sure. It's being inspired by an *act* that is awesome and incredible.

I'd also put the host of natural wonders that blow our minds in this category of inspiration. Whales singing, babies taking their first breath, the cosmos with its infinite sweep—these are moments of inspiration by "genius," whether we know the genius behind them or not. And let's also add the human-made wonders of the world to this category—from great walls to robotic hearts—these are displays of genius that dazzle us, that often inspire us.

While most of us are not (yet) Serena Williams or Jay-Z—or frankly, jaw-dropping, universe-busting excellent at very much, we could and should try. By all means, aim for genius—practice your thing, shine, and as you do, you'll inspire. But this kind of inspiration—*inspiring by genius*—is ultimately a "you" thing: *you* are working on *your* thing because *you* are called to do so; inspiring others is a *byproduct* of the excellence you produce. And so, again, as with inspiring by virtue, we'll learn so much from these practitioners of transcendent awesomeness, but the kind of inspiring that will really concern us is the kind you can practice every single day....

3. **Inspiration by Invitation.** Of course you should move people by the example of your *virtue*. Of course you should move people by the expression of your *genius*. These are the things that will make for meaningful lives and great obituaries. But most of the time, we need to move people with our words. Almost every day, we need to *ask* people to do something we want them to do. This is what I mean by *inspiration by invitation*. It's "inviting" people to commit to a cause, work hard, see things from your perspective, change their mind, buy something you believe in, or change their behavior. This is the inspiration of leadership.

It's also the kind of inspiring that we can plan and practice. We are standing (or sitting) before a person or a group of people, and it's our responsibility to move them to do something. We have all the tools of communication at our disposal—our words, our bodies, our tone of voice and attitude, the space itself—and we can use them to get people pumped to get the job done.

And here's the point: when we have to *inspire by invitation*, become a Muse. Don't mess around with the textbook bullshit of "motivation" and "persuasion." Don't try to logic your audience into changing their minds. Those bullet points are weak weapons. Learn from Rudy and Gandhi and Eleanor Roosevelt and your amazing cancer-crushing mom and those chainsaw-juggling lunatics and Dolly Parton and Steven Spielberg and sunsets and spaceships.

And when you crack *that* code—and you will!—your "invitations" will become irresistible.

CHAPTER 2

There's a Heart in Your Head

"Arguments convince nobody."

—MY FRIEND DAN'S GRANDMOTHER

Like it or not, for better *and* for worse, we human beings are each moved by our feelings. And so, if we want to move each other, we better get *fluent in feelings* fast.

The Eternal Struggle of Making People Move

Let's start big:

How do you make a happy young man sacrifice his life?

Imagine you're twenty-two years old in 1944, like my uncle was. On your shoulders rests a heavy burden. Your mother and father left their village in Calabria, Italy and, like so many other wide-eyed wanderers, made their way to New York through Ellis Island. These parents found an apartment in Greenwich Village and set up a vegetable stand on Bleecker Street. Selling vegetables wasn't their goal, however; family-making was. Two sons and four daughters carrying the burden of the quintessential American Dream: build a life, have a family, do better.[1]

And perhaps you, their eldest son, find yourself where your parents never hoped you would be: on the verge of sacrificing your life. You're in Slapton, a coastal town in Devon, England, a village that had its few hundred residents evacuated so that the Third United States Army could practice maneuvers for an invasion, an invasion whose details were unknown to all but a few of the 150,000 soldiers who would storm a beach and scale some perilous cliffs. When? Where? How? All a mystery.

But here's what you do know: you don't want to be here. You don't want to die. You want to be back home selling vegetables with your sisters on Bleecker Street.

And then you're summoned, you and your fellow soldiers are summoned to the hillside by the beach on June 5, 1944, because a general wants to speak to you.

Now imagine you're that general.

Imagine you're about to ask thousands of young men who would rather be anywhere else to wake up the next morning and set sail for a certain fight and a likely death. You need to move an army. You need to ask thousands of young men with all the promise of the world before them to fight—likely, to die—in an almost-suicidal mission for some sort of "greater good."

How do you do that? Do you remind them of the importance of the mission, of the nobility of the cause? If you could, would you take them through a PowerPoint presentation outlining the strengths, weaknesses, opportunities, and threats of the situation, and then send them off with a catchy, rousing slogan?

Of course not.

But what do you do?

Do you get dressed up in a funny old outfit and curse and bully and, in an ego-fueled rant, appeal to the basest instincts of your troops?

Yes, perhaps you do.

Now imagine a far less lethal scene. Your ad agency is pitching a new client, but it's not a particularly thrilling new client. It's not Nike or Apple or some technology company disrupting a broken old industry with ingenuity and cutting-edge design. But it's a pitch that matters, nonetheless. Millions of dollars can be gained for your firm, securing your job, maybe even offering the promise of a year-end bonus for your few hundred coworkers. For sure, winning this business means no layoffs.

But it's a conservative client with an insipid marketing leader, a blow-hard CMO with a track record of treating partners poorly. This isn't what you imagined or wanted your life to become. You studied English at a top-tier liberal arts school and hoped that a job in advertising could offer you a career cocktail of "creativity" and "commerce" that would both satisfy your soul and pay off your mortgage on your Montclair Tudor. You wanted to throw your talent to the entrepreneurs and the visionaries who would appreciate it, use it to build a better mousetrap and make a better world.

Yet here you are, Friday, 4:30 p.m., with no hope of catching the train to get you to your daughter's lacrosse game; no hope, in fact, of a weekend at all. Again. You need to muster the wherewithal to prepare this pitch to share with your boss on Sunday night for a meeting with the client on Monday morning. Harder still, you need to rally your team to do the same. Somehow, you need to motivate a substantial crew of men and women who would rather be at bars and barbecues and bar mitzvahs, anywhere except here in the office making work for a client who won't even appreciate their best effort. You need to get your team focused and stoked to do the mediocre work that needs to be done to win a prize that none of them really want.

How do you do that?

And while we're imagining...

Imagine you're a parent of a teenager who lost his focus and is second-guessing the value of college. His grades have slipped, and he quit the soccer team he used to love. Maybe he's losing himself in a swirl of drinking too much and sleeping all day. How do you save him?

Imagine you're the CEO of a start-up pitching the board of Silicon Valley's hottest venture capital fund. You know you've got an industry-busting idea on your hands, but you also know this board of investors will hear that same promise from dozens of other companies that very week. How do you unlock the critical second-round funding you need?

Imagine you're running for town council because you're fed up with a broken government and sincerely believe you can do better than the jackasses ruining everything. How do you cut through the toxic petty politics and actually enlist your neighbors not only to vote for you, but to join you in fixing the whole damn system?

Imagine you want somebody to spend the rest of their life with you, through good times and bad ones. Imagine you're in love with a beautiful, reasonable girl. How do you conjure a completely irrational life-long commitment when you don't even own a car?

And finally, consider the many times you've felt to urge to do better, to be better—to play more with the kids, eat healthier, drink less, exercise more, watch less TV. Your old habits are so strong. How do you turn your sincere but weak desire into real action? How do you move yourself to be a better version of yourself?

Behind all these scenarios is the very same question: How do we move people—including ourselves—to do *what they might not want to do?* How do we lead a family, a class, a team, a company, a congregation, or even a country?

The French philosopher Jean-Paul Sartre famously wrote, "Hell is other people," a quip which has come to represent a truth universally acknowledged: other people can be a pain in the ass.[2] They have their own ideas and ambitions and plans, often at odds with our own designs. Other people might not always be "hell," but they can certainly be a headache, especially when they're not inclined to do as we wish. And yes, yes, certainly the world is good *because* it is filled with these strong, stubborn human beings, but it leaves us with a persistent challenge: how do we move them?

In Neanderthal times, the strategy for moving other people was pretty straightforward: bone-breaking sticks and stones. With most matters, say hunting and gathering, a well-applied threat of force could do the trick of bringing others along: *See this club, Stan? Now go find me dinner, or I'll bash your skull!*

But from the beginning of words, people have tried using their mouth-sounds to make each other do things. Talking instead of hitting is a mark of being civilized, after all, and so we say: *Come here. Stop that. Touch this. Eat. Move. Don't move....* And occasionally we even add in a *please*. And in those simple prehistoric days, when a command was in the best interest of the commanded, obedience would generally follow: *Yes, I guess I'll help you gather some berries, Stan. I'm hungry too.*

So it went. Shared needs, self-interest, and, occasionally, sharp sticks were the coin that made the people of the realm work.

But today, we and our commands and our mouth-sounds have gotten infinitely stranger and more demanding: *Sacrifice yourself for your country. Work on this project over the weekend. Learn calculus. Marry me. Vote for me. Don't eat gluten, Stan. Buy these sneakers with the swoosh, not those with the stripes. Repent to receive eternal life.* These are strange requests, the kind that don't find a clean logic in the short-term arithmetic of pleasure and pain.

So how do we get each other to do things *today*? How, without resorting to sticks and stones, do we move one another when our hopes run into the wall of other people's wants?

Well, self-interest and brute consequences certainly have staying power. They're motivations that still work well. It's deep human nature, after all, to do what brings pleasure and repels pain, and so, if we couch our commands to others with promises of pleasure or threats of pain, we might find success. Arguably, the modern science of behavioral economics is an attempt to understand just how to apply these age-old motivators in a new-age world. Where once we smacked, now we "nudge." We exploit the biases that have been built into the human psyche over the centuries.

And "nudging" certainly works, especially on those issues that are matters of process and habit, like signing up for a retirement savings account or keeping your hands sterile in a hospital. But many of the decisions we face today require intellectual acrobatics that demand a much more engaged and thoughtful approach. We "think"—and think hard—about such matters: *Is my nation really worth my life? It sure feels good to love you today, Stan, but will I feel this same way after decades of marriage? I don't see why calculus matters. How much more are those sneakers with the swoosh really worth? Sure, I want eternal life, but I also want to stay home and watch the football game.*

This is the curse of our blessed non-Neanderthal lives: our brains have gotten our bodies all tangled up; doing anything important involves an awful lot of mind working on our muscles, weighing pros and cons, often at a very abstract level. It's a thicket of difficult decision-making, and cutting through it needs more than a nudge.

For centuries, philosophers and scientists have wondered what to do about this conundrum: how do we get free-thinking human beings *to do* anything? How do we lead? How do we command a team or an army or a nation or, heck, just our kids?

The great Greek thinker Aristotle offered a reasonable answer in the heady days of Athenian Democracy: persuasion. Persuasion, he claimed, is the art of getting people—"rational animals" in his formulation—to do as we ask. Persuasion is the use of words, often "elevated" words, to command action. In a series of lectures eventually published as *Rhetoric*, Aristotle laid out the rules for using words to move crowds.[3] There are three "modes of persuasion" he concluded:

1. **Ethos.** This is an appeal to authority, either the *bona fides* of a person or the shared values of a community. Essentially, it's a polite, eloquent way of saying, "Do this because I said so." Very caveman.

2. **Pathos.** This is the fun one, the appeal to emotions. Make 'em laugh or cry, give 'em hope or incite fear. The rationalists amongst us worry about these appeals to our feelings, dismissing them as the tweaking of mere flimsy emotions, but Aristotle understood that underneath each rational animal is an animal still.

3. **Logos.** This is the place for logic, for facts and figures and proof and evidence. This is courtroom rhetoric, the kind practiced by the high school debating team. Logos is actually the mode of persuasion with which we're most comfortable, because it seems so clear-cut and objective; and yet, interestingly, Aristotle was very skeptical of logos-based appeals, as he thought they were ripe for manipulation. Even in Ancient Greece, beware the propagandist bearing facts.

So there you have it: a variety of ways to use words to make people do things. And for the last two centuries, scholars have quibbled with some of Aristotle's work, debating the primacy of one mode over another, but, for the most part, we've all accepted that a strong cocktail of logic—delivered with authority and occasionally feeling—gets the job done. The debating team has triumphed. We've all agreed to *reason* with one another, to make our cases for action based on facts and logic with an occasional shake of emotional verve. *Think about it,* we say. *Facts don't lie. Let me give you a few good reasons.*

And, over these centuries, we've built a deep appreciation for soaring "rhetoric" and an admiration for those people who can give those speeches that move the masses. We've studied the greats, like

Lincoln and Churchill and Kennedy, the forgotten like Thucydides and Cicero and Macaulay, and even the fictional like Shylock and Atticus Finch and Coach Taylor from Dillon, Texas. These are great-speaking men, and women as well—though too often, they've been less chronicled in the dusty tomes—like Sojourner Truth and Virginia Woolf and Eleanor Roosevelt and Barbara Jordan and Malala Yousafzai who have spoken words that have changed the way the world would be.

While there's so much beauty and wisdom to be found in this study of rhetoric, it hasn't really resulted in very practical advice for our day-to-day needs. There are hundreds of books and thousands of essays teaching us how to "give a great speech," and the advice in them usually boils down to a trifecta of platitudes: prepare, practice, personalize.

Well, sure. Perhaps preparing, practicing, and personalizing your speech is the recipe to persuading your audience.

But what if you're not giving a speech? What if you're talking to a colleague in the parking garage or your kid on the telephone? How do you move people, day in and day out, in quiet conversations and family dinners and office meetings and team huddles?

And on those occasions when you do have to give something that resembles a speech, how do you do so in a way that works for a modern audience, one with ears un-attuned to the clank of classical rhetoric?

But mostly, what if persuasion is no longer the point? What if logic, be it delivered in a conference room or from a stage, has lost its power to move people? What if reasoning with each other no longer gets us very far? What if it never really did?

The Man Who Murdered Aristotle

We are living in a golden age of neuroscience, and if this brain-deciphering field is yielding one unifying lesson, it's the insight that we humans are odd, irrational ducks. You've probably read the books: we *blink*. We're *nudged*. We're *pre-suaded*. Our actions are the result of so many factors, from our environment to our cultural biases, most of which work on us unconsciously, short-cutting the rigor of deliberation. Very rarely are our decisions the result of pure, calcu-lated logic. Even when we *think* we're being oh-so-rational, we're often not even coming close. That's our brain giving us the false comfort that we're both aware and in control of our biases and impulses. Silly, hopeful us clinging to the myth that we're more rational than animal.[4]

You're likely familiar with Dr. Daniel Kahneman, the psychologist who won The Nobel Prize for illuminating how our minds *really* make decisions. In *Thinking, Fast & Slow*, he describes two types of thinking: System 1 and System 2.

System 1 Thinking is automatic. It's intuitive, emotional, and quick. This is "thinking" that swells and spurts from the mysterious seas of our unconscious mind. Let's think of it as the *"Fuck It!"* force behind those moments that feel so instinctual: *Fuck it, I'll buy the fast car. Fuck it, I'll tell him I love him. Fuck it, I'll quit my day job and open a bicycle shop.*

System 2 Thinking is its exact opposite: measured, careful, and well-reasoned. System 2 Thinking involves effort and an awful lot of classic Aristotelian logic—weighing pros and cons, analyzing advan-tages and disadvantages. Let's call this *"Hmmm..."* thinking: *Hmm, which car will be the most practical one for our family? Hmm, is he really the right husband for me? Hmm, I better shut up and get on with my work if I want to pay for my kids' college.*

This model of competing brain energies makes sense to most of us who, all the time feel, the need to "correct" our instincts (System 1) with our reason (System 2). We want the cake, but we know we shouldn't have it. We feel our desire to tell off our stupid boss and quit our stupid job, but we consider the consequences of doing so. Most of us rest assured that our System 2 superhero will swoop in and save the day before our System 1 rascal unleashes hell. We trust that our *"Hmmm..."* will rescue us from the disaster of impulse.

But we'd be so wrong to trust the power of that mild-mannered *"Hmmm..."*

What's really shocking about Kahneman's work is the conclusion that System 2 Thinking has very little chance of saving any day. As

Kahneman explained, "System 1 is really the one that is the more influential; it is *guiding* System 2, it is *steering* System 2 to a very large extent" (emphasis added).⁵ In other words, we've got it the wrong way around: our rational brain does not "correct" our emotional brain; no, our emotions *drive* our thinking. "*Fuck It!*" is in charge.

"Fuck It!" thumps "Hmmm."

Dan and Chip Heath, brothers, academics, and authors of many best-selling books explaining what actually moves people, borrow an old metaphor to explain this phenomenon: Imagine a rider on an elephant, they tell us. The rider knows the elephant is gargantuan and powerful, but the rider also knows he is a man—a smart man who has mastered the skills of directing a dumb, lumbering elephant with an expertly-applied mix of whips and treats. The man believes he can steer the beast.... But come on, people, it's a friggin' elephant! If that elephant really wants to go left or lay down or buck or roll-over, our rider is simply hosed. The man is a pipsqueak of System 2 Thinking, hopeless against the beast of System 1.⁶

Without going too much farther down this rabbit-hole of science, it's also worth noting that Kahneman's work builds upon the findings of another giant of modern neuroscience, Dr. Antonio Damasio, who runs the Brain and Creativity Institute at The University of Southern California. Damasio's first book, called *Descartes' Error*, takes that Enlightenment philosopher to task for his very influential belief that we human beings harbor separate systems for feeling and thinking. In Descartes' theory of dualism, our body and our mind are discrete organs, one base and emotional, the other noble and rational. This (flawed) thinking has found its way into modern beliefs about the distinction between our "right brain" (the creative side) and "left brain" (the logical one). But as Damasio proves, it's all nonsense, an error. While different regions of our brain exert *motor* control over specific parts of our body, thinking is a far messier process. In matters of decision-making, there is no "right brain" or "left brain"—there is only *a* brain, an integrated and complex organ in which feeling *informs* thinking; in fact, as Damasio demonstrates, *good* thinking is impossible without feeling. He uses some heavy-duty laboratory work to prove that what we consider "thinking" is really our brain's mostly-unconscious *reaction* to our emotions. Feeling is, in fact, how we "think" our way to decisions—and, without feeling, we're as likely to make bad decisions as we are without logic. Our best "decisions," in other words, are built upon sands of emotions.[7]

So the next time you hear somebody talk about "right brain" and "left brain"—or the tug-of-war between our "emotional" and "rational" selves, laugh. Whatever you do, don't try to reason with them. It's futile.

All of this is very difficult to swallow for an intelligent, educated reader like you. We resist the notion that the hard work of our brains so easily surrenders to the whispers of our hearts. We insist we weigh the pros and the cons of a given decision and mentally muscle our way to a correct answer. We pride ourselves on our human ability to be bigger and better than our base emotions. We scoff at the accusation that we're remotely controlled by the impulses hidden in the deepest recesses of our psyches.

But that's the weak, pesky whisper of System 2 Thinking. You really can't argue with science. It's factual.

And, of course, for our purposes, all of this science has one clear implication: reason doesn't move people; feeling does. Aristotle's faith in *logos*—the lawyerly logic of argument and evidence—is misplaced. It's *pathos*—the feelings—that really move our modern (and yet still Neanderthal) selves. As my friend Dan's grandmother used to tell him, "Arguments convince nobody." In other words—like it or not, resist it or not—if you want to move anybody to do anything, you'll have to figure out how to arouse their emotions. You'll have to figure out the language spoken by the heart in their head. You'll have to *inspire* them.

And when you do, oh boy, that's when the good stuff starts.

Campaigning in Poetry

Yes, feelings most always trump logic, and perhaps there's no better illustration of that like-it-or-not truth today than Donald Trump. Much has been written about his surprising victory in 2016 being borne of the steady refusal of politicians from either party to address the fractured state of working-class America. Steel workers and coal miners and the army of minimum-wage-earning laborers felt threatened and ignored by a world that was galloping on the back of technology to an automated, highly educated future, a future where the value of their skills was uncertain. These hidden Americans lost their footing, and when they looked to Washington, DC, they saw nobody with a helping, steadying hand to offer them.

Into that trauma roared Donald Trump with a fusillade of pronouncements that were shocking, if not scandalous: his pronouncements on immigrants and trade; his threats to rupture America's traditional role on the global stage; his fawning over international strongmen like Vladimir Putin. All of that was unorthodox enough, but on top of those policy—um—positions was a confounding instinct to dissemble, to contradict himself, to contradict the facts, to slide over reality into the realm of "alternative facts" (as his counselor would later call some of these falsehoods). And then came filmed footage of Donald Trump boasting about his assault of women. It was vulgar, vile, and confoundingly irrelevant to the outcome of the election.

So how did this middling mess best the "most qualified" presidential candidate in the history of our Republic? *How did he even get close?* Now, certainly, there are myriad explanations, ranging from the reasonable (Change!) to the nefarious (Russia!) to the structural (Damn, Electoral College!), but I would suggest that Trump beat Hilary Clinton, in large part, because he campaigned in poetry, as Governor Mario Cuomo once recommended all politicians should do. That's right: poetry. With Trump, it was angry poetry; he was emotion incarnate, campaigning in the bold feelings of nationalist resentment and bravado to a tune with a very catchy hook: *Make America Great*

Again. Discussions and dissections about how he would actually accomplish that—the prose of policy—were not just meaningless, but ineffective. Any rational indictment of Trump (or his policies) was impotent against the raging bull of his belting feelings. In fact, in his wake has been borne such anti-rational notions as alternate facts and "fake news"—literally and vividly, reasonable evidence has lost its power. Ultimately, this "poetry" revved up a meaningful segment of the population, swinging some critical states toward Trump, even while Clinton won the popular vote.[8]

As Dan Balz, the respected veteran journalist and chief national correspondent at *The Washington Post* put it, "Trump understood something that others did not appreciate.... Trump has traded approval for intensity.... It was that intensity that helped him win. And it was the lack of intensity for Clinton that helped doom her candidacy, allowing Trump to win the electoral college while losing the popular vote."[9]

And, lest we dismiss this election as a fluke, let's review the general trend of most modern presidential elections: Barack Obama beats Mitt Romney; George W. Bush beats John Kerry and Al Gore; Bill Clinton beats George Bush; George Bush beats Michael Dukakis; Ronald Reagan beats Walter Mondale and Jimmy Carter.

He who has campaigned in poetry has won. He who has summoned intense emotions—feeling pain, dreaming big, stirring anger—has won. He who has argued with the reasonable natures of our disposition has lost.

Pause for a second—but only a second—to be sad about this, if you must. You can certainly bemoan these "emotional appeals" as cynical and dastardly manipulations. And you can do so while the Muses continue to thump the Robots. But I hope we'll soon come to understand that, while moving people through their emotions *can* be a manipulation, it can also be the best and most beautiful way of communicating with each other, a way that honors the messy fullness of our humanity. If we want to be moved, as Lincoln said, by "the better angels of our nature," we'd be wise to remember that angels and devils are *the very same species*: they speak the same language; they just have different agendas.

You'd think marketing experts would have learned the power of appealing to our emotions instead of tinkering with our reason. After all, we think of them as the Don-Draper-like Svengalis who build big business on snowflakes of fairy dust but, oddly, beneath the occasional pop of a heart-tugging commercial, most of these experts cling stubbornly to the belief that logic moves markets—despite all the evidence to the contrary. That evidence came to light in 1957 when Vance Packard, a journalist who was worried the world was being duped by the wizards of Madison Avenue, published an exposé of their tactics called, appropriately, *The Hidden Persuaders*. The book makes the case that the best brands appeal to timeless human desires like security, power, and ego. And while some of his accusations, like the preponderance of "subliminal" advertising, are hare-brained, the gist of his argument was right: marketing moves people through their emotions.[10]

But bizarrely, even though *The Hidden Persuaders* was supposed to be a revelation of how the ad industry actually worked, the ad industry never really bought it. Oh, for sure, agency executives pay lip service to the power of "emotions" in their marketing, but at the heart of their craft lurks the persistent belief that people need "reasons" to buy what they buy. They call them "reasons to believe" (*Now with 3x the cavity-fighting power!*) or they divide them into "functional reasons" (like whiter teeth) and "emotional reasons" (like the self-confidence that comes from whiter teeth)—but *reasons* they remain. They celebrate a brand's "unique selling proposition"—the attribute that makes it a *better alternative* to the competitive product. This cereal that has more whole grains. This car with better fuel efficiency and comfortable seats. This bank that will make you richer in retirement. Even today's fad for brands to have "purposes" comes gauze-wrapped in the safety of logic: *You will like our winter jacket company more than the others because we really do care about the environment. And to prove how much we love the environment, we will donate more money to saving it than our competitors will.*

It's a world of *"-er"* marketing—better, stronger, faster, sexier, good-er. It's downright Aristotelian.

And this is not to say that marketers don't use emotions in their work. Of course they do. See, there's a mother holding an adorable baby. But generally, those emotional appeals aresprinkled on top of the arithmetic of argument. *Oh wait, where did that baby go? Why are they pouring blue liquid into Diaper A and Diaper B? I think I'll go watch some cute cat videos now.*

So what's the problem with this model of marketing—coherent "reasons to believe" delivered with an emotional punch? What's the problem with a brand—or a political candidate or a corporate leader—juicing up their logical arguments with some feeling flimflam? What's the problem when they pump up their "unique selling propositions" with some sex appeal or sentimentality or humor?

Well, simply put, that model, rational at its core, is a weak model. It just doesn't work as powerfully as the alternative can.

The Mad Men of the twenty-first century have begun to enlist the expertise of academics and neuroscientists to help figure out which bits of their work really move markets, and it turns out they had an awful lot to learn from Dr. Kahneman. Consumers—whom we'd be wise to remember are actually people—are moved by the unstoppable tides of System 1 Thinking.

A few British academics have landed a one-two punch to the face of reason-to-believe marketing. First, Professor Robert Heath, who teaches at the University of Bath, has demonstrated that advertising is processed by the brain with "low involvement"—in other words, people don't "think" about a commercial; they just let it wash over them.[11] Perhaps, every now and then, some act of marketing does create some salient and valuable associations for a brand. Maybe something catches our attention and maybe even share something a company does—but even those episodes are processed at very low levels of consciousness.

Robert Heath has demonstrated what most non-marketers have always known: most marketing, like politics and news, is literally background noise. And if it's background noise, it can't really *persuade* anybody of anything.

The next blow to the nose of the old hidden persuaders came from Les Binet, an ad man himself, who along with Peter Field, was commissioned in 2007 by the august Institute of Practitioners in Advertising (IPA) to review hundreds of "effective" marketing campaigns and divine their secrets.[12] They divided the campaigns into three categories, those with: 1. A Rational Approach; 2. An Emotional Approach; and 3. A *Balanced* Rational and Emotional Approach. And then they looked at marketplace data and sales results to judge which approach was most effective.

Now, if you, like almost every marketing professional, bet that the *Balanced* Rational and Emotional Approach was the most effective model, you'd be, like almost every marketing professional, wildly wrong. In fact, Binet and Field demonstrated that *purely emotional* advertising is *twice as effective* as any other kind. And, in case you need an example of purely emotional advertising, they provide one of the best: a completely nonsensical film of a gorilla playing the drums to a song by Phil Collins. Is this an ad for drums? Or gorillas? Not at all. This is a commercial for Cadbury's candy bars. Go watch the ad. It's preposterous. It's confusing. It's also utterly captivating. Best of all, it was a runaway success, driving a sales increase of almost 10 percent. Commercials don't usually do that for such big and well-known brands.

I'd add most fashion advertising to the category of purely emotional marketing as well. Just flip through the pages of any slick fashion magazine and you'll see some bizarre images, impressions really of strange worlds with glamourous people. In fact, I remember a high-profile ad for *Dolce & Gabbana* that had the most gorgeous Italian models standing around a forest, holding goats. Why were they holding goats? Who knows? Hardly ever does fashion advertising commit the cardinal sin of trying to explain anything to you.

It's all feeling—and it creates more visceral desire than any breakfast cereal ever has.

As Binet summarized it, "You can see clearly that the more emotional the strategy, the better it worked. People might think that adding emotions in to a rational campaign might be the answer, but pure emotion works better, even in categories that are supposedly rational, like financial services and computers.... People go by their gut feeling first."[13]

Alongside this confounding insight about the power of pure, anti-rational emotion, Binet and Field shared a related bit of wisdom: thinking gets in the way of *making* great advertising. As you'd guess, there's an awful lot of "strategy" that goes into the making of marketing, and much of that brain-work is fueled by market research. *Copytesting*, for example, is the market research methodology that involves showing ideas, a commercial or a new product design, usually in unfinished form, to a group of consumers and discussing their responses. *What do you think? What do you like or hate? What would you keep or change?* It *seems* like such a good idea: before you spend your marketing money, just ask real flesh-and-blood people what they think. In the industry, these exercises are sometimes called "disaster checks."

But according to Binet and Field's work, they ought to be called disaster-makers. Advertising that is copytested has an *inverse* relationship to real-world success. Think about that: asking people to judge your marketing is a *bad* idea. It makes the marketing more rational *and, hence,* less effective.[14]

The problem with copytesting is that it engages the "rational" side of a consumer's mind. It's very, very System 2. *Do you like this ad? What is its message? Do you find this message compelling? What would you tell your friends about this product?* And then, armed with those answers, marketers go on to create exactly the "rational" marketing we just learned doesn't work so well.

> "People go by their gut feeling first."

A focus group is a fraud: people rationalizing their feelings and, in the process, butchering the truth. And it's not because people are liars; no, the research *itself* is the problem. It's predicated on the twin false beliefs that people can both explain their own decisions and that those decisions are reasonable. We now know both of those premises are false.

Market research asks drumming gorillas to explain themselves and beautiful goat-cradling Italians to explain themselves, and yes, Donald Trumps to explain themselves—and, as it does, it sucks the very vitality out of the object it's examining.

And yet why does it persist? Why is market research a multi-billion-dollar industry, a required crutch of so many top-spending marketers? Well, no doubt MBA-armed executives and cable-news political prognosticators find comfort in the (false) confidence this kind of research provides. *Look,* they tell their boss, *I tested this idea. Look,* they tell their viewers, *suburban women voters hate Trump.*

But I believe there's something at play beyond the instinct to cover one's own ass, something that affects all of us, even those of us who will never make marketing. Perhaps the world of *pure emotion*— of "pure imagination," as Willy Wonka put it—is a scary place to be. Perhaps feelings are terrifying things.

EVIL LITTLE DOTS

-
-
-

The bullet point. It looks so innocent, like a period with a swell of self-confidence.

But, of course, a bullet point never exists alone. It's a herd creature. There you see it with its tribe, more bullet points, stacking themselves atop each other, justified left, perched on the outskirts of words and numbers, a safe, short distance from real meaning.

It's easy to see bullet points the way PowerPoint wants you to see them: an indispensable, unobtrusive *organizational* device. It's easy to use them as a tool to present our positions with impact. But did you know the creators of Power-Point had a hidden agenda? They wanted to give *power* to bullet points. They did. It's right there in the name.

And we've let them. Each day, we create more than thirty million Power-Point presentations. Imagine how many bullet points are contained within them.

Don't be fooled by the modest stance of these self-confident periods. They don't want to organize our thinking; they want to dictate it. They want us to believe that the "right" answer is the answer that's best supported by a multitude of compelling—well, bullet points.

Yes, PowerPoint has given the bullet point a fierce power, the power to give weight and credibility to any old thought. *How can this headline be wrong? It comes with so many bullet points! Bullet points win!* Be a consultant: add bullet points to your argument until their weight bends the will of your audience.

Bullet points are the last roar of a world clinging to the false comfort of System 2 Thinking.

Let's silence them. Let's put a knife in the back of bullet-point thinking.

Take the pledge, readers: swear off bullet points forever. Promise yourself that you will never again try to move people by the muscle of evidence and the weight of reason. They are false, weak weapons. From here on, you will inspire with ideas too beautiful to be broken into bulleted bits. From today on, you will move people with stories that stoke their passions. From now on, you will be a Muse.

Unless you're a data scientist. Then you can use bullet points.

The Radical Act of Sharing Our Feelings

So here's the bottom-line: to be inspiring, you'll need to *practice* being emotional. To get anybody—including yourself—to do good, grand things, you'll have to learn to *express* your deepest feelings. It sounds so easy. After all, you *feel* emotions constantly, swings from ecstasy to melancholy, with the usual suspects of joy, sadness, anger, boredom, frustration, determination, hate, and love thrown into the mix. *Sometimes* our feelings are intense, but all the time, they're present, as deep a part of who we are as our very breath.

Being emotional *should* be an everyday breeze.

But it isn't. The world conspires to suppress our emotions. Our institutions, especially the corporate ones, treat emotions as a distraction from the important business of productivity and progress. I once suggested to the CEO of a *Fortune* 100 company that, as awesome as daughters and sons are, maybe we should also have a "Bring-*Yourself*-to-Work Day." He shook his head. He, like most leaders, prefers the cold currency of universal, impersonal logic.

Oh, there's certainly a new breed of "enlightened" leaders who worship at the modern church of "corporate purpose" and send their executives to mindfulness retreats. There are certainly some who believe—and many more who want us to believe that they believe—that our work is best when it's most personal. But even these buttoned-up managers betray their bias when feelings walk into the office: *Don't be so emotional! Let's look at the facts! Let's put our "personal biases" aside and examine the pros and cons of the situation!* Those are the rules of work. And school. And most of life. And we know they're the rules, because when they're breached, when a person comes along and is all razzle-dazzle eruptions of feeling, we tut-tut and wag our fingers. *Chill out.* That's what we say. *Chill. Out.* Two ugly, mean, dehumanizing words hiding behind a sensible appeal to reason.

There are moments for "chill," for sure. An always-apoplectic world would be a noisy nightmare, but after a career of working with dozens of corporations, I've come to believe that we're squashing too

40

many feelings—and we're doing so at our own peril. Sure, you can "mobilize teams" and "get things done" on the back of well-polished arguments and elegant analysis, but *emotions* are the super-fuel for progress, the energy that inspires us to be our super-human best selves. When we're stoked, furious, determined, enraptured, in love, bursting with joy or ambition—when we *feel*, we do, and we do with an awesome conviction. Feelings are the energy of action, a radical competitive advantage to accomplishing anything. Feelings are people-moving magic.

Which might be why they terrify us.

Emotions are so powerful, so combustible, that we only allow them in certain "personal" situations and, even there, they need to be leashed and tightly controlled. In fact, a best-selling self-help book suggests that whenever somebody asks how you're doing, you should reply, *"I'm wonderful, thank you very much!"*—because sharing any other emotions might bum out the person who asked.

The only safe space for emotions, it sometimes seems, is the imaginary world of art: music, movies, books in which we "lose ourselves." Ah, another terrible phrase. Maybe those are actually the creative places where we *find* ourselves—and maybe, when we do, we ought to bring ourselves to work and everywhere else we happen to go. CEOs be damned!

Maybe, rather than trying to box up our emotions and shove them in the corporate attic, we ought to let them stampede like wild horses through our sad beige conference rooms.

Woah, you might be thinking. *Chill out! Are you suggesting that we throw out facts and ignore logic all in the service of our own emotional agendas? Are you suggesting we let our passions run roughshod over reason?*

Well...

Sorta, kinda, sometimes, yes.

I am *not* suggesting we lie. This is not a book promoting psychosis. I believe in facts and science. I see the value of firm logic and clear thinking.

But, as we'll come to see, exercising those virtues of logic and clarity comes at a price: they cost us the opportunity to arouse ourselves, to inspire each other. They stick us in the "Strategy Trap," where bullet points become baby steps. And who wants to step like a baby?

So, by all means, exercise all of your sharp, fact-filled, analytical, critical, reality-based thinking in figuring out *what should be done*—and then stop making so much sense. When it comes time to *getting it done*, well, that's the time to muzzle your sensible side and unleash the kraken of your wildest feelings.

Sensible readers will have two more objections:

1. *Balance! What about balance? Aren't you setting up a false dichotomy? Can't we turn up the dial on our System 2 thinking and make things happen using both logic and emotion, both reason and passion?*

   No, no, no, unfortunately, we can't. As Binet and Field demonstrated in the realm of marketing, reason ruins the passion party. And, as we'll see, neuroscience has confirmed what you intuitively know: analysis paralysis is a real phenomenon. The more we think hard, the less we do hard. We can't get people to move with determination while we're making them think with deliberation. So, no, critical thinking is not an ally to inspiration; it's an enemy.

2. *Isn't this what bad people do? Don't lunatics and tyrants dissemble facts and manipulate the feelings of the mob? Isn't "arousing people's emotions" the playbook of cult leaders, charlatans, autocrats, snake-oil salesmen, and exploiters?*

   Yes.

   Please, don't be a bad person.

As I was saying: to be inspiring you'll need to practice being emotional in a world that doesn't really want you to be. You'll need to be an *emotional rebel*—which is a dangerous thing to be. After all, the person who shares feelings is an instant target of worry and ridicule. At best, he's odd; more often, she's unprofessional or unhinged.

I, instead, choose to pity the robots. Their fear of feelings is scar tissue on their soul.

We're going to explore the **Six Skills of Inspiration**, which are techniques for infusing your communications with people-moving emotion, but you can begin exercising your "emotion muscle" right now with two daily practices, two daily habits that will help you become fluent in the awesome and exotic language of feelings. Think of them as Muse Practice:

1. **A Daily Muse Outburst: I Feel...**

   Starting today, find an opportunity every day, to express your feelings in a place, at a moment, where you ordinarily wouldn't. Maybe it's in a meeting with serious colleagues or in an exchange with a customer. Maybe it's with your friend or partner or neighbor, while you're discussing something important. Maybe it's to yourself, when the engine in your head is working hard to figure something out. At that moment, pause, figure out what you're feeling, and express it very directly by starting a sentence with the simple phrase, "*I feel...*" Maybe you feel excited or terrified or frustrated. Maybe you feel like something is silly or stupid. You feel like it's the same-old, same-old boring routine. Maybe you feel thrilled and confident and you can't wait to get cracking. Maybe you feel a combination of feelings, a natural swirl of emotions, like hope *and* worry or excitement *and* anger, that doesn't make easy, explainable sense. That's okay. Just share it. *I feel...*

   And when you share how you feel, notice what happens to you. Be perceptive to your body language. Do you lean forward and speak more quickly? Do your shoulders sag? Do you look away, unable to make eye contact? Are there some feelings that are more difficult to spit out than others? Do you feel anxious or relieved? And, of course, be mindful to how others respond.

Expressing our feelings is a powerful, radical act, and so sometimes, people have difficulty dealing with them. They might ignore us, or even get defensive. You might bring a conversation to an awkward pause. That's okay. Then again, others might respond in kind, sharing their own feelings. The discussion might just lead to new and more satisfying places. (Of course, you have to be careful here. Don't tell your boss you feel like she's an idiot. Be generous. Don't hurt anybody. But, by all means, try to be as honest as you can: take stock of your feelings, understand them, and spit them out.)

If you keep a journal, record these daily acts of expression, but if you don't, just try to look for any interesting patterns that emerge over the course of a few weeks. The following worksheet might help:

MY DAILY MUSE OUTBURST

TODAY, I THOUGHT

_____

_____

_____

I SAID, "I FEEL…"

_____

_____

_____

WHICH MADE ME FEEL…

_____

_____

_____

AND HERE'S WHAT HAPPENED

_____

_____

_____

With this exercise, you're building a muscle—the muscle of expressing your feelings—and, like building any other muscle, there will be days when you feel the strain and days when you feel the power. But, over time, your ability to identify your feelings and share them—with your language, your body, and your tone—will develop into a powerful skill. This ability will become a critical tool as you set about the task of inspiring.

2. A Daily Muse Snack: Feed on Feelings

We all know the best way to learn a foreign language is to immerse yourself in a place where that language is spoken, daily and naturally. The same is true as you learn to be *fluent in feelings*—and the foreign land to which you should travel is Creative World, the place where movies and songs and books and poems provoke a wild range of feelings. As I mentioned, art seems to be one of the few "safe spaces" for feelings. When we see a movie or attend a show, we're allowed—we're even expected—to feel a wild range of emotions. The more we feel them, the more comfortable we'll be expressing them. And so, I urge you to feast on a daily diet of creativity. Each day, find a piece of art that makes you feel something, anything—and feel it.

Throughout this book, I'll provide examples of inspiring art that I've culled from a survey of thousands of people, asking a simple question: "What inspires you?" You'll see the classics, like "Eye of The Tiger" and Dead Poet's Society. You'll find the new standards, like Hamilton, "Roar," and Eat, Pray, Love. You'll see the Gettysburg Address and hear some choice bits from JFK's most arousing speeches, but you'll also read a recipe for radishes with butter and the instructions from an ice bucket that left a hundred million people soaking wet. Sprinkled amongst these selections will be gems you know but might have forgotten, but also some new treasures waiting to be discovered.

And, at the end of this book, I've provided thirty examples for 30 Days of Muse Snacking—not all of it is art that will necessarily inspire you, but all are acts of creativity that should help you feel something.

So use these examples—or don't. But commit to experiencing one act of creativity every single day. Make it a habit, a morning ritual or an evening unwinding. Set a reminder on your phone. Use Spotify and Google, ask your friends what they love, or just wander the world, real or virtual. There's just one rule: find something new or, at least, something that's not totally familiar. If you're anything like me, you've got a well-worn road of go-to favorites. Enjoy them, of course, but search for something different. Perhaps even challenge your tastes: if you don't think you like modern art, spend five minutes looking at a Mark Rothko painting. If you hate hip-hop, give Kendrick Lamar one shot to change your mind. Watch a video of the Comme des Garçons fashion runway show or crank up some Dolly Parton on your commute and pretend you're in a pickup truck. Whatever you find, listen to it, look at it, feel it, cook it, watch it, read it—do whatever it demands and, as you do, try to identify what feelings it arouses in you. Try to give those feelings a name, a name as specific as possible. Maybe a movie makes you feel sad, but what "kind" of sad, the kind that comes from a broken heart or the kind that comes from seeing your own shortcomings? Maybe a song makes you feel "great," but interrogate that feeling: do you feel powerful or understood or just delirious and dizzy?

So then, two daily habits which you can begin to practice immediately. They won't always be easy, but they'll likely be fun: one will help you express feelings and one will help you absorb feelings. Together, they make an emotional give-and-take that'll help you start to learn the language of the Muses, the language of feelings, the language that'll get you what you want.

Chapter 2 Key Terms

People: (noun) A pain in the ass; difficult to move, but essential for accomplishing almost anything you dream of doing; a group that includes yourself.

Aristotle: (proper noun) Greek philosopher who believed that we could move each other by talking in a way that was logical and persuasive (see: *Rhetoric*); even though he acknowledged the power of feelings to influence people, he's our short-hand for the triumph of logic and reason.

System 1 Thinking: (proper noun) The automatic, unconscious "thinking" that drives most of our decisions; described and named by Dr. Daniel Kahneman, Nobel-prize-winning psychologist who has gotten us all to think about the limits of our thinking.

Cadbury Gorilla: (proper noun) A marriage of a primate and Phil Collins; an example of a purely emotional commercial, the kind that is twice as effective as any marketing that tries to rationalize with you (*see also:* goat-cradling Italian models).

Emotions: (noun) Everything.

A Metaphor:
Muse, DJ, Bouncer

Think of the Muse, think of yourself, as the host of a party. And congratulations—you've put together the very best party anybody can imagine. The room looks perfect, awash in the kind of light that makes everybody beautiful. The stress of the long work week has slipped away on currents of fancy cocktails, scrumptious snacks, and the kind of music that makes everybody move. You've planned a perfect playlist: heart-pumping dance tunes, rousing sing-alongs, and sultry slow songs—each seems to be played at exactly the right moment. Even when you grab your phone and start to improvise, you can't seem to make a mistake. Every song you pick *works*. Everybody feels like their very best self—energized, interesting, sexy, and connected.

You know this party. You've been to it—even if only for a few minutes, at that part of the night when everything is good and gold and glittering, when you are exactly a worry-free, thought-free, fully-feeling-amazing spirit.

Tonight, this is your party. You've planned it, created it. You're making it work. You are an ideal host. You are an ideal DJ.

And then you hear it: a faint *knock, knock*. You ignore it, but it gets louder and then louder still. Luckily, it seems like only you can hear it. *Knock, knock, knock.* You know exactly what's happening. It's your neighbor banging on the door. It's your neighbor who thinks the music is too loud and the hour is too late. And maybe it is. But if you open that door, lower the music, ask your guests to "keep it down"—well, that's even worse than an angry neighbor. That's the end of the party, the moment when the revelers look at their watch, remember themselves, and reckon they can still get home for a proper night's sleep.

Inside is magic and energy and the party-induced possibilities of an anything-goes perfect night. Outside is the end of all that—the prick that pops the party. And make no mistake: it's a zero-sum proposition; there is no reasonable compromise that won't snuff out the magic. Everything is so perfectly-calibrated, that any change—a brightening of the lights, a softening of the music—breaks the spell.

As the Muse, you are both DJ and bouncer, the one who must stir the hot feelings of the crowd and keep the cold wind of reason barred tightly behind the door. The worst thing you can do is answer the door. Let the bastards knock it down.

CHAPTER 3

The Inspiration Advantage

"You can't wait for inspiration.
You have to go after it with a club."

—JACK LONDON

Q: Okay, I'm buying it. Emotions move us. Too much thinking seems to get in the way of doing. But *what do I do* with that insight?

A: inspire (verb): to arouse the emotions of your audience to the point of action; to create an energy that brings out the very best effort in people; to transform ordinary people into superheroes, who will be more committed, more powerful, and, ultimately, more successful.

True facts.

God's Strong Breath

In-spi-ra-tion.

It's a good Latinate word, with a very Catholic, mystical *spiritus* at its core. Literally, it means "to inhale breath or spirit," but as the word became used in the thirteenth century, it didn't refer to any old errant spirit; no, inspiration referred to the inhalation of a divine spirit, *the* divine spirit. It's the word used right in the big book at the beginning of it all, *"And the Lord God formed man of the dust of the ground and breathed into his nostrils the breath of life; and man became a living soul."*[1]

That's inspiration, then: the breath of God (or sometimes, Bono), the divine force that makes us living souls. Without it, we're lost and lifeless. With it, we are Adam and Eve, the first men and women, ready to birth a new world.

Indeed, inspiration has created nations, started religions, won wars, and changed the course of history. It has hatched economy-growing businesses and birthed soul-stirring masterpieces. Inspiration is the energy that moves the world by moving its people.

In quieter ways, inspiration is a force that makes magic happen in our everyday lives. We've all felt it: the pep-talk of a coach or the tender words of a teacher that have turned our lives; perhaps a book or a movie or even a conversation has steeled our resolve to eat better, exercise more, quit a frustrating job, or pursue a crush with romantic abandon. Inspiration can be the whisper in a child's ear that blossoms into an unimagined future. Inspiration is escaping poverty, quitting drugs, starting a business, sharing your treasure, and learning to love.

We've also seen inspiration: somebody do something so perfectly, with so much heart, often against the odds—a deaf singer on a reality television show belting out a song like a diva; an entrepreneur sacrificing everything to follow her dream; a veteran with one leg running harder on the treadmill than anybody else at the gym. We witness these heroic acts, and we want to do—*to be*—just as good. That's inspiration.

It's no wonder we crave inspiration, hunting for it in TED talks, television shows, and quippy refrigerator magnets. Inspiration feels so good. Its delusion-tinged energy grows us into giants, invincible beasts, cutting a path through any obstacle, striding in the direction of our very best selves. Inspiration whispers, "You can do it!"—and we jump.

And when we jump, amazing things can happen. The German poet Goethe said "Leap! And the world will conspire to break your fall," while the consultants at Bain & Co. reported that inspired employees are 225 percent more productive than their unmoved colleagues.[2] Think about that: an "inspired" employee is capable of producing more than twice as much work as an uninspired one. In fact, many studies show that employees who start their shifts by listening to inspiring songs like Survivor's "Eye of The Tiger" actually get more done.[3] That's weird! Listening to a song makes you better at your job? But, of course, it does! You've likely experienced the phenomenon yourself. You don't mind working late nights and long weekends if—if—you feel inspired by your boss or your project. You're pumped, psyched, stoked—and it couldn't be more different than the dull drag you feel when your toiling on a task that hasn't carbonated your spirit. And yes, likely, you've listened to "Eye of The Tiger" or "Roar" or "Lose Yourself" or "Uptown Funk"—and the energy of those songs has pushed you farther and faster than you had been going. One psychologist describes this kind of music as a "legal performance-enhancing drug."[4]

But you don't need Bain & Co. or any old philosopher to tell you what you already know. You've felt strange power in the inspired moment: the laws of physics seem to relax and anything you desire—the win, the victory, the masterpiece—hangs right in front of you, ripe for the plucking. When you're inspired, you feel unstoppable, like a giant striding across the land, crushing any irritating obstacles that stand in the way of your desire.

This is **The Inspiration Advantage**—the *extra* power that inspiration creates, the superior results achieved by a team or a person when they are "emotionally engaged," driven by conviction and commitment. To borrow a line from an old ad campaign: *This is your work. This is your work on inspiration…*The difference is profound.

Inspiration Breeds Advantage

Most of us can think of a personal Muse, a person who has inspired us to work harder, a person for whom we'd do almost anything. For me, it's been a handful of teachers, a few men and women who I *felt* saw something special in me. Their belief in my ability stoked my desire to work harder—and fueled the many late nights and long weekends of actually doing so. They were emotional caffeine. They were also loving and supportive.

Not all Muses are.

One of my favorite examples of a professional Muse is Elon Musk because, well, by many accounts, he's not a very nice man. He's a visionary, no doubt, having created two of the most exciting companies of the century: Tesla, which is spearheading the electric car revolution, and SpaceX, the world's first company to commercialize space travel, having developed reusable rocket technology. His plan is to colonize Mars, and the market believes he can. Tesla alone is valued at more than $60 billion—more than any automaker in the world. Even though his companies have struggled with operationalizing their visions—and in 2018, the man himself seemed near a personal breakdown—Elon Musk seems to have earned his reputation as our century's Thomas Edison, a big-thinking science whizz turning his dreams into commerce. My kids think he's amazing.

And yet he's also earned a reputation as a complete jerk. The stories of horror among his employees are legion. He's a never-satisfied boss, humiliating his employees and constantly questioning their loyalty, despite the fact that many of them pour in more than eighty hours of work a week. In a much-shared anecdote about his enormous ego, his ex-wife reports that, *as they danced at their wedding reception*, he looked into her eyes and reminded her, "I'm the alpha in this relationship." Eek. As I said, *ex*-wife.[5]

And yet, as one former executive at SpaceX noted, Musk still manages to inspire deep and powerful loyalty. Dolly Singh, who ran human resources at SpaceX, tells the story of the bleakest day at the company, August 2, 2008. For *the third time*, SpaceX's Falcon 1 Rocket failed to launch. This was a massive setback and a genuine humiliation for a man who had promised to commercialize space travel. Musk watched the failure from a control room at SpaceX headquarters outside of Los Angeles, and when the loss of the rocket became obvious, he cut the video transmission feed his employees had been watching, and he marched out to address the assembled company. There's not a transcript of his remarks, though he likely riffed a few phrases that would make their way into his official statement, like the defiant, "I will never give up—and I mean never." Singh records the response of the devastated employees:

I think most of us would have followed him into the gates of hell carrying suntan oil after that. It was the most impressive display of leadership that I have ever witnessed. Within moments the energy of the building went from despair and defeat to a massive buzz of determination as people began to focus on moving forward instead of looking back. This shift happened collectively, across all 300+ people in a matter of not more than 5 seconds. I wish I had video footage as I would love to analyze the shifts in body language that occurred over those 5 seconds. It was an unbelievably powerful experience.[6]

That's The Inspiration Advantage. It's following a guy—*even an asshole*—"into the gates of hell carrying suntan oil."

There's an old Roman phrase for this feeling of inspiration, this feeling of being possessed, gripped by a spirit that won't let you go: *furor poeticus*, they called it—a madness or divine frenzy. A sweet movie on the Hallmark Channel might swell your heart and make you weepy, but that's not inspiration. No, real inspiration is *furious*. It grabs you by the shoulders and shakes your body *until you act*.

You've felt it: a convicted determination; a focus, a flow; but one that distorts reality: time no longer applies its brutal cuffs; energy seems to come in inexhaustible supplies, priorities are re-arranged; courage dominates; and the practical, quotidian objections that stump our dreams are felled. When you are inspired, you are powerful, unstoppable, and, yes, a little crazy as well. You're singing in your car.

Beats by Dre, the company that has made their headphones the hottest gear for listening to music, captures the disorientating feeling of inspiration in a brilliant set of commercials that profile athletes before their big games. To pump themselves up, superstars like LeBron James, Tom Brady, Serena Williams, and Conor McGregor tune out the world and turn up their tunes. In these ads, sounds fade away. The world almost disappears. There are no crowds roaring or coaches instructing. There's only the athlete and the music, the Muse, existing in a surreal mental cocoon, focusing maniacally on the battle brewing. Beats' slogan says they're "Above the Noise"—operating on a plane higher than the petty distractions of reality. Take a moment to watch these beautiful ads where the world seems to slip away and our hero prepares for the battle of a lifetime. Reality is, in fact, forgotten.

This touch of focused madness has been described as many things: the zone, flow, pumped up, psyched, or stoked. But whatever the words, the feeling is the same: an intense determination to do something grand coupled with a seeming-suspension of the laws of physics. Tennis superstar Roger Federer says that he sees a 2.7-inch tennis ball as "big as a bowling ball or basketball" before he hits it, which is a description that echoes the writer Annie Dillard's particularly evocative description of what it feels like when she's inspired:

> *You search, you break your fists, your back, your brain, and then—and only then—it is handed to you. From the corner of your eye you see motion. Something is moving through the air and headed your way. It is a parcel bound in ribbons and bows; it has two white wings. It flies directly at you; you can read your name on it. If it were a baseball, you would hit it out of the park. It is that one*

pitch in a thousand you see in slow motion; its wings beat slowly as a hawk's.[7]

Balls grow bigger. You can't miss. The laws of physics change. It's like Neo seeing the Matrix and, with crystal clarity, understanding how to control everything. When inspired, you feel completely capable, almost as if the world has conspired with your deepest talents to make failure genuinely impossible.

Inspiration is crazy like that.

The Professor X of Exercise

Dr. Michael Joyner runs a laboratory at the Mayo Clinic where his team of "human performance experts" investigates how our bodies perform under stress, sometimes brutal physical stress like the kind endured by elite athletes, the kind that makes you gasp for breath and clutch your heart and collapse in a pool of your own sweat. It's good, strong, and useful science.

But in 1991, Dr. Joyner did something extraordinary: this nice doctor from Minnesota invented a species of superheroes.

That year, Dr. Joyner published an article in the *Journal of Applied Physiology* with a very precise conclusion: a human body *could* run a complete marathon in one hour, fifty-seven minutes, and fifty-eight seconds—almost nine minutes faster than the standing world record, an inconceivable ambition, given that leaps in shoe design and training methods were only able to shave a mere *two-and-a-half* minutes from the record set in 1965. But here was Dr. Joyner, armed with science, laying down an audacious challenge: it was *physically* possible for a human being to run 26.2 miles in less than two hours. This seemed like delusional stuff. In fact, as Dr. Joyner remembers, "People thought this was nuts and it took a while to get the paper published."[8] *Nuts!*

As Ed Caesar describes in his gripping book, *Two Hours: The Quest to Run the Impossible Marathon*, Dr. Joyner's science was an inspiration to Matt Nurse, who ran the Nike Sports Research Laboratory, the cutting-edge R&D department for the company, the place where designers and engineers had reign to dream big. And Matt Nurse, buoyed by Dr. Joyner's science, dreamed big indeed: In 2014, Nike launched a special project called *Breaking2*, a multi-million-dollar global mission to make Dr. Joyner's theory a reality, to turn runners into superheroes.

And they *almost* succeeded.

On the morning May 6, 2017, at a car racing track in Monza, Italy, three marathoners, Olympians and record-breakers, supported by a phalanx of pace-setters, nutritionists, and physiotherapists, set out to break the two-hour barrier. One of them, Eliud Kipchoge, an Olympic Gold medalist from Kenya, came close, clocking a final time of 2:00:25. He missed the goal by less than the duration of a Nike commercial.

"By the terms of its mission, Breaking2 was a failure," writes Caesar, "Nike tried everything to help a runner break two hours, and they couldn't do it—not quite. But nobody who knows the sport, and who was at Monza to witness the attempt, could have seen Kipchoge's run in such terms. Kipchoge's 2:00:25 was one of the most impressive displays of distance running in history."[9] More than impressive, his run was catalytic, redoubling the efforts of elite runners and their teams to cut twenty-six seconds from that finish. And nobody doubts it will happen; there's an army of runners who believe it will, who believe *they* can.

On May 6, 2017, Eliud Kipchoge ran like a superhero. He did what had been thought to be physically—emotionally, spiritually—impossible. And he did it, because twenty-five years earlier, Dr. Michael Joyner asked the question you should ask yourself: How great can we possibly get?

Muses Make (Super)Heroes

Inspiration, then, isn't just a feel-good feeling. It's not watching *Rudy* or seeing a sunset and "believing" you can do anything. No, inspiration—real, valuable inspiration—results in *action*, the kind that yields better results. It moves people to do specific things—and often, difficult things that once seemed out of reach.

Inspiration turns ordinary people into extraordinary people.

When psychologists study achievement—be it in business, arts, sports, or education—they find that successful people are marked by an "intrinsic motivation" to do what they do. In other words, their motivation comes from *within* themselves. It's personal—and proven to result in both greater success *and* greater happiness. It's why we're all told to find jobs doing what we love. We'll be happier (and likely richer) than if we just chase a paycheck.

Extrinsic motivation, however, is the carrot-and-stick way of the world. It's when we do things because some "external" force is nudging us to do so. We do it for money. We do it for our parents. We do it because we think "society" wants us to do it.

Now, none of those are bad reasons for doing anything, necessarily, but they're also not the kinds of motivation that garner the best results. They feel like "obligations"—and obligations only get us so far, certainly short of the 225 percent greater productivity that Bain & Company measured in inspired employees.

Obviously, most of what we do is driven by a mix of "intrinsic" and "extrinsic" motivations. *I do like my job, but if money weren't a factor, I wouldn't be doing it. I do love my children but, sometimes, I just need to power through the parenting and get to the chardonnay.* If, however, we can shift the balance of our motivation—from extrinsic to intrinsic, from external to internal—we'd increase our chances at both success and fulfillment. The more we exercise, for example, because we *want* to be fit—and not just because the doctor is telling us to lose twenty pounds—well, the more productive and enjoyable exercise time will become.

The ways in which motivations become "internal" is a great mystery indeed. Why do some of us love running—and others of us hate it? Why do some of us know we were born to open a bakery—and others of us still haven't found the job that seems to fit? Like Shakespeare said about greatness, some us are born runners or bakers; some of us become runners and bakers along the way; some of us have runners and bakers thrown upon us.

Inspiration is one way in which external motivations can become internal ones. We've all had the feeling of an inkling inside us growing and deepening into a real desire. I've always had a vague sense, for example, that I should quit my job and "do something good for the world"—but when I watch *Dead Poet's Society*, that vague sense becomes a clear calling: Ah, I want to teach high school literature! You don't really want to exercise and eat healthy, but when you see the face of your newborn granddaughter, you feel the drive to stay alive to see her grow. Yes, moments like these—seeing Robin Williams as John Keating awaken a *carpe-diem* zest in his students or holding your new granddaughter in your aging arms—these moments take mere extrinsic notions and transform them into real, intrinsic desires.

And sometimes, inspiration actually *creates* that desire. While it's very unlikely anybody can be inspired to do something they actually detest, inspiration often softens an initial resistance and births a new urge: as Bono did to me or Patton did to an army of soldiers who certainly didn't want to die on beaches in Normandy.

This is inspiration then: the creation or strengthening and deepening of an *intrinsic* motivation. This also helps us understand the role of a Muse: to create, strengthen, and deepen the intrinsic motivations of an audience—and thereby, help an audience *achieve* the great things that are the fruit of their strongest, most personal desires.

Joseph Campbell, the man who explained myths to the modern world, famously defined a hero as "somebody who has given his or her life to something bigger than oneself."[10] It's a criterion that stretches from Superman to Dorothy Day, from Harry Potter to John McCain and also includes the many "heroic" acts the rest of us sometimes commit, from the girl who stands up to the bully on the playground to the family that shares their beliefs on lawn signs, even when those beliefs might be unpopular in the neighborhood. These are obviously do-gooder examples, but heroes don't have to be so generous. The "bigger cause" can be an ego-driven one as well: money, power, or fame, for example. (Though, as we'll see, selfishness is ultimately an inspiration-killer.) Either way, heroes commit to a cause, an ambition greater than the preservation of their comfortable status quo. They risk what they have for something better.

As Campbell sees it in so many myths, heroes follow a remarkably similar journey. From Odysseus to Luke Skywalker, with knights and caped crusaders and bespeckled wizards thrown in the hero stew, these characters trace a path from being ordinary to accomplishing the improbable—and it generally (though not always) happens through the instigation or tutelage of another wise person, a Merlin or Yoda or Dumbledore. You can read about the rites of the hero journey in Campbell's classic book, *The Hero with a Thousand Faces*, but for our purposes, there are two stages of the hero's journey to study: "The Call To Adventure," which is the moment our hero is *called or asked* to do something, something important and uncomfortable; and "Crossing The Threshold," the moment our hero *commits* to the daring adventure and enters the treacherous world where both battles and glory await.[11]

This moment—this space in between being called to adventure and committing to that adventure—is the moment of inspiration. It's where the Muse works. In that space, you must transform your audience from skinny, lost orphans to indomitable crusaders; you must awaken the power *within* them. It's when extrinsic motivation becomes intrinsic motivation. It's when *your* desires become *their* desires.

In other words, inspiration makes heroes of us.

This simple chart helps illustrate the point:

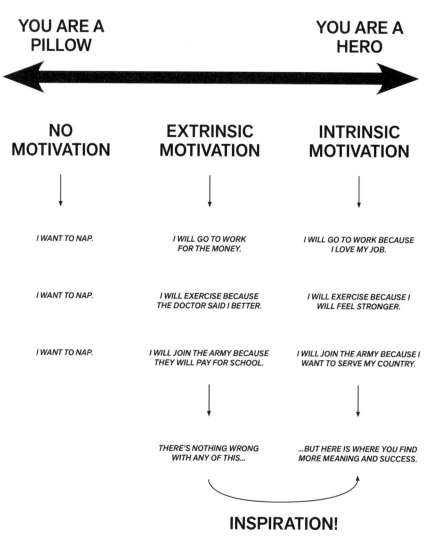

**YOU ARE A
PILLOW**

**YOU ARE A
HERO**

**NO
MOTIVATION**

**EXTRINSIC
MOTIVATION**

**INTRINSIC
MOTIVATION**

I WANT TO NAP.

*I WILL GO TO WORK
FOR THE MONEY.*

*I WILL GO TO WORK BECAUSE
I LOVE MY JOB.*

I WANT TO NAP.

*I WILL EXERCISE BECAUSE
THE DOCTOR SAID I BETTER.*

*I WILL EXERCISE BECAUSE I
WILL FEEL STRONGER.*

I WANT TO NAP.

*I WILL JOIN THE ARMY BECAUSE
THEY WILL PAY FOR SCHOOL.*

*I WILL JOIN THE ARMY BECAUSE I
WANT TO SERVE MY COUNTRY.*

*THERE'S NOTHING WRONG
WITH ANY OF THIS...*

*...BUT HERE IS WHERE YOU FIND
MORE MEANING AND SUCCESS.*

INSPIRATION!

*(THE MUSE CREATES AND STRENGTHENS
INTRINSIC MOTIVATION.)*

The rest of the book will be filled with lessons for helping you move people across that divide and, yes, they will involve some Dumbledore-level magic, but essentially, the Muse offers an audience the gift of conviction. The Muse stokes a sense of *agency* in an audience, an awakening to their powers: *You have the power to save the world. You have the power to colonize Mars. You have the power to run like lightning.* The refrain of the Muse, like Rob Schneider in Adam Sandler movies, is an emphatic, *"You can do it!"* Or as Barack Obama told his young supporters in 2008, *"We* are the ones we've been waiting for!" It's what my eighth-grade son's teacher did for him when she sent him a note sharing her conviction that he would crush his math final. To him, that seemed like a Delusional Ambition, one demanding the effort of the hero he wasn't sure was inside him, but a hero that she saw so clearly.

And when this conviction is given with passion, with intensity and instructions—which are the see-it-through tools that get the job done—inspiration ensues, heroes are made, and worlds are changed.

Chapter 3 Key Terms

Inspiration: (noun) Arousing a person's emotions to the point of action; not just a feel-good feeling, but a force that gets things done (*see also* inspiring: producing inspiration, an everybody skill).

The Inspiration Advantage: (noun) The extra-awesomeness that happens when a person is inspired; more focus, more determination, more winning; more happiness; use in a sentence: *Thanks to The Inspiration Advantage, I crushed my enemies and achieved my dreams.*

Hero-Making: (noun) One way of thinking about what a Muse does; by creating and strengthening *intrinsic* motivations, a Muse stokes a person's can-do conviction, helps them feel and use their superpowers (see: Dumbledore/Harry; Dorothy/Scarecrow; your favorite teacher/you).

Nonsense:
The Eye of the Thai Girl

Dum. (Pause.) Dum-dum-dum. Dum-dum-dum. Dum-dum-duuuum.
Those opening bars of Survivor's "Eye of The Tiger" still turn my hands into fists and make me want to run, run anywhere, harder and faster, punching the air all the way. As the band explained it, they timed those "slashing chords" to the punches in the climactic fight scene of Rocky III. Some musicians might be bothered by the slightly off-tempo beats as the song starts, but the rest of us don't mind at all. For us, it just works: guitars and fists and heartbeats and hope all seem to coalesce in those irrepressible notes.

But this perfect song almost wasn't.

Originally, Sylvester Stallone wanted to use Queen's "Another One Bites the Dust" to punctuate his hero's triumph, but when that band refused to grant their permission, Stallone sent his unfinished edit of the film to Survivor, asking them to replace Freddie Mercury's hit with an original composition. "Something with a pulse, something for the kids," he asked the band.[12] And that's exactly what he got. I remember seeing Rocky III as a ten-year-old and rushing home to box the neighborhood kids on our front lawn. I was blonde, so I was Drago, the Russian super-bruiser—but my heart was all-American tiger. That song became my spiritual soundtrack.

And not just me. If you grew up in the 1980s, that song was an anthem, a hymn to gritty resilience and the kind of determination that can't be stopped even by the whizz-bang slickness of Soviet science. And the song also seems to possess some sort of magic productivity power. Studies have shown, for example, that workers who listen to "Eye of the Tiger" before their shifts work harder and better. Now that's a song!

But the tune's massive and enduring popularity makes it all the more puzzling that the lyrics themselves are so often mangled. Go ahead, see if you can sing the refrain with the right words. Most people can't. The last known survivor is supposed to be stalking his prey in the night, but often, he's not. He stomps his way, starts to pray, starts to spray, soaks his bread, toasts his bread, starts to spread, smokes his bird. And, even though the name of the song is a strong clue, some people insist on singing "Ivan the Tiger" or "High with the Kaiser" or, bizarrely, something about a Thai Girl.

In fact, "Eye of the Tiger" is one of the most mondegreen-heavy songs of all time.

A mondegreen is the common phenomenon in which a listener mishears a lyric from a song and makes up an alternate set of words. We hear a garble, but our brain, insisting on finding meaning and creating clarity, proposes a set of words, even if those words are completely nonsensical in the context of the song itself. It's an unconscious process (like a Freudian slip in our ears); our brains, desperate to make sense out of nonsense, can't accept not knowing, not completing a lyric, and so Jimi Hendrix sings, "Excuse me while I kiss this guy," Madonna is living in a "Cheerio World," and in Toto's "Africa," Mt. Kilimanjaro rises above Estelle Getty. And speaking of sitcom stars, what exactly was Elton John thinking when crooned, "Hold me closer, Tony Danza?"

The amazing thing about mondegreens, however, is that no matter how nonsensical our invented lyrics become, they hardly ever change the *effect* of the song we're experiencing. Somehow, even in your muddled jumble of lyrics, you still "get" the idea or the feeling of the song. Even as you sing about Ivan the tiger smoking his bird in the night, you feel that song's sense of ferocious determination. As you sing about the kaiser who toasts his bread in the night, you still run harder and faster on that treadmill. None of the word-nonsense seems to matter. None of the butchering of the lyrics affects this song's ability to rouse our spirit.

Why is that? In the case of "Eye of the Tiger," is it the propulsive beat? Is it the other lyrics you do understand? Is it the movie, the association with Rocky Balboa, the quintessential underdog with the never-quit spirit and the knock-out hook?

Yes, it is. It's all of those things. This song, like all songs, is the sum of many parts that create a particular mood: sounds, tempos, and tones all create vibrations that make their way through the air, to your ear, and into your brain where they trigger the release of chemicals like oxytocin and dopamine, chemicals that genuinely alter our mood, causing us to be more aroused or relaxed, for example. These musical vibrations also work on our heart, the literal one: fast beats increase the speed of our heartbeats; slow beats slow them down. Some of the "sensations" in songs have literal meaning: they are words that tell stories, that connect to your own memories and experiences. But even these literal nuggets of meaning within a song take on an emotion-stirring quality based upon how they're sung. When Whitney Houston belts out "I Will Always Love You," it sounds like the firm promise of a lover as she leaves the man who adores her; but when Dolly Parton sang those very same words in her original recording, I hear something very different: I hear pity. "I Will Always Love You" sounds less like a promise and more like a kindness, like the tonic she thinks her man needs as she smashes his heart. The very same words, but very different sounds—and in matters of music, sounds win. That's why "Eye of the Tiger" "works" even when you don't know the words themselves; the song sounds like determination. Like "Yesterday" sounds like regret. Like "In Da Club" sounds like a party. Like "Shape of You" sounds like sex. There are so many factors that make all of this so but, in the mental temple of our brain, the Music Muse sorts it out with ease and elegance. And she does so because Miles Davis is right: the notes—the lyrics, the beats, the technical aspects of music-making—are a small part of the magic; attitude is everything.

CHAPTER 4

Beware the Muses

"There is a muse, but he's not going to come fluttering down into your writing room and scatter creative fairy-dust all over your typewriter or computer. He lives in the ground. He's a basement kind of guy. You have to descend to his level, and once you get down there you have to furnish an apartment for him to live in. You have to do all the grunt labor, in other words, while the muse sits and smokes cigars and admires his bowling trophies and pretends to ignore you. Do you think it's fair?"

—STEPHEN KING

The Muses aren't sweet singing spirits. They're a pain in the ass. They toss us and turn us—and yet, somehow, leave us better than they found us.

The Irresistible Pull of Passion

"Being a fan, like being in love, is giddying, it's as personal as skin, it connects you with others in a particular way, and it sets you up for a fall.... 'Fan' as a label is a slur on your critical objectivity and even your maturity, but if you weren't a fan of something or someone, wouldn't life be a little bland?"

—DAVID MITCHELL[1]

Think about the people with whom you've fallen in love. And maybe it's a romantic love, but it doesn't have to be. Think about the people to whom you've developed a powerful attachment. You care about them in a deep and personal way. Maybe they're friends you see all the time, maybe they're superstars you only see on TV. But, in some way, you love them. You root for them. You're on their side.

Now see if you can isolate *the moment* when it happened, when your heart first stirred. Of course, we fall in love for a variety of reasons—hormones, geography, shared experiences, childhood preferences, and a host of mysteries that would take a lifetime of therapy to identify—and maybe it was a Cupid's-arrow moment across a crowded room. But most likely it was during a moment in which she or he was expressing their *passion* for something in particular. They were telling you about something or somebody they loved: a book, a movie, a parent, a food, a memory from childhood, or a fantastic vacation. Maybe they were sharing a desire or a dream. Or maybe you *saw* them expressing their passion: the *way* they sing on stage, the *way* they cook, the *way* they dance or laugh or tell stories, the *way* they play. Listen to a kid describing what he wants for a birthday or a friend telling you about his new boyfriend. They're besotted. Their words come more quickly. Their gestures are more animated. If you could measure their pulse, you'd see their heart rate is literally elevated.

Passion definitely has many looks—but all of them are intense. Steely resolve, quiet determination, manic enthusiasm, and sometimes a state that seems like a spiritual possession. It can be hoots and cheers and painted faces at a football game. Or sometimes passion is deeper, a quiet intensity, like a sprinter crouched in the starting blocks or somebody praying, really praying, as if their soul literally depends upon it.

And maybe, when you see somebody express their passion, their passion "matches" your passion. You both love *Les Misérables* and goat cheese ravioli. It's kismet. You've found your ravioli-loving soul mate and you're off to your castle in the clouds.

But not always. Sometimes we fall for people who are expressing a passion that *doesn't* so neatly match our own and, yet, somehow, we still find them irresistible. They're gaga for sushi or heavy metal or soap operas—and that gaga-*ness* is infectious. They're doing their thing—and we're pulled along for the wild ride. Why? How does that work?

Well, passion is always emotional, for sure, but it's an emotion about *longing for* something or somebody. Happy and sad are states of *being*, but passion is a state of *wanting*. It's desiring, craving, all forward momentum. And, in its wanting, passion shows its convictions, its beliefs. Behind every passion is an implied point of view: this thing I desire is desire-worthy.

But that's debatable, of course. Passions are, at heart, opinions—and opinions can be argued. Maybe *Les Mis* sucks. Maybe goat cheese is gross. Maybe Tarantino is better than Scorsese. Maybe he's ugly. Maybe you're an idiot.

This *maybe-ness* of passion might be exactly what makes it so irresistible, so captivating. The passionate person is both confident and vulnerable, so sure of their own perspective and quite possibly, foolish. It's like they're walking fast on a tightrope—so full of certainty and so totally exposed.

And sometimes, the passionate person is downright pained. You sometimes hear people refer to the *"Passion* of Christ" when they're talking about Jesus's torture and crucifixion. The Latin root of the word passion is *pati*, a verb that means "to suffer," which passion sometimes feels like. Have you seen a teen in unrequited love? Have you *been* a teen in unrequited love? Have you seen a Jets fan in January? Indeed, longing and suffering are bedfellows.

So passion is a hot emotional mess. It's desire, determination, confidence, vulnerability, and, now and then, pain. Real passion is a person splaying themselves open before you.

And how do we react in those situations, those moments in which we're trusted with a heart's confession of its radically pure passion?

Well, it's awkward. At first. We're disorientated. We're not used to such raw expressions of feeling. But generally, that disorientation lasts for only a little time. As humans, we've evolved to be an *empathetic* species and, when somebody opens themselves up in front of us, we lean in, and mostly, with kindness. We engage. We fall forward and, sometimes, we fall in love. We follow.

Passion stokes empathy. And empathy creates connection.

When you express yourself with passion, you're *literally* building a team. Passion is *the primary energy* the Muse must summon. And then comes the strange part.

Out On a Hillside

When you close your eyes and imagine Muses, you likely think of spirits who travel on the wind, showing up with a flourish to inspire artists, to crush writer's block and make masterpieces. Muses, we believe, unstick creativity. For centuries, artists have prayed to these spirits, desperate for the touch of inspiration they might bring. Shakespeare himself wished "for a muse of fire that would ascend the brightest heaven of invention" and, even today, Taylor Swift credits her love song hits to the man who had been her "Muse" for one hot summer, the strapping actor Tom Hiddleston. Artists have always turned to the otherworldly, the beautiful, the better-than-human, for the inspiration they can't seem to find within themselves.

71

MODERN MUSE—NIKE: PASSION BEATS PRODUCTS

If you work in marketing, you're forbidden from using Nike as an example of any-thing great. Almost all of the experts would agree that the brand born in Portland is, in fact, the very greatest marketer of all time, but it's exactly that consensus which makes eyes roll when anybody says, *"Well, Nike..."* They're the George Washington of advertising: so good that most folks feel they're in a class by themselves with very little to teach the rest of us mere mortals.

But I disagree. Nike is referenced so much because they *are* the greatest marketer of all time. Unlike Apple, who has invented whizz-bang products, or McDonald's, whose secret sauce is the automation of their supply chain, Nike's success can *all* be chalked up to their marketing—the advertising, promotions, partnerships, and experiences they've created to stoke desire for their sneakers. *That* marketing has created a company valued at more than $100 billion.

So what, then, is the secret of their marketing success?

Nike has never tried to argue anybody into believing their shoes were better made than any other athletic shoes; no, they've used their hundreds of millions of dollars to do the almost impossible: inspire people to play sports, to exercise, to move from the sofa, to *Just Do It*. And they've done it with a preponderance of passion. They use their marketing to show us how much they love athletes and the sports they play.

According to Mark Fitzloff, who was Chief Creative Officer at Nike's long-time ad agency, Wieden+Kennedy, "Nike always knew the athletes were their product. The ground-breaking move was in building those characters: The Jordan Character. The Tiger Character." He explained to me that, in their mar-keting, they were certainly "trying to move people to feel the chills, to feel tears of joy, to feel the triumph of the human spirit," and that they did so by celebrating the *adversity* even, especially, the greatest athletes face. "Every Nike story is a story about overcoming imperfection. It's not about perfection at all." [2]

So Nike has shown us Michael Jordan and Tiger Woods not only break-ing the bonds of physics, but struggling with late-career comebacks. They've shown us Lance Armstrong on his bike fighting back at cancer and shame. They've shown us tubby tweens jogging down endless roads, taking one step after another in search of their own greatness. And yes, they've shown us how athletes like Serena Williams or Colin Kaepernick can use their perch to inspire change away from the arena, even when popular opinion might be against him.

And as you see the world through Nike's eyes, as you see their genuine empathy for real athletes who struggle and succeed, something very magical

begins to happen in your brain: you start to believe that a company that loves athletes that much would never make crummy shoes for athletes; that a company
that loves sports that much will always serve those sports with their very best
effort. By sharing their passion for sports, Nike leads us to believe they make
great products. The opposite approach—the dominant approach in the needy
world of marketing—is all chest-thumping claims of greatness that, ironically,
only engender skepticism. Where other brands protest so damn much, Nike
protests not at all: they just share their passion. In fact, they are the greatest marketer of all time because they are the most passionate marketer of all time. Nike
isn't just a goddess; she's a Muse as well—all passion, no reasons.

All that lyrical Muse-worship might fool you into thinking the
Muses, like fairies, are a sweet crew who swan into your life and charm
you with songs that set you on your way to doing great things.

You'd be wrong.

Muses, like fairies, are trouble-causing badasses.

The very first mention of the Muses comes from a guy named
Hesiod, an old poet who lived in Greece around the time of Homer
about three thousand years ago. You probably haven't heard as much
about Hesiod as you have about Homer—but you definitely know his
best stories. He wrote *Theogony*, which is a collection of the origin
stories of the Greek gods, the stories that explain the creation of the
world and introduce us to Zeus and the other Olympians who would
rattle the affairs of humanity forever. These are the stories of lust and
revenge and feuding divinities that have entertained and educated
audiences for centuries. They are the enduring myths of western civilization. And Hesiod told them first. Without Hesiod, no Shakespeare,
no Harry Potter, no *House of Cards*.

In the very opening scene of *Theogony*, Hesiod tells the tale of the
night he *learned* those stories. I'm warning you: it's a horror story. [3]

Hesiod is a young shepherd, cranky, poor, and unsure of his
place in the world. He's tending his family's sheep in the foothills of
a deserted mountain range in the middle of a cold, misty night. *He's
tending sheep all alone in the middle of the misty night!* And there,

under the stars, in a clearing, he comes upon nine strange and beautiful spirits—sexy nymphs, in fact, who are bathing. They're naked and laughing and singing.

This could be very, very good, Hesiod imagines as his teenage body swells with excitement.

But it's not.

Clio is the spirit who seems to be in charge of the others. She spots Hesiod first and steps closer, closer still, now circling him, and with each circle, moving closer and closer until she's close enough to whisper in a voice so low it almost sounded like the breeze, "*You... piece...of...shit. You poor, pathetic boy. You dirty peasant who has to dig and kill for his food.*" She was quiet and ferocious. (Okay, she doesn't actually call him a piece of shit, but the original Greek is close and just as insulting: "Shepherds that camp in the wild, disgraces, mere bellies."[4])

Any arousal Hesiod felt is quickly dampened. He's afraid now, terrified by what this strong, strange woman and her sister-spirits might do to him. This is the moment Hesiod should politely moonwalk away. But he can't. He's captivated.

And here's what Clio and her sisters do next: they breathe. They breathe on him, around him, in him. This is the breath of inspiration. In an instant, they give him his songs, his stories, stories about how it all began and where it all could go, stories about people filled with lust and rage and ambition, people who set off to foreign lands and create new civilizations and those who undo those civilizations through their petty jealousies and pricked feelings. These are tales of love and ego and war and kids killing their rotten parents and parents killing their children to spite their ex-lovers. These are stories of nations battling because rulers had no choice and countries warring because they made the wrong choices. These are the stories of Clio and her sisters and their family and friends from God-knows-where—but they're also stories that are mysteriously familiar to Hesiod. He has never heard them, but he *knows* them, as if they'd been trapped inside his head forever just waiting for his voice to find the words to set them free. At that moment, as he later writes, he feels full. He has all that he ever needed.

But the Muses bestow this gift with one utterly bizarre warning. They tell Hesiod, "We know how to say many lies like they are the truth, and whenever we wish, we know how to tell the truth." Remember, Clio continues, our mother is the goddess of memory. Our power is that we can help you remember and we can make you forget.

The Muse helps you remember and makes you forget, blurring the distinction between truth and lies.

Wait, what? Everything you just told me might be a lie? Or it might be true? Or it might be part-lie and part-truth? And you'll help me remember some things but you'll make me forget others? WTF? WTF, Muses?

And then Hesiod is alone with his memories that might be true or might be false.

Remember how you feel when you're inspired: like you can accomplish anything, even the most grand and delusional things. In fact, they seem not only likely, but easy. You can *see* yourself finishing the marathon, opening the restaurant, giving the victory speech.

But are those truths—things that can be, that will be—or are they lies, fictions cooked up by our imaginations to help us feel good?

When Bono dreams he can eradicate malaria, is it a truth or a lie? When you feel like you can accomplish anything, is it a truth or a lie?

Muses tell us things that *sound like* lies. We probably *can't* run a mile in less than four minutes. We probably *can't* land a man on the moon in the course of this decade. We probably *can't* organize all the world's information on one single website. Lies. But the Muse makes those lies *sound* like truths, like they just *might* be possible.

Yes, according to the mythology, the mother of the Muses is indeed Memory. And memory has a slippery relationship with inspiration. On the one hand, memory is a stumbling block to courage. We remember our limitations. We remember the low odds of success. We remember the people who depend upon us to be reliable and reasonable. We remember all this—and we pause. But memory also gives us proof that great things *might* occur. There are stories of heroes and examples of pioneers. There are the residual feelings of being young and free and capable of anything, everything. *These* we remember—and we leap.

The Muses know which memories to suppress and which to awake. They know what we should forget and what we must remember.

But what exactly is it that the Muses help us forget?

Reality, I think. The laws of what is likely.

Think about your own experiences of inspiration. We've all felt it: coaches, teachers, athletes, books and movies, and, occasionally, a preacher or politician have roused our emotions and changed the course of our lives. What's happening in those moments of magic?

We feel conviction, for sure—the belief that we are capable of doing something—and the feeling of commitment to achieving it. By nature, though, *the thing*—the starting a business or making a free throw or giving up drugs or writing a screenplay—is special, is extraordinary. After all, nobody is really "inspired" to brush her teeth or eat his bowl of cereal.

So the Muses help us forget our limits, our limitations, the likely outcomes. They chase away the reasonable, rational voice that whispers, *"You can't do that!"* and replace it with a siren-like, *"You can do anything!"*

The first act of inspiration, then, is to erase doubt—right at the moment it instills belief. The Muse makes us feel like we can accomplish what all of our reasonable instincts say is just too far out of reach.

And there's a word for that phenomenon, for that refusal to accept the limiting truth of reality: delusion.

That's right: the Muse makes you delusional.

The Muse makes you believe you can accomplish things that your reasonable brain suggests are just too hard, just too far out of reach. And the Muse does that by disorienting you in a frenzy of feelings. When Clio calls Hesiod a "piece of shit," it's a disorienting upper-cut to his brain—a surprise, a shock—that resets the rules and clears the way for new possibilities, for any and every possibility.

You certainly don't have to curse and insult to inspire your audience, but you do need to show up in a way that surprises, that breaks the plane of the perfect picture. Lin-Manuel Miranda recast our image of Hamilton as a Latino hip-hop artist. Coaches ask players to "take a knee." Managers lower their voices and say, "Shut the door and sit down, please." Rock bands wrap their audience in total darkness before taking the stage. Patton stood before the troops the day before the invasion of Normandy in an oddball uniform with the filthiest mouth. All of these are acts—tactics, even—to re-set a scene and alter the expectations of your audience. We're going to explore a wide variety of techniques you could employ to do just that but, for now, know that The Muses show up to stir up some trouble. Inspiration isn't a pretty business. It's messy and passionate, and it needs to be, because it's trying to move that giant heart in our head.

LESSONS FROM THE ORIGINAL (GANGSTA) MUSES

1. **Make an Entrance.** Clio and her freaky sisters sprung themselves on Hesiod in the middle of the night. Muses make dramatic entrances, the kind that signal the "ordinary" course of events is about to get interesting. Think about how you enter a situation in which you want to inspire—a conference room, a classroom, a family meal—and find ways to surprise your audience. What you wear, where you sit, the language you choose are all tools that will help. What rules do you want to break or expectations do you want to defy? Are you a manager who should sit at the head of the conference table? Don't. Are you a preacher who shouldn't ever drop an f-bomb? Think again. Are you a coach who wears a suit—or a coach who suits up with the rest of the team? We'll explore more techniques that'll help you "Show Up To Stir Up" in Chapter 7 but, for now, know that the only "wrong" way to show up is the one that's totally expected.

2. **Keep Them Guessing.** The fundamental, totally transparent promise of the Muses is that you'll never know if they're telling the truth or lying their ethereal asses off. This does not mean that modern muses should purposefully dissemble, making up facts and statistics. No. It does mean that we should tell stories that capture the imagination of our audience, stories with *just enough* mystery and delusion to get people wondering. That's the beauty of stories—of myths!—after all; they are truthful at the core but fantastical in their spinning. In Chapter 6, we'll look at how our ambitions themselves can "Get Delusional" in a way that plants powerful "question marks" in the minds of our audience. Is that possible? Can we really do it? When these are the questions your audience is asking, you're on to something big.

3. **Be Divine.** The Muses never once forget where they came from: Mt. Olympus. They are goddesses. They have the power and all the swagger that comes with it. It's become fashionable these days to talk about "servant" leadership—the kind of leading that prioritizes serving the needs of the team. That's fine, but not when the leader actually forgets to lead, forgets that she has something to impart that is more valuable than what already exists. The Modern Muse knows she's been to Olympus, knows she has something worth telling—and dammit, with swagger and power, makes sure the audience is riveted.

The Inspiration Equation

It's not easy, but it's effective. The Muse arouses the emotions of others by expressing a profound passion in a way that breaks the stranglehold of reason.

And I hope you're seeing how it works. When we express our passion, we stoke empathy and create connections. Passion builds bonds. And then, when just a little bit of the ordinary rules of reason are extracted from a situation, great possibilities blossom. The hard things become easier, conviction grows, and commitment plunges our team ahead.

Now, to be clear, I'm not suggesting that the Muse is incoherent or strips *all* reason from her communications. No, that would be nonsense (which is only *sometimes* inspiring). But the Muse does need to extract some logic from her communications to slip around an audience's "analytical stance" that's waiting to pounce with an argument.

But the problem with this equation, I have to confess, is that it makes it seem like inspiration is some sort of two-step process: *First,* express passion. *Next,* get weird. And poof, out pops an inspired crew.

Not exactly. Like almost everything we're discussing, it's stranger than that. Inspiring is *simultaneously* passionate and unreasonable, *simultaneously* full of conviction and delusion.

The Inspiration Equation:

PASSION – REASON = INSPIRATION

When Thoughts Become Feelings

Growing up, I had never really been a sports fan, but I did, late in my twenties, fall hard for Roger Federer. He was the first athlete I ever really loved. I loved watching him play. I loved talking about his skills. I wanted him to win every single time he stepped on the court.

And I think what I loved about Federer was the *perfection* of his tennis playing—each shot, each step, was elegant, beautiful. Commentators like John McEnroe can only reach for metaphors and similes—poetic devices—to describe the way he moves across the court: *Like a tiger. Like a wizard. Like he's floating.* The greatest tennis player of all time seems to break the rational rules of physics, distorts the space-time continuum as he flies after a ball to one-hand, back-hand it across the net at an impossible-to-return angle. To me, this was art, so different from the sweaty muscle sport Rafael Nadal was playing.

In the many moments ESPN replays a blazing Federer forehand in slow motion, you can see how he follows the textbook-taught formula for "proper" hitting: he keeps his head down; he watches the racquet hit the ball; he follows through; and he does it all with steady, solid feet beneath him. It's a perfect display of "proper" technique. Pros and coaches would be proud. It's rational.

And yet, of course, that's not the source of his genius. Atop that functional tennis machinery, Federer adds art. It's hard to spot: the unusual flick of the wrist on the backhand; the three-step charge when hitting a service return; but then, something else, something ineffable. Like Mozart, at some point, a different spirit, a divine spirit, the breath of God, seems to animate Roger Federer. That's his genius. He manages to transcend the physics of his sport.

Or, heck, if you think I'm insane, look at any great athlete in any sport. Messi, Manning, Muhammad Ali, Michael Jordan. They do things that no one should have the ability to do. Children and many a weekend warrior watch what they do and imagine they might do it themselves, but they can't.

Many enthusiasts have studied the "10,000-Hour Rule" that Malcolm Gladwell introduced us to in *Outliers*, the theory that achieving excellence in any endeavor requires ten thousand hours of "deliberate practice"—ten thousand hours of hitting serves or baking cakes. And, although some critics have challenged its veracity, nobody really impeaches the notion that mastering a skill of any sort requires a great deal of practice, perhaps on the back of some natural talent. But what does that practice really help you achieve? What does ten thousand hours of practicing guitar or performing surgery or public speaking really accomplish?

The opportunity to do it with feeling, with passion.

When the rote mechanics of an act are so ingrained that they become as second-nature as breathing, you're freed not to focus on those mechanics, to let yourself go, to swing, to sing, to commit.

The late novelist David Foster Wallace wrote an essay that's become a prayer book for me. In "Roger Federer as Religious Experience," he describes the transformation that happens from so much perfect practice:

Hitting thousands of strokes, day after day, develops the ability to do by 'feel' what cannot be done by regular conscious thought. Repetitive practice like this often looks tedious or even cruel to an outsider, but the outsider can't feel what's going on inside the player—tiny adjustments, over and over, and a sense of each change's effects that gets more and more acute even as it recedes from normal consciousness.[5]

In a footnote, Foster Wallace describes this journey from careful practice to *unconscious* genius as being "like a thought that's also a feeling."[6]

Antonio Damasio would like the image: no left brain or right brain, just a brain where thoughts and feelings make beautiful things. Roger Federer is unreasonable passion incarnate, passion which, at points, leaves its reason behind and soars a little higher than the laws of physics should allow.

Inspired artists talk about flow, a state of working that is effortless because you're so deeply plugged into the action itself. They describe being "lost" in their work,

A thought that's also a feeling.

the moment in which it doesn't feel like work at all, just a self-sustaining cycle of positive, productive energy. "They couldn't do anything wrong if they tried," goes the obviously false *and* totally true cliché.

Have you ever witnessed somebody in that moment of flow? Have you ever seen an actor lose herself in a character? Have you seen a child sit for hours playing make-believe with cars or dolls? It's like seeing somebody sing, with feeling, in a way that slips you from the surly bonds of your sticky arena chair and deposits you somewhere strange and far away.

Witnessing flow, witnessing mechanical perfection performed with deep feeling is transportive. It's inspiring.

But, of course, Federer and Streep and Obama and Yo-Yo Ma are passion that lives atop perfection, the kind that is the privilege of those who have *mastered* their art. The kind of passion in the realm for the rest of us mere mortals, however, is the passion of striving, of desire.

When you talk about something you want, something you really, really want, you start to break the bonds of mere logic. Your voice changes. Your gestures become more animated. And all of those characteristics—the voice, the tempo, the urgency, the enthusiasm—conspire to create a connection with our audience. You become beautiful, as beautiful as Roger Federer playing tennis or Adele lost in a spotlight.

But, of course, this isn't just a phenomenon that happens with words. Once, at the gym, I saw an incredibly obese man running on the treadmill—breathing hard, dripping sweat, all to the point where I worried what might happen to him. This was him expressing his passion—living his desire—to lose weight, to be healthy, to prove naysayers wrong, to achieve some sort of goal that was present in his heart. Words weren't necessary: he wore his passion on his huffing body.

That's inspiration: sharing your passion, with words, with your whole being; on top of perfection or in spite of imperfection.

The Muse flies on the wings of crazy wanting.

MEET THE REASONABLES

The Reasonables are an ancient species that are everything the Muses aren't: clear, logical, straightforward, and dull. The Reasonables trade in numbers by day, not songs by night. You find them everywhere you find civilized society. They're smart and reasonable. They trust reality. They tend to be organized and unfailingly polite. They're—well, logical.

And lest we begin to stereotype them as droopy dogs, The Reasonables have certainly done great things for the world. Isaac Newton, George Washington, Bill Gates—all members of The Reasonables. And so, too, are most of the CEOs who have run *Fortune* 500 companies, as well as the tens of thousands of managers and executives who report to them.

It's an age-old tension between the Muses and The Reasonables, between the voices that point us toward heaven and those that remind us of gravity. It's a battle that likely rages within each of us as well—System 1 versus System 2, *"Yes I can!"* versus *"Wait one second."*

And for much of the course of human history, The Reasonables have been in charge. They are the corporate climbers and bureaucrats. They are the steady-as-you-go establishment. They are dads who tell their kids to work hard and choose a sensible major in college that'll prepare them for the "real" world. They are the musty teachers in *Dead Poet's Society*, telling Robin Williams's Muse-like Professor John Keating to get a grip and behave himself.

In fact, so many of the stories we love are stories of the epic clash between the Muses and The Reasonables. Rudy's father who tells him he'll never play football at Notre Dame and, in fact, he doesn't even belong at such a place. Aaron Burr who tells Lin-Manuel Miranda's Hamilton to keep quiet and be charming. The wizened political wizards who tell Barack Obama to wait his turn. The Muses consort with the underdogs and the brave hearts.

And that can't be an accident of evolutionary biology. There must be a reason that, every time the Muses clash with The Reasonables, we take the side of inspiration.

The accumulating evidence shows the Muses have the upper hand, at least in the world of commerce. Jim Stengel, the former marketing leader of Procter & Gamble—a very logical company, mind you—studied more than a thousand businesses across every conceivable company and came to a very definitive conclusion: companies that lead with emotion outperform the rest of the market.[7]

"Muses Win" is a story of styles we see play out in so many industries today: Jeff Bezos at Amazon beats Walmart. John Mackey at Whole Foods beats big food companies like General Mills and Kraft. Reed Hastings and the wizards at Netflix beat every television executive around. Certainly, Bezos and Mackey and Hastings and, heck, Elon Musk are smart, sharp, informed, and astute—but they have a facility their competitors don't have: they're each slightly unreasonable. They've "forgotten" the rules of their respective industries and inspire their teams with possibilities that, at one point, sounded awfully crazy: *What if everything we wanted could be delivered to a home? What if food weren't processed? What if we could watch what we want when we want to? What if no cars needed gasoline?*

And this dreamy ambition isn't just limited to the world of business. Coaches like Duke's Coach K (a thousand wins!) and religious leaders like Pope Francis who employ emotion get better results from their teams and congregations. Even parents. Recent studies show that when a parent appeals to love, not logic, they're more likely to get their kids through difficult situations.

The Muses, it seems, have a competitive advantage. They have unreasonable passion.

Chapter 4 Key Terms

Clio: (proper noun) The leader of The Muses; a fierce spirit; her super-power: blurring the distinction between what's real and not real, what's possible and impossible; also known as: delusion-maker.

The Reasonables: (proper noun) The logical, reasonable, analytical, feeling-fearing folk who are the eternal enemies of the Muses; they're not bad people, they're just sad people.

Choose Your Own Adventure

If all of this is feeling a little fluffy to you, and you're aching for some hard, scientific proof (including a story about monkeys, ham, peanuts, and watching sports in silence), turn to Chapter 5 on page 88.

If, however, you're all good and roaring to get practical, turn to page 99 and let's get cracking on the **Six Skills of Inspiration**.

Science!

"The face is the mirror of the mind,
and eyes without speaking
confess the secrets of the heart."

—ST. JEROME

Mirror neurons are the mechanism in our brain that help us learn by replicating—"mirroring"—what we witness. And news flash: mirror neurons don't just mirror actions; they mirror emotions. They transmit empathy. They are the pathways of inspiration.

But wait, cutting-edge science is also proving what we've been discussing: reason, analysis, and logic "smudge the mirror." They're inspiration-killers.

Science, Not Shrines

What exactly, biologically, did Bono do to me on that fateful night in East Rutherford? I know he aroused my emotions, but what does that actually mean, scientifically speaking? What actually happens to a person's body and brain when the Muses show up and work their Muse-magic?

I was raised Roman Catholic, baptized in the same Greenwich Village church where my parents were married and although, in my childhood, masses were no longer spoken in Latin, the Church was still a place of profound mystery for me, a place where spirts and saints would come and go, giving us what we wanted, if we were worthy. And so we prayed, we prayed for life after death and an Atari under the Christmas tree.

By fourth grade, I had become an altar boy, a rather devout one who made a shrine to the Virgin Mary in my bedroom using some of my mother's Tupperware and pebbles I found in the driveway. This makeshift chapel was the focus of all my longing before I hit puberty. Any feeling I had, I shared with Our Lady of The Tupperware Grotto. I confessed my sins, but I also shared my hopes. I'd pray to be better at baseball, to be a better break dancer, and also for my parents and my brother, for our health and for the money that we needed. And I prayed for these things with the firm conviction that a divine spirit would indeed swoop from the heavens and deliver my dreams.

Perhaps it's this lingering faith in supernatural spirits that keeps me clinging to the hope that inspiration is a heaven-sent mystery. It feels good to believe in magic, and it's certainly much more dramatic when we do: just close your eyes and pray for Clio to appear. Cross your arms and pray for Bono to make you a believer. Maybe, maybe nudge the spirts along by reading some poems or watching *Rocky* or summitting a mountain at sunset and soaking in the grandeur of it all. But ultimately, the strategy to being inspired remains: be open and be patient.

I think this is what some people mean when they say that inspiration is inherently "beyond control." It's a force we're lucky to feel when the Muses deem us worthy.

But, alas, science has a way of complicating our myths and, in matters of inspiration, the professors have been putting puzzle pieces on the table at a furious rate these past few years. Let's see if we can arrange them in a way that begins to make *neurological* sense of what happens in those magic moments when it feels like spirits are working on our spirit.

A Monkey-Inspired Model of Inspiration

Dr. Giacomo Rizzolatti looks a lot Einstein, which might just be a fantasy for many male scientists. He has unruly wisps of white hair and doesn't seem too bothered by his tailoring. He flashes the kind of grin that suggests he has a giddy delight in discovering the mysterious workings of the human mind and, in the early 1990s, Dr. Rizzolatti and his team at The University of Parma did, in fact, discover a group of neurons in the mammalian brain that might just be the key to unlocking how inspiration works.[1]

And it was an accident.

The scientists were looking for the specific neurons in a monkey's brain that linked to the monkey's hand movement. If they could figure out exactly which neurons controlled grabbing and grasping, they might be able to develop treatments for *people* who had lost the ability to control their hands. This approach held great promise for curing all sorts of muscular maladies: if scientists could isolate the exact neuron that controls grasping, they'd also be able to isolate the neurons that control walking, for example.

By Dr. Rizzolatti's admission, they were using a very "informal process." They hooked up the monkeys to *fMRI* machines—brain-mapping machines—that would display exactly which parts of the monkeys' brains would be activated as they performed a variety of movements. They would then offer peanuts to the monkeys and watch electrical currents ripple through their minds while they grasped the treat. By doing this, Dr. Rizzolatti and his team were able to identify the exact neuron in the pre-motor cortex that was activated every time a monkey grabbed a peanut: the F5 neuron. That F5 neuron, it seemed, was the neuron that helped our hands grab and grasp. A monkey grabs a peanut, F5 lights up. A man grabs a slice of cake, F5 lights up. Clear, simple, and useful science.

But, one day, the clear and simple science became infinitely odder.

Some of the scientists on Dr. Rizzolatti's team were eating lunch, but they were doing so in the laboratory, steps away from the monkeys, still hooked up to the mind-mapping *fMRI* machines. This was Parma, so there was likely ham and cheese involved in the meal, but there were also peanuts. As the story goes, the team, in fact, dipped into the same stash they were using for the monkeys and, as they did so—as *the scientists* reached for the peanuts and grabbed a handful—they were startled by the beeps behind them. The *fMRI* machines whirred alive. To the astonishment of the researchers, the monkeys' F5 neurons were firing—even though none of those monkeys were grabbing or grasping a single peanut.

This made no sense, especially to scientists who believed that each of the millions of neurons in a mammalian brain performed a unique function. The neuron that fires when you grab a peanut should *not* be firing when you *witness* somebody else grab a peanut. One is doing. The other is seeing.

And yet that's exactly what had occurred. And it occurred again and again with experiment after experiment. As Dr. Rizzolatti explained, they had discovered neurons which "fire both when the monkey does something specific and when the monkey observes something of the same kind done by an individual."[2] From a neurological perspective, seeing and doing were starting to look like the very same thing.

Scientifically, this is a bizarre occurrence, but when we think about the experience of our own lives, it becomes more familiar. How many times have we watched sports, for example, and felt our bodies twitch with the movement of the athletes. We see a team jump off the bench to celebrate a goal and our body lurches off the couch as well. How many times have we seen somebody cry and felt a swell of sadness ourselves? In our lives, we've felt the connection between what we see and what we feel and what we do, but here in Parma, Italy was scientific proof of that mysterious chain of stimulation.

Dr. Rizzolatti called these neurons "mirror neurons"—because they copy or "mirror" the action we see another person perform even when we are not performing that action ourselves. And it's no exaggeration to say that, over the past twenty years, mirror neurons have helped scientists explain so much of how our mind works.

Mirror neurons play a critical role in helping us learn, for example, by *watching* what another person does. A baby sees her mother mouthing a word, her own mirror neurons fire, and, eventually, she copies that mouth movement. A kid sees a basketball player shoot free throws, his own mirror neurons fire and, eventually, he copies those body movements. This is why most discussions of mirror neurons inevitably include the phrase "monkey see, monkey do." It's ridiculous, but true: our brains "do" what we witness, even if our bodies don't budge.

For our purposes, however—and without making this an elaborate science lesson—there is one aspect to mirror neurons that might have great relevance to inspiration: mirror neurons mirror emotions, not just actions.

Through fascinating studies, including some with autistic children (who, according to one theory, have impaired mirror neurons that make it difficult for them to understand and mimic others), scientists have demonstrated that mirror neurons don't just mirror actions; they also mirror feelings. Simply witnessing the *emotional expressions* of another person triggers those same emotions in us. This explains why we feel sad when we see somebody else cry or we smile when we see somebody laugh, regardless of our baseline feelings. It also explains how performance works: when we see Jennifer Lawrence heartbroken, we feel heartbroken as well, and, yes, when we see Bono enraged and indignant, we, too, feel enraged and indignant.

Dr. Rizzolatti explains that there's a "mirror mechanism embedded inside our emotional centers," and he uses a fun, gross example to explain it: When we see somebody smell rotten eggs and make a face of disgust, our very same mirror neurons are activated as when we actually smell rotten eggs. Smelling rotten eggs and seeing somebody make a face *like* they're smelling rotten eggs generate the same response in our brain—and the same scrunched-up nose on our face.[3]

Now the implications of this biology get pretty cosmic. Mirror neurons are the mind's instrument for "putting ourselves in the shoes of another person," explains Dr. V. S. Ramachandran (TED talk superstar), which is why he calls mirror neurons "Gandhi Neurons."[4] He argues that they dissolve the barriers between people and help us share each other's most intimate sensations. He identifies mirror neurons as the key to human empathy and, hence, the driver of human civilization itself. From monkeys stoked to see their doctors eat peanuts, mirror neurons have now become the biological basis for human relationships, the pathway for our passions.

Or think about it this way: mirror neurons are the "heart" of our brain, the place where we feel our emotions.

In fairness, the study of mirror neurons is still in its infancy, and there are some scientists who challenge some of these grandest claims, pointing out, for example, that human empathy is still possible in people with damaged mirror neurons. And yet most scientists have accepted the basic point we all experience: we feel what we witness.

As I learned about mirror neurons, I wondered if they could be the scientific explanation for how inspiration really works. Remember, scientists had avoided the study of inspiration for many years, but perhaps here was a laboratory-proven key to unlocking the mysterious process of the Muses. Are mirror neurons the "pathway" of inspiration? Is inspiration as "simple" as the transfer of emotion from a Muse to an audience—and, if so, does that give us a blueprint for inspiring each other? Does witnessing Bono become passionate about injustice trigger our mirror neurons to feel the very same sense of passion? Does seeing Steph Curry execute a steady series of three-pointers makes us feel motivated to do the same? Does hearing the conviction a teacher has in our ability to succeed activate the same faith in ourselves? Perhaps passion is literally infectious; it enters and possesses a person, changing the operations of her mind, determining her behavior. It's a simple, chemical logic.

I was excited by my theory, but I knew I ought to run it by an expert. That led me to a giant in the field of modern neuroscience, Dr. Marco Iacoboni.[5] Dr. Iacoboni doesn't look like Einstein. He's actually a bit of a jock—a passionate tennis player and an obsessive fan of the sport, which he described to me as his "daily meditation." He collaborated with Dr. Rizzolatti and the team in Parma, bringing the study of mirror neurons from monkeys to humans, and at UCLA, he leads a laboratory that has done groundbreaking work to explain how mirror neurons work in a broad range of activities, from sports to music and video games to political advertising. But in his official biography, he makes his prejudices clear, "To be honest, I really don't give a damn about the brain. I care about the human soul." This was my guy.

And I was thrilled when Dr. Iacoboni agreed to talk to me. I explained my interest in inspiration, shared my conversion story about Bono, and clumsily communicated my layman's theory that inspiration is the transfer of emotion through our mirror neurons.

"Right," he said.

Well, that seemed simple.

But then, Dr. Iacoboni went on to talk about the critical factor I was missing in my formulation: intensity. He makes his point using the example of one of his favorite athletes, who, happily, happens to be *my* favorite athlete: Roger Federer. If you're a fan of Federer's and you're lucky enough to watch him play live on the Centre Court of Wimbledon, you will feel a more intense "mirroring" of his performance than if you're not a fan, watching the match on television while a million distractions buzz around your living room. In fact, Dr. Iacoboni sometimes watches tennis on television with the sound turned off so that he can *feel* the performance more intensely. As he explains it, "Silence allows you to tune into the athletic gesture, which allows you to feel the action more dramatically."[6]

"Feel the action more dramatically."

That last word contained the idea I needed: inspiration is the *dramatic* display of emotion. Inspiration is emotion expressed *so dramatically* that it stimulates an intense arousal in the audience.

The Color Commentary Conundrum

"Musicians sort of knew this already—that the emotional center is not the technical center, that funky grooves are not square, and what sounds like a simple beat can either be sensuous or simply a metronomic timekeeper, depending on the player."

—DAVID BYRNE, *How Music Works*

Well, then, that seems easy enough: if you want to inspire, share your passion, show your emotions—and the magic of mirror neurons will do the trick of arousing your audience. If you believe—*really believe*—in the mission of your company, your team will feel that conviction and toil all weekend. If your kids *feel* your passion for their success and happiness, they'll shut off the video games, hit the books, and rack up stellar grades.

Ah, if only it *were* that easy.

Scientists have also begun to discover what *impedes* the activation of mirror neurons—and, unfortunately, it's exactly the thing we're tempted to do instead of sharing our emotions: explaining.

Remember Dr. Iacoboni's curious habit of watching tennis on television with the sound turned off. It was his strategy for creating a more "dramatic" mirroring of the superstar he was watching. His could "learn" to move like Federer if he could "plug in" to Federer, without distraction, guaranteeing the strongest mirroring of the activity he was witnessing. In some way, the commentary was a distraction, an inhibitor of mirroring. Now, certainly, there are times when he *enjoys* John McEnroe's musings, but for matters of inspiration, that play-by-play analysis and explanation gets in the way.

The Reasonables don't just subvert the Muses; they murder them. Which brings us back to where we were: Passion – Reason = Inspiration

---

Dr. Iacoboni's laboratory confirmed this phenomenon with an experiment they did that mirrored what happened with the monkeys in Parma. At UCLA, the scientists divided people into two groups and asked both groups to watch a video of a person grabbing a cup. Simple enough. But with one group, they asked the subjects to "think about" what the person might be using the cup to do after they grasped it—to drink it, pass it, clean it, smash it, whatever.[7]

The result surprised the team. Those people who were asked to think—to consider the possibilities, weigh the evidence, deduce a conclusion—exhibited less arousal in their motor cortex (one of the sites of their mirror neurons) than those who simply watched the video without any instructions. As Dr. Iacoboni explained it in an email to me, "The 'analytical stance' was truly shutting down the motor cortex of the observers" who were asked to think.[8]

Analysis paralysis, it seems, is a real biological phenomenon, a way of describing the antagonistic relationship between our prefrontal cortex and our motor cortex, the part that thinks things through and the part that gets things done.

Could it really be that "thinking" gets in the way of feeling? Could it be that "analysis" gets in the way of inspiration?

Of course, it does. And you don't need a sophisticated justification from science to believe that. You've felt it. Your most exciting, inspired thinking generally happens when your brain is taking a break from its hard work of analysis—when you take a hot shower, a long walk, or when you're in that hazy state of waking up in the morning and possibilities are strange and unlimited. We are at our most imaginative when our brains are relaxed from the hard toil of figuring things out.

Or, said another way, persuasion and inspiration are opposite energies. The more we try to persuade, to reason and marshal evidence, the more we engage our audience's prefrontal cortex—and that seemingly benign act is exactly the thing that makes us less able to engage and arouse their emotions. You can't argue somebody into eating an apple pie. If you want to inspire, you'll need to turn down the volume on your own play-by-play commentary.

Chapter 5 Key Terms

Italian Neuroscientists: (collective noun) Rock stars; discoverers of mirror neurons, which just might be the neurological basis for human learning and empathy, as well as the mechanism by which inspiration occurs.

The Analytic Stance: (noun) A logical, rational approach; thinking about something, weighing pros and cons; a massive obstacle to inspiring.

PART 2

THE INSPIRATION PLAYBOOK

Let's Do This!

In this section, we'll explore the **Six Skills of Inspiration**. They're not a magic formula but, practiced together, they'll help you execute the Inspiration Equation. With these skills, you'll be able to express your passion in a way that subtracts *just enough* reason to rile up your audience, without sounding completely insane. These skills can be practiced by you personally—or they can even be employed by a team or an organization or a brand. They can be expressed in person or through writing or any other kind of art you want to practice. Each individual skill is valuable on its own but, obviously, when all six are practiced together, the greatest inspiration ensues:

The first two skills—**Get Delusional** and **Aim For Action**—are about your goal. They are about the *what* you want to accomplish, the *what* you want your audience (or yourself) to actually do. You think you might know this already—*I want to run a marathon! I want to inspire my team to beat the competition! I want to get people to buy my thing!*—but we'll explore how we can transform straightforward goals like those into perfect expressions of unreasonable passion, the kind of exhortations that get an audience both excited to move and crystal-clear about how to do so. These first two skills require deep thought and preparation. They are your inspiration *strategy.*

The next two skills—**Show Up To Stir Up** and **Talk Like Music**—provide advice for the *moment* of inspiration. You're with your team—in the room, on the stage, all eyes are locked on you. Now what? With these two skills, we'll explore *how* you can communicate to inspire, to break the sad bonds of the same-old, same-old situation and invite your audience to do something fresh and wonderful. These skills are about *dazzle.*

The final two skills—**Love, For Real** and **Be True You**—are the most critical and difficult. They are about *you*, the kind of person you'll need to be if you're going to become a Muse. You don't prepare for either; you practice for both, day in and day-out. Ultimately, these skills are about summoning the *empathy* and *authenticity* you'll need to move anybody to do anything.

Unfortunately, none of these skills are party tricks. You can't just show up and "do them" and expect to arouse your audiences. But they will help you refine and practice the characteristics of being a Muse. They will help you *become* a more inspiring person and a more inspiring leader.

And, as I've been stressing, the challenge of practicing these skills is that they each demand you express yourself emotionally. And that, as we discussed, isn't always easy in a world that often prefers our feelings to be tucked safely away. You'll have to expose yourself, make yourself vulnerable. You'll have to be dramatic—and, by doing so, you'll run the risk of being rejected.

Our Drama Problem

Drama, in our world, has become a dirty word. She's stirring up "drama." He's being so "dramatic." We're fine with "drama" on screens and stages; in fact, we crave it—but, in our everyday "real" life, we avoid it and condemn it. Human drama seems so silly and overwrought. And *sometimes* it is.

But not always. Not when you're trying to stir people to action.

Drama was, of course, central to life in Ancient Greece, where plays were as much a religious experience as they were a form of entertainment. They were dedicated to gods and goddesses, and it was assumed that playwrights—through the Muses—were speaking the lessons of the divine. Drama comes from the Greek word *dran* which means "to act"—and so, we have actors and actresses acting. But that very same root carries a double-meaning in Greek. It also signifies "to do"—in the sense of "to take action, to achieve." Drama is as much about "acting" as it is about "achieving"—and it's the connection between those two activities that I think is at the heart of inspiring. In other words, if you want to be a Muse, you'll have to embrace some disruptive "drama" and practice the craft of acting. You'll have to Unleash Your Inner Drama Queen—or King.

And this is where our hackles might rise, for we've come to think that "acting" is fakery, pretend, and make-believe. I can't imagine most CEOs—most of The Reasonables in any field!—embracing the idea that leadership demands *acting*. But I think that would be a very narrow understanding of acting indeed. As Alfred Hitchcock said, "What is drama but life with the dull bits cut out." That works for me: drama distills life to its most essential truths—and acting expresses them with moving authenticity. Sure, we see that practiced with polish by Judi Dench or Rami Malek, but we also see it masterfully exhibited by each other every single day. When our child cries because he's afraid of his dark bedroom. When our lover touches our waist with one hand as he reaches up toward the cupboard for a coffee mug with his other. When our boss tells us, "This is serious. If we don't make our numbers, we're hosed." What is all this but *drama*, but life distilled to its most precious and important elements? Real drama, as great actors know, is raw truth.

So our first obstacle to inspiring is getting over our silly prejudice that "drama" is a bad word—or even something that's just appropriate for special occasions on certain stages. For the Muse, the ground beneath her feet must become a stage. If you're approaching a moment that demands you are inspiring, you need to approach it as if you're stepping into a spotlight. What you wear. How you speak. How you gesture. These are all the critical tools of inspiration—*just as much as the content of your ideas*. And please, get over the hang-up that these elements are somehow superficial. They can be, but they don't have to be. In fact, as we'll learn in Chapter 11, your ability to inspire hinges on your authenticity. Yes, be dramatic, but don't ever be fake. You'll know when you cross that line.

But if the first obstacle to becoming inspiring is beating back a silly mental hang-up, the second obstacle is far trickier: act. Yes, inspiring is, like it or not, a *performative* act; a Muse must think of the people he wants to move as his *audience*, as a person or a group of people who need to be *transported* from one emotional point to another, often from apathy to excitement. And that demands a consciousness—an acceptance—that you are "working on" that audience in some respect; yes, you are *manipulating* them. And if you're a jerk, that's a terrible thing—but you are not a jerk. Your aim is true. Your ambition is noble. And so you must manipulate the emotions of your audience to get them to behave in a different and better way.

And remember, none of this is about being a great public speaker, in any traditional sense of that phrase. No, inspiration can come from mumbles and bad posture and people who struggle to speak loudly enough for the back row to hear. Inspiration can come from people who don't pepper their talk with "personal anecdotes" or make direct eye contact as they position themselves in the perfect place and use rounded hand gestures. These are the contrived tricks of "public speaking coaches." These are techniques that ironically rob speakers of the very rough authenticity that makes for the best Muses. As we'll see in Chapter 7, even Abraham Lincoln's genius as a public speaker was rooted in his awkwardness, even his ugliness, his tattered clothes and beat-up hat, and his refusal to form sentences that always made "sense" to the people hearing them. Lincoln was a great actor and a terrible pretender.

So, if "public speaking" lessons aren't the answer, what is?

Keep practicing the Daily Muse Skills introduced in Chapter 2 to help you become fluent in feelings: a Daily Muse Outburst and a Daily Muse Snack. Like so many people have developed a daily ritual of mindful meditation, try to form a habit around both the expression and consumption of feelings. Before you know it, the fear you face from sharing your truest feelings in social settings will begin to disappear.

But knowing there is a "performative" element to inspiring as well, I have another piece of (unlikely) advice: practice improv comedy.

Funny enough, I hate "improvisational" comedy. I just don't find it as funny as the brilliantly scripted bits in stand-up or sketch comedy, bits that actually hold up to repeated viewing. Have you ever re-watched an improv act? It's dreadful. The shelf life of improv is minutes. But, while I don't find improv particularly funny, I do think it's a brilliant craft for aspiring Muses to practice. Improv demands that you are both spontaneous and truthful at the very same time. You must open yourself so that your most-inside instincts tip out of your body, but it only "works" when those "offers" (as improvers call them) ring genuine, when they feel human. The motto of Upright Citizens Brigade is "Don't Think."[1] And it might as well be an instruction for the best kind of inspiring—don't think; feel.

And, interestingly, at the root of improv is practicing the craft of listening, of "accepting" the offers around you. This is what separates bad acting from great acting. The latter responds to the environment with intention, rather than just overwhelming the audience with emotional bluster. Public speaking coaches sometimes tell speakers to ignore the audience or, even worse, to imagine them sitting there naked. These are tricks meant to reduce nerves, but they have the awful effect of diminishing the real humanity of an audience. Instead, when you speak to an audience, please see them as the flesh-and-blood human beings they are. Listen for their laughs—or snores. Try to feel when their energy lifts—or sags. If you see arms crossed or throats clearing in a way that feels like they're not "picking up" what you're putting down, stop and address the issue. Improv classes will help you master these skills, will help you learn how to be in the moment, in communication and communion with your audience, in a genuine way.

Go to an improv performance, and I promise you'll see as many "misses" as "hits"—and, hopefully, witnessing that imperfect art will have you feeling like you could step onto that stage yourself. Because, of course, you can.

Exercise: Douse Your Ambition in Drama

Take a look back at Page xxiv on which you articulated your Ambition, the goal you most want to accomplish right now. No doubt, it's a terrific, worthy goal, a goal about which you care very deeply. The time has come, however, to douse that ambition with passion. Do you want to find funding for the film you want to make? Do you want to start a business? Do you want to become a triathlete? Do you want to lead your team at work to new heights of success? All of these are worthy goals—but they'll only become inspiring when you start to express them with unreasonable passion.

The worksheet on the next page will help you do just that. It's a series of questions—prompts, really—that are designed to dress your ambition up with emotion. Even if you know exactly *why* you want to do what you want to do, answering these questions will help you communicate your desires in a way that moves people. And, although it might be awkward, I'd suggest you speak your answers out loud before you write them down. In fact, if you have somebody you trust nearby, make that person your audience-of-one. And, as you speak, pay attention: When does it become easy? When do the words just flow out of you? When do you lean in and speed up and gesture wildly? *Those* are the good things, the genuine things, the things to capture.

And, if your ambition isn't exactly about you, personally—but about your company or your brand or your team—that's fine as well. Just answer the questions from the perspective of that team or company or brand.

But mostly, have fun with this exercise. While our passions might sometimes lead us to suffering, sharing those passions should be an act of liberation, a moment of joy.

YOUR PASSION PLAY PROMPTS

MY AMBITION: _____

WHEN DID I FIRST KNOW THIS WAS WHAT I WANTED TO DO?

WHAT–OR WHO–INSPIRED ME?

WHAT–OR WHO–KEEPS ME GOING? WHAT'S MY FUEL?

WHY AM I THE PERFECT PERSON TO DO THIS?

WHY DO I THINK THIS MATTERS?

HOW MIGHT MY LIFE–OR THE WORLD–BE DIFFERENT, BE BETTER WHEN I SUCCEED?

WHAT TERRIFIES ME ABOUT THIS ADVENTURE?

WHAT WOULD I SACRIFICE FOR TO ACHIEVE THIS GOAL?

WHAT'S MOST EMBARRASSING ABOUT THIS AMBITION?

HOW WOULD I EXPLAIN THIS TO A KID?

HOW WOULD I EXPLAIN THIS TO GOD?

HOW DO I FEEL WHEN I'M DOING THIS, WHEN I'M TAKING STEPS TOWARD MY GOAL?

You should now have your Ambition and, alongside it, you should have a page of notes that add some passion to it, some stories and feelings and hopes and fears. There should be some heroes and some villains—and a moment of inspiration and something wonderful at the end of the rainbow that you can describe with a good deal of clarity. You should have a story about your ambition, but don't worry if it's a messy story. Don't worry if it doesn't have a neat beginning, middle, and end. That's fine. In fact, that's better. Just keep your clear ambition and its jumbled story in mind as we explore the skills you'll need to get practicing as you morph into a Muse.

CHAPTER 6

The First Skill of Inspiration: Get Delusional

(How Delusional Ambitions Makes Superheroes of Us All)

"We are the music-makers,
And we are the dreamers of dreams."

—ARTHUR O'SHAUGHNESSY, "Ode"

You might be familiar with that quote from the movie when Willy Wonka grabs Veruca Salt by her snotty little face and reminds her that "pure imagination" can create almost anything, including lickable wallpaper on which snozzberries taste like actual snozzberries!

It's permission to dream.

But what most of us don't know is that Wonka is quoting from a poem by Arthur O'Shaughnessy that, just a few lines later, introduces another phrase, one that has become even more famous: "movers and shakers." For O'Shaughnessy, music-makers and dreamers are not airy-fairy artists; no, they are the "movers and shakers of the world forever," the ones who get the big work done.

Nobody is inspired to do small things.

Small, easy things, by their nature, don't arouse emotions. They're routine and unremarkable. Watching a wounded veteran, adjusting to life with prosthetic legs, pull herself across the occupational therapy room at a hospital is awe-inspiring. Watching any old *you* walk across that same room is not.

Therefore, if you seek to inspire, stretch your ambition—stretch it beyond reason, stretch your ambition as far as you can imagine, stretch it to the point of absurdity and delusion. Don't beg your team to work the weekend. Tell them to save the company. Don't tell your kid to finish her homework so she can watch YouTube. Tell her you believe she has it in her, through her hard work, to be the scientist that maps the hidden landscape of subatomic particles. Don't tell yourself to lose five pounds before beach season begins. Imagine you'll be the one turning every head on that shore, an audience of beach-combers admiring what you've done by dint of your awesome discipline.

And don't worry about the mockery of small, cynical minds—or the whisper in your head that what you propose just might not be possible, that it might be crazy. Those objections are the evidence you're onto something grand and world-tilting.

A reasonable ambition, a measured and measurable ambition, gets stuck in the tangle of that persnickety prefrontal cortex. A reasonable ambition is a duck sitting for an argument.

Dreaming is the first step to doing.
Dreaming big is the first step to doing big.

Muses must dream. Fantasy pulls you toward its own reality.

Delusion Confusion

When I was helping Heineken with their marketing strategy, the team decided we needed to know our "core consumer influencer," inside and out. We called these people "The Social All Stars." They were the movers and shakers amongst their friends, always one step ahead of their crew, knowing what clothes and clubs were cool. If we could understand them—their values and their preferences—we'd stand a better chance of connecting with them and influencing their friends, of helping Heineken become one of their favorite beers.

We did all the traditional market research. We held focus groups and commissioned surveys, but we were most excited by the "ethnographic" research we'd undertake. We would meet "The Social All Stars" on their terms, in their places, and we would study them until we understood them. So we went to bars and clubs and art galleries. We discussed music and fashion and graffiti.

One of my tasks was to head to Queens, New York, for a conversation with a music producer at his studio. I took the subway, followed the directions, and ended up at what was clearly not a professional music studio, but an apartment. I knew it was somebody's home, because this Social All Star's *mom* let me in and pointed me toward her son's bedroom. This wasn't right. I was supposed to be meeting a music producer of *legal drinking age*—and, here I was, face-to-face with a kid I would've sworn was a teen-ager who was spinning records on a deck in his bedroom.

> **"You've got to get delusional, man."**

I have no idea how this kid made it past the professional screeners we hired to organize our market research, but the jig was up. I asked him if he was, in fact, of legal drinking age. *No.* I asked him if he was, in fact, a music producer. *Yes, well, sort of.* I probed. Did he work with musicians? Did he make any records? Did he sell any albums?

I'll never forget his reply: "If I don't believe I'm making music, I'll never be making music. If I don't think I'm a music producer, I'll never be a music producer. You've got to get delusional, man."

We all know that Muhammad Ali said, "I am the greatest." He said it and sang it again and again. But, years after, he had proven his boast, he copped to a confession, "...I said that even before I knew I was."

Even Ali. Especially Ali. You've got to get delusional, man.

Delusion is a force that inspires. In fact, a Delusional Ambition is the embodiment of the Inspiration Equation: it's an *unreasonable* expression of passion, an *irrational* proclamation of what you want you or your team to accomplish. *It's crazy. It's mind-blowing.* And that insanity is exactly its power. The dictionary's definition of "delusion" is instructive:

> *An idiosyncratic belief or impression that is firmly maintained* despite being contradicted by what is generally accepted as reality or rational argument *(emphasis added)*[2]

Delusion—as a clinical pathology—is a scary affliction. But delusion—as a tool to boost inspiration—is a treasure. It's exciting. It is a belief that is "contradicted by what is generally accepted as reality or rational argument"—which is precisely what you're trying to do when you're trying to inspire, to contradict rational argument. *Breaking a two-hour marathon? Colonizing Mars? Getting into Harvard? Starting the most important company of the twenty-first century? Shedding a hundred pounds?* That's delusional, unreasonable, irrational, and, ultimately, wonderful stuff.

The Irresistible Terror of Big

In 2000, the Oscar-winning actor Anthony Hopkins starred in a brilliant commercial for Barclays Bank, which, at the time, was the largest bank in Britain. Hopkins, playing himself, walks through his mansion and speaks directly to the camera:

> *Seeing the big picture, having the big idea, clinching the big deal. Nobody wants to clinch the little deal. Who wants to do that? You'd be a little deal clincher, a small shot...When I was growing up I wanted to be the big man. I never wanted to be the little man. Even the little man wanted to be the big man...When you go to America you want to go to the Big Apple not the little apple...I've got a big day today, a big meeting with the big chiefs from a big studio. It's the big time with the big bucks....*

Nobody wants to clinch the little deal. It's a curious human truth: more often than not, we crave what's big; we lean in to the large; we desire what's grand.

Why is that? Why, so often, in so many areas, is bigger better?

Indulge me for a few pretentious moments while we get a little heady dusting off some old books.

Edmund Burke, like Bono, was an Irishman who knew how to turn a phrase (One of my favorites: "To make us love our country, our country ought to be lovely."). Burke was an eighteenth century politician serving in the British Parliament, but he was also a philosopher fascinated by the way our minds respond to the physical world around us. He wrote a very dense philosophical treatise with a mouthful of a title: *The Origin of Our Ideas of the Sublime and the Beautiful.* It was an explanation of aesthetics—what attracts us, what repulses us, both in the world or art and in the world at large. He wanted to explain how seeing things—or hearing or reading things—makes us feel.

According to Burke, there are two great categories of stimulus: the sublime and the beautiful.

The "beautiful," for Burke, is very pleasing indeed. Harmony and order and proportion that is soothing to the human senses. Pretty pictures, perfectly symmetrical faces.

The "beautiful" is very nice, certainly, but for Burke, it isn't particularly *powerful*; what is beautiful might *please* us, but it rarely moves us, hardly arouses us.

The "sublime," however, is beauty's get-it-done stepsister. The sublime doesn't please our senses; it excites and arouses our spirit. It creates "astonishment," which Burke describes as a state in which your soul is suspended and all reason ceases. The sublime, for Burke, is the off switch to reason that leaves you in a state of *sheer feeling*. Sound familiar?

Burke's examples of the sublime are telling: the vastness of oceans, the steep sheer face of mountain cliffs, and his favorite passages from his favorite poet, John Milton, whose *Paradise Lost* is the classic telling of the battle between God and Satan. Burke loves the descriptions of the giant black void of hell and the epic clashes of angels warring in boundless skies. This is big, *Game-of-Thrones*-like stuff.

I'm sure you've felt the effect of the sublime yourself when you've gazed upon grand canyons and giant oceans. You've felt the sublime when you've stood in the surf and been rolled head-over-feet by a wave that could never be stopped. You've felt the sublime when you gazed into the eyes of a lion, even a lion on the other side of the zoo's glass barrier. You've felt the sublime when you laid on your back in a field and lost yourself amongst the sky full of stars in the dark heavens above.

And, when you do feel what's sublime, it transforms you, even if only for a moment. You're captivated.

But that's *what* the sublime does. The real freaky insight is *how* the sublime does it. According to Burke, "No passion so effectually robs the mind of all its powers of acting and reasoning as terror."[3]

Wait, what? Terror? How'd that horror-show stuff get into this lovely discussion of mountains and oceans and poetry? What does terror have to do with inspiration?

Well, almost everything.

We fear what we don't know: the dark, the anonymous heavy breathing on the other side of the phone call, the far away, whatever lurks under our bed in the creepy night hours. *This* is where Burke locates the power of sublimity: in its mystery, its hazy shadows, its unknowable-ness. *That's* the scary stuff: what we can't see clearly. In fact, for Burke, the opposite of sublimity isn't exactly beauty; it's clarity. As he puts it, "To see a thing distinctly is to see its bounds, and cut it off from infinity."[4]

When we see a thing *clearly*, we see its limits, its limitations, its boundaries, its endings. But when we can't quite see a thing clearly, our imagination takes flight. And this is thrilling. Think about the moment the lights turn off before a band takes the stage at a concert. In that moment, anything is possible, anything might happen. Darkness might foretell disaster—or it might foretell wonder. Either way, it's arousing.

So are we to conclude that, in order to inspire, we must arouse fear?

Well, yes, I believe so.

A clear idea is an idea that isn't trying hard enough. It's grasp-able. But a sublime idea—a delusional idea that makes you a little nervous because you can't quite totally see how it will come to be—well, those are the ideas that inspire.

And I know that's awkward for sweet people like us, but there's good news for our kind hearts: we can arouse the kind of sublime fear that inspires without resorting to terrifying threats. We have a handy and generous way of doing so: big, grand, delusional ambitions, the kind of ambitions that make us gulp and worry right before they pull us toward our very best selves.

My Small Big Business Moment

A few years back, I left ad-agency-land to become a marketing executive at a very serious global company worth billions of dollars. This was a place of *business*, a place for The Reasonables. In fact, I'd be the only vice president at the company *without* an MBA, the only vice president who never studied statistics. I was prepared to feel dumb. In fact, I wanted to; I had so much to learn.

So, with freshman-like enthusiasm, I settled into our corporate auditorium for my first leadership meeting, a meeting of the "Top 40" executives in our company. The walls were wooden, the carpet was plush, and the mood was tense because the business was struggling. There was worry that our company was suffering a slow death as the world's values shifted to our competitors' brands. There was even talk we might be taken over by hostile raiders! But we were ready, ready to hear our CEO's vision, the sophisticated analysis and gutsy strategy that would save this hallowed company.

And then it came. It came in bold-faced type on a PowerPoint slide with a heading that said "Strategy"...

Grow.

That's what we would do, our CEO told us. We would grow—I mean, *Grow* the business. And, while we were *Grow*ing, we would "control costs." But mostly, we would *Grow.*

The rest of the presentation included some specific numbers and a host of ideas about how we would "innovate." There was a plan to make granola bars less crunchy, for example. But mostly, we would *Grow.*

I was sure I missed something. Grow *must mean something quite special and specific in business school,* I imagined.

As we were shuffling out of the auditorium, I found a new colleague who had quickly become a friend and asked her if she had a few moments to spare. At the risk of sounding stupid, I wondered, what did all of that actually mean? She explained it so elegantly: *The "market" thinks our only chance to make money is to cut costs and pump up our margins. We believe we can still stoke demand for our brands. We believe we can grow our top-line sales.*

Now I got it. Investors believed we were finished. We believed we weren't.

Grow, in that context, *did* mean something. It was an optimistic strategy, perhaps even an admirable and courageous position to take. But it was also, ultimately, a modest, well-reasoned ambition.

I couldn't help but compare this corporate strategy to some of the famous visions at other companies. Bill Gates wanted "a computer on ever desk and in every home." Elon Musk wants to colonize Mars, and the leadership at Uber is aiming for the day when nobody needs to own their own car. These are grand ambitions.

At my company, we wanted to, well, *Grow*.

That might have been a pragmatic strategy that focused my fellow executives on the hard work at hand, but I'm certain it *inspired* none of them. It was a *small* ambition, which might just be worse than no ambition at all.

And it didn't work. Two years later, that company's goal was to *Decline 2 percent.*

Compare my meeting to the famous one some Apple employees were lucky enough to attend in September of 1997. Steve Jobs had returned to the company just a few weeks earlier, a grand return after he was ousted nearly a dozen years before from the company he had founded, fired by a corporate board of Reasonables who would go on to grind Apple into unprofitability with a me-too strategy aping Microsoft.

The company was in a world of hurt when Steve Jobs took the stage in their dingy auditorium, eyes blurry, confessing he had been awake until 3 a.m. the previous night working on the advertising campaign he was about to unveil.

There was no PowerPoint slide. No bullet points. Just Steve Jobs, in black mock turtleneck, shorts, and sandals. The company had "suffered from neglect," he said, but he had a plan to reverse that decline, a plan to grow. It wouldn't be touting their expertise at "making boxes for people to get their jobs done" or talking about "why we're better than Windows." No, it would be reminding the world *why* Apple exists, which was, as the ad he eventually played declared, to "push the human race forward." *To push the human race forward.* Like Einstein did. And Gandhi and Alfred Hitchcock and Rosa Parks and Jim Henson, all of whom had marquee billing in the new marketing.[5]

To push the human race forward. That's what Apple set about doing. *That's* what Steve Jobs asked his team to do and, in so asking, he called them to a greatness as grand as Gandhi's and Einstein's. If Steve Jobs asked his team to work their tails off to "beat Microsoft," he'd be treating them as mere managers. But, in asking them to change the course of human history, he was seeing them as magicians, martyrs, and masters of the universe.

And that team responded. On that day, Apple's fortunes turned around, putting them on course to be the world's first company valued at one trillion dollars.

The Reasonables pray for growth.

The Muses push the world forward.

The Reasonables see people as the job they can do.

The Muses see people as the heroes they can become.

The Muses win.

In the corporate realm, we're often a long way from Burke's sublime. Here, it's a world of Reasonables, with their annual plans and quarterly presentations that start with such serious-sounding objectives: *Grow share. Extend the brand. Launch in a new market. Outperform last year.* Consultants parrot these objectives back to their corporate executives, believing it gives them credibility as informed and serious partners; and maybe it does, but it also quite certainly keeps the conversation stuck at sluggish modesty.

It's difficult to be a Muse, egging your audience toward the big sublime, especially in buttoned-up corporate environments that prize reason and "strategy." To too-many MBA-addled brains, grand, delusional ambitions seem like silly diversions, or worse, the fairy dust the marketing team sprinkles on advertising.

Every now and then, a business aims higher. Nike certainly wants to grow share and expand the brand to new markets, but they also want to inspire the athlete in *every single body*. Dove wants to make *all women*, no matter their shape or size or color, feel beautiful. Perhaps Old Spice has tackled the most daunting of challenges: to make every pimply-faced fifteen-year-old boy smell and feel like a swaggering man, man.

Being the most interesting thing in a bar. Bringing humanity to air travel. Creating spaces for everybody to belong. These are big brand purposes—for Dos Equis, JetBlue, and Airbnb, respectively. These "purpose-driven brands" don't only make people feel good; they deliver better results as well. Jim Stengel, Procter & Gamble's former marketing guru, has assembled a virtual mutual fund of brands like these that transcend their commercial goals and pursue a meaningful role in the world at large. His fund of ambitious brands outperforms their competitors by a factor of three.[6]

MODERN MUSE: DOS EQUIS
I Don't Always Think Big, But When I Do...

I was lucky to work at the ad agency that created "The Most Interesting Man in the World" ad campaign for Dos Equis beer. The "MIM" (as we called him) became a beloved, iconic character, a cultural sensation and an internet meme, driving market-busting sales for almost a decade. The story of his creation is a story of Delusional Ambition.

Our client had a very tight, reasonable brief: They wanted to make Dos Equis "the second-best-selling premium imported Mexican beer in America." Corona held the top spot, which we'd have to accept, while aiming to be "the second-best-selling premium imported Mexican beer in America." That's right: we'd go for number two.

And the client's market research team even had a conviction about how to achieve that not-so-lofty goal. Corona, they concluded, "owned" the daytime in consumers' minds. They were about sunshine and letting yourself relax on soft, sandy beaches. They were yellow and chill. Dos Equis, however, would be the opposite of that mellow summertime vibe. We'd "own" the nighttime—adventure and daring. We'd be "active"—a beer brand for people who wanted to engage life, not escape it.

As a strategist, that all felt right and reasonable to me.

And yet, as one of one of our creative directors pointed out, perhaps that *reasonable* logic suffered from one fatal flaw: a beer brand doesn't really get to choose its competition; no brand does. Nobody walks into a bar and asks for a Corona or "the second-best-selling premium imported Mexican beer" available. No, they walk into a bar and are confronted by dozens of exciting choices—all sorts of beers, domestic and foreign, cheap and expensive, craft and mainstream, plus vodkas and whiskeys and cocktails and shots. A bar on a Friday night is a beverage buffet, not a binary choice, and so, simply being an alternative to "the next drink on the shelf" wouldn't get us very far.

In the course of our work, which involved many hours drinking in bars and talking to strangers, one of the strategists on the team uncovered a curious insight: bars are filled with guys who lie. Well, sort of. Bars are filled with so many twenty-five-year-old guys so desperate to impress that they exaggerate the truth; they pump up their adventures to sound more exciting, more interesting. The gravest sin for a young guy to commit on a weekend night prowling the bars and clubs looking for umm, company is to be dull. You'd rather be dead.

So, instead of being "the second-best-selling premium imported Mexican beer in America," maybe Dos Equis could aim higher. Maybe we could be *the most interesting thing in the bar.* We could be the very thing our twenty-five-year-old consumers desperately desired to be: the *most interesting thing in the bar*—more interesting than any beer or drink or, heck, any person or conversation. *That's* how you birth "The Most Interesting Man in the World" and not just "another interesting guy in another interesting beer commercial." It's ambition that made the difference. It's aiming grander than a reasonable business objective that gets the greatest results.

The Ambition Makes the Super-People

While Delusional Ambitions are uncomfortable aspirations for many businessfolk, who are often desperately muscling their way to results and bonuses, we tend to be slightly more wide-eyed when personal matters are at stake: *Lose twenty pounds. Win the state championship. Launch my own business. Get into Harvard.* We find it easier to dream big when we're dreaming about "life" and not just clunky commerce. Perhaps that's because we feel looser, less restrained by the burden of short-term results, what business consultant David Weinberger calls "accountabalism"—the counter-destructive process that values measurement over meaning.[7] It's rampant in corporate conference rooms, because it's easier to measure sales than "interesting-ness" or "love."

But, in our personal lives, from the time we were young, we dreamed in superlatives: the best, greatest, biggest, strongest, most beautiful. *That's* the language of kids dreaming, the Muse-like language of inspiring ambition. To the title character of *The Little Prince*, everything, the entire universe, was both grand and accessible, vast and intimate, at exactly the same time. The Little Prince could stand on a planet and almost touch the stars.

Kids possess the invaluable ability to imagine, to imagine unencumbered by the physics of day-to-day drudgery. For a spell of youth, anything is possible.

Perhaps kids feel this nothing-is-impossible instinct because they've been coddled by parents telling them they could, in fact, do anything. But perhaps it's just a matter of time. They haven't lived long enough to run into the walls of negativity that eventually bruise ambitious instincts. Either way, kids dream. They can be presidents and movie stars and running backs and billionaires. They can be astronauts and chefs and they can marry their dogs and they can be happy. They can, in fact, be heroes.

As we discussed earlier, one way to think about the role of a Muse is as somebody who makes heroes of others, like Steve Jobs did with his team at Apple. He enlisted them as soldiers in the great march of human progress.

It's important to keep in mind that ambitions, by their nature, are *relative* goals. What might be a breeze for one person is an absurd effort for another. While one team aims to finish the season with just one victory, because they never have, another aims for a National Championship because last year, they won their State Tournament. It's difficult to objectively label an ambition as "small" or "grand" or "delusional"—but, as with love and fear, the best guides are your feelings.

Or maybe this tool.

Meet **The Ambition Spectrum**. On the near side are the Humdrum Ambitions—the ones that hardly stir us, the ones we can accomplish as easily as any of our everyday tasks—but on the far side of the spectrum are the Hero-Worthy Ambitions, the hard ones, the ones that require almost super-human effort but, in so requiring, arouse our fiercest emotions. The Humdrum Ambitions set the bar low. The Hero-Worthy Ambitions are the ones that inspire.

And now, look at *your* Ambition from page xxiv and ask yourself where it might fall on this spectrum. Where your Ambition lands will certainly be relative to your own personal situation. For example, for somebody struggling with depression, just waking up and getting to work might be a Herculean 9—and, for others, like Iron Men, biking a hundred miles might be a breezy 3. But look at your Ambition, and understanding the feelings it evokes in you, try to plot it in the appropriate place:

THE AMBITION SPECTRUM

1–3. These are **Everyday Ambitions** that can be achieved with effort, but ease. For most of us, these are "accomplishments" like getting to work on time, not getting fired, and managing to keep the kids safe and alive while helping them finish their homework and get to soccer practice on time. These might also be the day-to-day steps—"the baby steps"—toward reaching a loftier goal: get to the gym, eat well, read more, drink less, turn off the phone and actually play with the kids, tick off everything on the "to do" list.

For a business, these Everyday Ambitions are the ones that simply keep the doors open, the ones that avoid the disaster of bankruptcy: make what you make; serve your customers well; don't break any laws; and think about growth.

These Everyday Ambitions are important, for sure. They are the goals you need to achieve to do whatever it is you do. But they are no more than that. They certainly don't keep you awake at night, either fretting with anxiety or imagining a glorious future. They just *are*.

4–6. These are **Big Ambitions** that take *uncomfortable effort to achieve*. They demand a change in our behavior that doesn't always feel so great. They involve risk. They're often goals that are expressions of passion that lead to a change in the way we've been leading our life: run a marathon (which means exercising regularly), write a book (which means no more Netflix), open a cheese shop (which means quitting your job), travel the world (which means spending your savings), become the boss (which means stepping out of your comfort zone), start dating after an ugly divorce (which means opening yourself to the possibility of more heartache). Ambitions like these demand that we "put ourselves out there," exposing our dreams and our vulnerabilities.

For a business, these Big Ambitions are "moderate stretch" goals: grow, for sure, and do so with an intentional strategy: innovate a new product, find a new market, reorganize the team, improve customer service, revive the brand. These are the goals that reverse declines and beat expectations, the ones that'll get the attention of your competitors and the approval of your investors. And, as with the personal Big Ambitions, these are ones that carry some risk. They demand investment. They might fail.

These Big Ambitions stir our feelings. They evoke worry: *What am I thinking? Is this really a good idea? Can I do this?* But they also get us jazzed, pumped, and stoked: *I can see it. I can't wait. It feels right and good.*

7–9. These are **Grand Ambitions**, goals that we can only achieve with great difficulty. They demand *significant change in behavior,* change that will certainly be risky and definitely be uncomfortable. There will be many days when we don't want to bother and others days when we fall short. These goals are often amplifications of "moderate" goals: lose thirty pounds and run a marathon in less than four hours; create an empire of cheese shops (not just a sweet little café), write a best-selling book or win an Academy Award; become a foster parent; become a *good* politician; become the scientists who discovers stem-cell solution to cancer; recover from alcoholism and stitch your life together again.

And, for businesses, these Grand Ambitions are the ones that change the trajectory of a company and rewrite the rules of a category: radical purpose-driven innovation, like Apple or Starbucks; transformation of a corporate culture; reversing a dramatic decline by inverting your strategy; reshaping your business by selling significant assets and acquiring new ones. These are the Ambitions that get companies profiled in *The Harvard Business Review*—for their success or their failure. They are the ones that make and ruin careers.

These Grand Ambitions flirt with impossibility: *Can it really be done? Can I really do it?* But, because they do so, they also swell our hearts and feed our imagination. These arethe fantasies that we might have had as wide-eyed kids—and if, as you ponder your Ambition, you feel a nostalgic sense of child-like possibility, you've probably got a Grand Ambition on your hands. These are the Ambitions that become the stuff of our dreams.

10. Finally, there are **Delusional Ambitions**, ones that, by *almost* all rules of reality, are *impossible* to achieve. Be the next Steve Jobs. Be the next Meryl Streep. Run a marathon in less than two hours. Travel to Mars. Be President. Win the US Open. Cure cancer, all of it. Live to see your great-grandkids graduate from college.

For businesses, these Delusional Ambitions are often expressed in their *brand* visions: inspire the athlete in every single body; bring peace to an angry world; empower a generation to cure cancer or end poverty or clean the oceans; stamp out bigotry; make everybody their very best self; feed the world. But these brand goals can also be hardcore and commercial: be the world's first *two* trillion-dollar company; quintuple sales; bankrupt all of the competition; be a startup that becomes a *Fortune* 5 company in a decade.

The Delusional Ambitions often feel so nice and lofty but are, generally, quickly dismissed as naïve wishful thinking. They're more likely to be dismissed than debated.

So where do you think your goal falls on The Ambition Spectrum? Is it nudging its way into being a *Big* Ambition? Is it stuck in the humdrum land of *Everyday* Ambitions? Or have you already rocket-shipped to *Delusion*-land?

Keep in mind that, no matter where your goal lies on this spectrum, it's probably a very good goal. Everyday Ambitions and Big Ambitions, even though they tilt toward the humdrum, are critical and worthy. They can organize behavior and even motivate others by providing clear destinations.

Everyday Ambitions, even Big Ambitions—these are great goals. They're just not particularly inspiring.

Only once we cross the threshold to Grand Ambitions do we begin to see *unreasonable* displays of passion. That border, that fuzzy border between Big Ambitions and Grand Ambitions is the Muse's starting line. It's exactly the point where The Reasonables begin to tut-tut and wag their heads and roll their eyes. It's also exactly the point where heroes are born.

The Muse then, to birth heroes, must move her Ambitions *toward* the delusional.

And how do we do so? How do we create childlike heroes on the wings of Delusional Ambitions? Well, here are three techniques for— but wait, it's probably best if we first handle those pesky Reasonables waving their hands in the back of the room...

THE AMBITION SPECTRUM

INSPIRATION LIVES THIS WAY!

EVERYDAY AMBITIONS	BIG AMBITIONS	GRAND AMBITIONS	DELUSIONAL AMBITIONS
I WILL DO A GOOD JOB AT WORK.	*I WILL HELP MY TEAM HAVE THE BEST QUARTER EVER.*	*I WILL RISE UP THE RANKS, RUN MY COMPANY, AND LEAD US TO GREAT SUCCESS.*	*I WILL LEAD THE MOST INNOVATIVE COMPANY ON EARTH.*
LET'S BE THE SECOND-BEST SELLING MEXICAN BEER IN AMERICA.	*LET'S BEAT CORONA.*	*LET'S BE THE MOST LOVED BEER IN AMERICA.*	*LET'S BE THE MOST INTERESTING THING IN THE WHOLE BAR.*
		I WILL KEEP THE UNION TOGETHER.	*I WILL ABOLISH SLAVERY.*
	WE'LL MAKE MONEY AS A ROCK BAND.	*WE'LL BE THE BIGGEST ROCK BAND IN THE WORLD.*	*WE'LL BE A "LIFE CULT" THAT ERADICATES POVERTY IN AFRICA.*
I'LL WALK TO THE STORE.	*I'LL START JOGGING.*	*I'LL COMPLETE A MARATHON.*	*I'LL COMPLETE ANOTHER MARATHON 25% FASTER.*

AND REMEMBER, AMBITIONS ARE ALWAYS RELATIVE. WHAT'S "BIG" FOR YOU MIGHT BE DELUSIONAL FOR ME.

A Note to The Reasonables

"But, but, but," I can hear The Reasonables protest the value of Delusional Ambitions with two objections:

First, the silly one: *"These delusional goals might make people feel nice in the moment, but they're ultimately distracting from the hard work at hand. They can't be achieved. They take our eyes off the ball in front of our face."*

Well, as I've written several times throughout this book, I am not rejecting the ability of rational strategy and reasonable measures to help a team or an individual progress. Smart, small steps have always worked and always will. They just won't take you as far as giant leaps might. As we discussed in Chapter 3, inspired teams get *dramatically* better results—double the success of uninspired teams, according to Bain & Company. Everyday Goals make everyday progress—and, if that's your aim, bless you. But, if you're selling a genuine competitive advantage in your personal or professional realm, you'll be well-served aiming higher.

The second objection of The Reasonables, however, doesn't come from a place of small ambitions, but a place of sincere compassion: *"What's the good in having a goal so delusional that it's unattainable? At what point does delusion become deflating?"* Some of you might worry that setting such audacious, delusional goals—goals which are often simply unattainable—is, ultimately, *de-motivating* to an audience. Does asking a high school sprinter to shave 25 percent off her fastest time cause only stress and heartache as she realizes the impossibility of the ambition? Does asking your sales team to *double* their results in the next quarter lead to frustration and burnout?

You'd think it might and, yet, some recent studies suggest exactly the opposite. A team of scientists at Concordia University examined what happens to athletes when they come face-to-face with "unattainable" goals—in this case, an impossible-to-achieve cycling challenge.[8] There are two obvious, natural responses: when face-to-face with the prospect of failure, an athlete can reject the goal (disengagement: *it's a stupid goal, anyway.*) or reframe the goal in a manner that makes it more achievable (reengagement: *I'll at least beat the rest of the team.*) The scientists at Concordia University concluded that *both* reactions have positive benefits, leading to "lower depression, stress," and negative thoughts.[9] The very act of bumping up against a Delusional Ambition is "healthy."

And yet, as your intuition probably indicates, one of the two responses—reengagement—is better than the other. In fact, "reengagement can help renew athletes' sense of meaning and purpose in life."[10] Staring down a Delusional Ambition until it confesses its vulnerability is a therapeutic act of optimism and will.

The trick for The Muse then is to help people *re-engage* as they struggle with the grandeur of a Delusional Ambition, to help them find their own attainable goal within the challenge of the one you've set for them. This reengagement is more likely to occur as motivation shifts from "extrinsic" to "internal," as we discussed in Chapter 2. Remember Eliud Kipchoge, who *almost* broke the two-hour marathon goal. As that goal becomes *his* goal—not just Nike's goal—his "failure" will vault him to ultimate success.

This transfer works best when a person feels understood and supported, when a personal, emotional connection is made or, in the words of the team at Concordia University, "liking, warmth, and interest" are expressed.[11] We'll cover that notion in depth when we discuss the Fourth Skill of Inspiration: Love, For Real but, for now, it's important to understand that delusional goals—even impossible goals—are arousing if—*if*—they're delivered with a sense of love. Fear not setting the bar preposterously high if you're also pushing a trampoline into place.

Behind both of these objections, however, is the same worry: Aren't Delusional Goals just too hard to achieve?

Of course, they are.

Remember JFK (Of course, there's JFK. There's *always* JFK in a discussion of inspiration). He's the American face of Grand Ambition, all emotional ideals and a do-do-do spirit. As he said at Rice University, inspiring the throng of students gathered for a football game to set their sights on a higher plane:

> *But why, some say, the Moon? Why choose this as our goal? And they may well ask, why climb the highest mountain? Why, 35 years ago, fly the Atlantic? Why does Rice play Texas? We choose to go to the Moon!... We choose to go to the Moon in this decade and do the other things, not because they are easy, but because they are hard; because that goal will serve to organize and measure the best of our energies and skills, because that challenge is one that we are willing to accept, one we are unwilling to postpone, and one we intend to win.*[12]

Pure Burke. Mountains, oceans, and inevitably, the moon—all sublime, all scary from this side of the journey. It's the degree of difficulty in accomplishing these endeavors that makes doing so both simultaneously terrifying and thrilling.

DELUSIONALIZING AMBITIONS

SELL SNEAKERS .... INSPIRE THE ATHLETE IN EVERYBODY (AND EVERYBODY WHO HAS A BODY IS AN ATHLETE)

BE A GYMNAST .... BE ON A BOX OF WHEATIES

WIN THE CIVIL WAR .... FULFILL GOD'S DESTINY FOR AMERICA

LOSE TEN POUNDS .... BE THE HOTTEST THING AT MY 20-YEAR HIGH SCHOOL REUNION

HELP MY KID DO HIS ENGLISH HOMEWORK .... HELP MY KID FALL IN LOVE WITH SHAKESPEARE

WRITE A BOOK .... CHANGE SOME LIVES

START A BUSINESS .... CHANGE THE WORLD

BE A GOOD PARENT .... CHANGE THE WORLD

WIN THE GAME .... PROVE THE HATERS WRONG

BE KIND TO MY NEIGHBORS .... ACHIEVE ETERNAL LIFE

So then, how do we move our ambitions along the Ambition Spectrum, pushing them toward the kind of goals that set people in motion? Here are three Techniques for Making Ambitions Delusional:

Technique 1: Superlativize

Yes, I know Superlativize isn't a real word but, for some reason, it reminds me of the Beastie Boys' song "Sabotage" (*Listen, all y'all, Superlativize!*)—and hip-hop is actually relevant to this tactic. Hip-hop, in general, is filled with boasts—the greatest, the best, the biggest, the toughest, the bad-ass-iest. As Kanye West rapped in "So Appalled," he would be on the big guy's playlist if the divine creator had an iPod! It's a contender in the heated debates about best hip-hop boasts, many of which serve a dual purpose: positioning an artist in a crowded field *and* raising the bar on the value of hip-hop itself. For Run-DMC, rapping was "tricky"—but, for Kanye, his music is God's music.

So a very straightforward way to nudge your goals toward Delusional Ambition is to *strive for superlatives* in your articulation. Find the highest degree or expression of your goal. Make it big. Double your numbers and use words that end with -*est*... Best, Fastest, Kindest, Strongest... Remember, Dos Equis wanted to be *the most* interesting thing in a bar. Microsoft wanted a computer on *every* desk in the world. Eliud Kipchoge wanted to be *the fastest marathon runner in human history.*

You might even use *preposterous analogies* to give you or your team a sense of just how delusional your goals really are. I remember when I was on the high school debate team, to calm my nerves before big bouts, I'd chant to myself (usually hunched over somewhere with anxiety pains in my stomach): *Be "The JFK" of debate. Be "The JFK" of debate*...I set my goal at the highest level of rhetoric I could imagine. Do the same: Be "the Ali" of the office. Be "the Beyoncé" of the PTA. Be "the Oprah" of your neighborhood. If you find the most successful person, you can aim to beat that person. Delusion indeed.

And a tactic for making these superlatives more concrete is the very simple exercise of inflating your numbers. Shoot for 10 percent growth when the projections tell you 5 percent is realistic. Aim to lose fifteen pounds when ten seems reasonable. Write two thousand words a day when you had been churning out a thousand. Jiggering up your measurable goal right past the point of your comfort begins to gin up feelings and, yes, sometimes dark feelings, like fear and anxiety. Can I achieve that? Are we signing up for too much? Will I feel like a failure? When those worries kick in, you're likely on the right track toward an ambition with a tinge of delusion. Fear, remember, lives closer to success than reason does.

Technique 2: Find Your "Mightier Purpose"

Abraham Lincoln won the Civil War *only after* he proposed a Delusional Ambition. Scholars have noted how Lincoln's feelings "evolved" over the course of the war, but Nancy Koehn outlines it dramatically in her book, *Forged in Crisis*. When Lincoln entered national politics, he was not a radical abolitionist. He was opposed to slavery, but content to forge a compromise that would allow its continuance in the southern states. Koehn describes Lincoln's tortured journey from simply wanting to work out a status-quo-maintaining compromise with (a modest 3 on The Ambition Scale) to waging a war to hold the Union together (an ambitious 6) to, ultimately, emancipating slaves and making real the foundational promise of the Declaration of Independence (at least a 9!). "In early 1863," Koehn writes, "Lincoln realized that his work had become bigger than saving the Union, as essential as this was. His responsibility now encompassed *transforming* the country..."[13]

Which is exactly what Lincoln set about doing when he issued the Emancipation Proclamation, against the counsel of his most senior advisors, and honored the fallen at Gettysburg by committing the country to the then-radical idea of racial equality. He was moving his ambition from the reasonable to the delusional. He was transforming a political goal to a spiritual goal. And, at that moment, Lincoln became our national Muse, rallying the beleaguered, ambivalent North to ultimate victory. As Koehn says, the Emancipation Proclamation was:

MODERN MUSE: JIM CARREY

The Art of Self-Musing

In 1982, Jim Carrey was one of the dreamy wannabes who arrived in Hollywood with great ambitions.[1] He was twenty-four years old and had nothing to his name. And he was used to that. When he was twelve years old, Jim's father had lost his job in the Ontario steel-mill town where the family lived. The Carreys lost their home, sardined themselves into a camper van, and slaved as janitors and security guards at a local factory. Jim would pull eight hour shifts after school. But through all the hardship, Jim clung to his goal: to be a famous comedian, to make the world laugh. It's all he ever wanted to do.

And here, in 1984, Jim Carrey was in Hollywood, penniless and struggling to catch a break. He was struggling with depression and would spend hours driving his old Toyota around the city's hills.

It was on one of these drives that Jim committed a now-famous act of audacity. He wrote himself a check for $10 million—a personal check which he dated for that very same day ten years into the future. This would be payment for "acting services rendered," as he wrote on the memo line.

And, ten years later, as you know, he was able to cash that check. His account was plump with the millions he earned from *Dumb & Dumber*. He never did cash it, though. Instead, he would slip the check into his father's coffin, a token of gratitude to the man who always supported him and, perhaps, also a token of pride: *Look, Dad. I made it. Thank you, Dad. I made it.*

Where would you put Jim Carrey's $10 million check on the Ambition Spectrum? I think it's certainly a Grand Ambition. It was a near-delusional act of optimism, considering his background, his complete lack of opportunity. Jim Carrey didn't play with Everyday Ambitions (get a job that pays for my groceries) or even Big Ambitions (land a series, get a movie). No, Jim flirted with delusion— and won.

Did Jim Carrey become the highest-grossing comedic actor in Hollywood history because he wrote himself that check, because he articulated a Grand Ambition for himself? Did that $10 million check inspire a struggling Jim Carrey?

Yes, I *believe* so.

...a watershed moment for Lincoln's leadership. In signing it, he left behind his own carefully nurtured plans for a gradual, peaceful end to slavery. He walked away from the position he had held since first entering national politics in 1854: a solution the problem of slavery that opposed its extension while recognizing its constitutional legality.... The new law gave the president a mightier purpose than that he had assumed when he took office.[14]

A mightier purpose. As Lincoln's goal leapt toward delusion, his ambition created heroes. *Literally.* His *moral* stand rallied northern troops, abolitionists, and slaves themselves who were now fighting for a goal much greater than the preservation of a country that had enslaved them. They were fighting for everything.

From the earliest days of humankind, we've been gazing at the stars and asking ourselves "Why?" *Why are we here? Why were we put on this earth with these talents? What are we supposed to be doing?*

Certainly, some cynics might think our existence is just one cosmic accident that carries no grander purpose, but most of us have embraced the notion that we have a job to do while we live and breathe.

The Muses cast that job in the *grandest* terms possible.

The Reasonables do not. They toil with "next steps" and modest goals. Interestingly, even the best intentions usually serve up sad ambitions. Think of all the parents (myself included) who have asked their children to "just do your best" or the coaches who tell athletes to "go out there and have fun." Knowing what we know now, you can see what pathetic instructions these really are. Could you imagine Harry Potter wanting to "neutralize" Voldemort? We are inspired by the grandest stakes: eternal life, for example, or fame.

One of the constraints that limits our thinking is our inability to get beyond the situation at hand, the one staring us in the face. The *immediate* business challenge. *Tomorrow's* game. *Last night's* homework. It's quite natural to want to address the impending situation or looming crisis, but we often do so at the peril of a grander achievement. The short-term snatch is a trap that often befalls marketers, especially, who spend a lot of resources arguing for why their product is better than the other guy's product: *Now with 5 percent more yada-yada!* After my encounter with Bono, I shifted the question I asked about the brands I nurtured from "Why are we better?" to "Why do we exist in the world?" It's a question that forces you to articulate your "what" or "why" in grand terms. It's a question that drives you to put your ambition on a cosmic stage, to figure out the effect your action will have on the wider world.

One way of doing this is what's called laddering—take your ambition, imagine it's the first rung of a ladder, and to climb to the higher rung, you need to ask yourself the *most* annoying question, the query that repeatedly comes from the mouth of wide-eyed seven-year-olds: *Why?* The worksheet at the end of this chapter can help, but imagine you want to inspire yourself to lose some weight and tone some muscle. A modest 3 on the Ambition Scale. Okay, why?

Well, that's a relatively easy step to the next rung of the ladder. You want to get fit and healthy? Great.

But why? Why do you want to get fit and healthy?

To have more energy? To live longer? To keep up with my kids? To fulfill my dream of running a marathon? Now we're inching toward a healthy 5 on the Ambition Scale.

Now we're starting to get to Grand Ambitions—but perhaps they're still recognizably reasonable. Ascending to the next rung is when we start stretching to Delusional Ambitions: *Why do you want more energy and health and quality time with your kids?*

Maybe because you feel like you've got something special, something unique, that only you can provide your kids? Maybe only you see the strength behind your daughter's insecurity? Maybe without you, your daughter will be crushed by self-doubt? Maybe you want to save your own life to save her life...and then some! A 7 on the scale?

Let's climb another rung: *why do you want to save her life?*

Perhaps it's because she's the kindest creature you've ever encountered, a budding she-Gandhi whom you suspect might bring peace to a world careening to the brink of disaster.

Could it be? Could your ability to get to the gym, lose weight, eat well, love your daughter, propel her through childhood with confidence, and support her as she begins to stride the world be the very thing that brings peace to warring nations? Could it?

That sounds delusional. A solid 9 on the Ambition Scale.

It also sounds awesome.

Perhaps it'll get you to the gym tonight.

So, yes, I'm asking you to ask yourself the ultimate existential question: why do you exist in the world? What's the point of your life? It certainly can't be to "increase market share for your company"—and I hope it's more than to "be good" at something. Express the stakes at play—and make them epic. Explore the far-out effects of success and the cataclysmic consequences of failure. Answer the ultimate question: *why does this matter?* As Marianne Williamson reminded us all, "Your playing small does not serve the world." And it certainly doesn't serve an audience you're trying to inspire.

Technique 3: Seize the Underdog Advantage

Every hero has an enemy, and the very best heroes have the very worst (or maybe best) enemies. In fact, there's likely a proportionate relationship between the two: the more evil and insidious the villain, the more strong and noble the hero must be. The hero must rise to the occasion of her nemesis. It's a phenomenon charted so dramatically in the Harry Potter saga. In the beginning, Voldemort is a weak parasite, unable to even maintain his own life without the body of a human host, the obsequious Quirrell. And Harry, too, is far from wielding his greatest powers. He's a mere wizardling. But, as the story develops, they each grow in strength, one becoming more vicious and destructive as the other becomes more, well, heroic.

So then, one technique for a Muse to inspire is to create an awful enemy, a villain that demands a heroic effort to conquer. How can you create a fearsome—a sublime—challenge for your audience? It'll be relative, of course. The rival football team might be the greatest squad of talent the state has ever seen, or the competitive company might be gunning for your company's very destruction. But maybe the loathsome enemy is the lack of faith your peers have in you. President George W. Bush described the "tyranny of low expectations" that plague low-income African-American students, the collective dismissal of their dreams. That's an ugly enemy. So, too, might be the comforts of bed or Netflix or chocolate cake. Apparently, Phil Knight once described Nike's enemy as "gravity"—not *adidas* or the couch or laziness, but gravity, the seemingly-unconquerable force that keeps us all locked in place. I want to fight gravity. I want to fight it every time I feel the tug of complacency.

The Underdog Advantage is the extra power you grant to your audience when you put them on the thrilling side of beating big competition. We all want to be David, nimble with slingshot, not Goliath, oafish and clumsy. Underdogs are aspirational and irresistible.

I remember the summer's night in 1982 when I stood on my front lawn and got socked in the jaw by my best friend. It didn't hurt as much as it should have, as I was hyped up on adrenaline and Cherry Coke. We had just seen *Rocky III* and, in a fit of patriotism-fueled delusion, decided we were boxers fighting for Cold War triumph.

Rocky Balboa epitomizes the Heroic Underdog. From the shoddy side of Philadelphia, he can hardly afford weights with which to train. And, at every turn of every movie, his opponent—his nemesis—seems to have all the trappings of the good boxing life. There's Apollo Creed with his shiny champion shorts and, yes, in *Rocky III*, there's Drago, a perfect specimen of Soviet Science (and perhaps steroids). When Drago tells Rocky matter-of-factly, "I will crush you," there's no reason to doubt the boast—except for the fact that it's *Rocky III*, and in this movie, like all the movies, the underdog wins.

We can draw a bold straight line from Rocky Balboa to Jimmy "B-Rabbit" Smith Jr., the battle-rapper in *8 Mile* both played by and modeled on Eminem. He lives in a trailer with his drug-addicted mom and his little sister, working hard, life of violence, all a shambles. But he's got a dream, an ambition to be a rapper, and he flexes those talents in lyrical battles at the local hip-hop club. He's Rocky with words. And, oh, he's white, which, only in the world of hip-hop, marks him as an outsider underdog. And like Rocky, he loses, and loses hard—before he wins, of course. The anthem of the movie is the song "Lose Yourself," an epic poem about an underdog's humiliation and eventual salvation. You know the lyrics that narrate his humiliation: a tale that starts with choking and joking and then our hero seizes his one shot, his one opportunity to make his life matter. I can't be the only person who turns up that tune when flagging at the gym. It's inspiring, like Rocky is inspiring. These are people with steep stakes on the line, with a demonstrated ability to fail—and they're giving their dream every fiber of strength they can muster.

Both Rocky and Rabbit are so inspiring, in part, because they faced Goliaths who beat them. Initially. These defeats, like Eliud Kipchoge's failure to break the two-hour marathon, contained the super-seeds for future success. They gnawed at our protagonists and, in so doing, they burnished ambition. To be a Muse, celebrate defeats—especially those defeats at the hands of the most formidable enemies. If you're a CEO, remind your team they were out-innovated by a competitor. If you're a coach, dwell on the other team's buzzer-shot basket that sent your crew to second place last year. If you're dieting, remember the day you slipped with half a pizza and a few beers. But don't do any of this to linger in the moment; do it to fuel your sense of vengeance.

Shakespeare-Style: Gulp!

In *Henry V*, Shakespeare shares his version of a speech that English king gives his disarrayed troops before they battle the polished French army at Agincourt. It's a long speech, and it's written in archaic language—but I urge you to read it and read it out loud. It's an amazing example of seizing the Underdog Advantage. As the scene begins, Henry's cousin was just bemoaning what few troops they have. They'll be slaughtered, he suggests, because they just don't have the right stuff. But Henry won't hear any pitiful complaints. He shines a spotlight on exactly the thing that worries his soldiers the most, their greatest vulnerability. In fact, he adds to the worry, reminding them

that they also don't have the right armor or equipment. We're fucked,
he might as well be saying, and he does so like this:

I pray thee, wish not one man more....
No, faith, my coz, wish not a man from England.
God's peace! I would not lose so great an honour
As one man more methinks would share from me
For the best hope I have. O, do not wish one more!
Rather proclaim it, Westmorland, through my host,
That he which hath no stomach to this fight,
Let him depart; his passport shall be made,
And crowns for convoy put into his purse;
We would not die in that man's company
That fears his fellowship to die with us.
This day is call'd the feast of Crispian.
He that outlives this day, and comes safe home,
Will stand a tip-toe when this day is nam'd,
And rouse him at the name of Crispian.
He that shall live this day, and see old age,
Will yearly on the vigil feast his neighbours,
And say "To-morrow is Saint Crispian."
Then will he strip his sleeve and show his scars,
And say "These wounds I had on Crispin's day."
Old men forget; yet all shall be forgot,
But he'll remember, with advantages,
What feats he did that day. Then shall our names,
Familiar in his mouth as household words—
Harry the King, Bedford and Exeter,
Warwick and Talbot, Salisbury and Gloucester—
Be in their flowing cups freshly rememb'red.
This story shall the good man teach his son;
And Crispin Crispian shall ne'er go by,
From this day to the ending of the world,
But we in it shall be rememberèd-
We few, we happy few, we band of brothers;
For he to-day that sheds his blood with me

Shall be my brother; be he ne'er so vile,
This day shall gentle his condition;
And gentlemen in England now a-bed
Shall think themselves accurs'd they were not here,
And hold their manhoods cheap whiles any speaks
That fought with us upon Saint Crispin's day.[15]

It might just be the greatest example of an inspiring battlefield speech ever. Henry embraces the underdog status of his troops in tattered clothes; in fact, he doesn't want a single more soldier to balance out the fight. They're a band of brothers precisely because they are a few—and in that disadvantage lies the opportunity for honor. In the struggle for which they are woefully outmatched is the prize of standing tip-toe one day hence, ripping off shirts, exposing scars, scars that proclaim courage and manliness.

Watch Kenneth Branagh deliver those lines in the 1989 movie and see if you don't want to saddle up and kick some French-army ass. There are so many lessons on inspiration to mine in this speech:

1. Acknowledge the odds stacked against your team. Look the reality squarely in the eye. Don't sugarcoat; in fact, de-sugar. Ratchet up the danger. Make Goliath bigger and brawnier.
2. And then laugh at that enemy. Display brazen insouciance. Shake off the desire to even want to balance the battlefield.
3. Paint a visual picture of what victory will look like. Locate your audience in the glory of eventual victory. Transport them to the part of the story where Luke and Han get their medals, where they get to—er—"hold their manhoods."
4. Name names: Bedford, Exeter, Warwick, Stan the Point Guard, Suzie in Accounting. Make it personal. Let your team know that you know them, and you believe in their power.

NOT-SO-MODERN MUSE: JESUS OF NAZARETH
How Does He Do It?

I know, it takes a lot of audacity to profile Jesus—Jesus *Christ*, to some of you—in a book that divines the inspiring techniques of folks like Bono, Oprah, and Elon Musk. It's a strange Mt. Rushmore of Muses, for sure. And yet I can't imagine a better representative of Delusional Ambition than that temperamental peasant who spawned a religious movement spanning two millennia, creating converts of billions of people. By some estimates, one-third of people who have lived on our planet in the past two thousand years have called themselves Christians.

And how did he do it? How did that guy inspire so many?

Well, an army of scholars has competently answered that question in myriad ways—lucky timing; a despised enemy; strong "first-generation" leadership. Perhaps you even believe the hand of God played a little role.

But what strikes me is the central promise Jesus made to those who would follow him, in John 14:6: "I am the way, the truth, and the life." *Eternal life. Forever life. In the happiest place imaginable.* Jesus didn't inspire followers by promising them temporal power or riches; no, his "ambition ladder" extended to the heavens. His Delusional Ambition was to give every man and woman alive a shot at the ultimate prize: forever-and-ever bliss.

GET DELUSIONAL WORKSHEET

MY AMBITION: _____

HOW CAN I SUPERLATIZE IT? HOW CAN I MAKE IT BIGGER AND GREATER?

_____

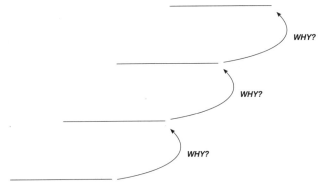

LADDER TO MY MIGHTY PURPOSE

WHY?

WHY?

WHY?

MY ENEMY IS: _____

AND THEY TERRIFY ME BECAUSE:

_____

And now, with all the delusional fodder from the previous worksheet, reconsider your Ambition from page xxiv. Restate it in more ambitious terms, words that stretch as far along the Ambition Spectrum you can imagine, comfort be damned:

MY AMBITION DELUSIONALIZED

THE ONE THING I REALLY WANT TO ACCOMPLISH AT THIS STAGE IN MY LIFE IS:

_____

_____

_____

_____

_____

CHAPTER 7

The Second Skill of Inspiration: Aim For Action

(How Changing Behavior, Not Thinking, Gets the Hard Jobs Done)

*"A decision is not made in your head.
It's made when you move."*

—MEL ROBBINS

Well, now you've done it. You've gone and cracked a Delusional Ambition. You want to change the world. You want to vanquish the fiercest Goliaths. You want to transform your team, shift politics, live forever, cure cancer, become the oldest kick-boxing champion in history, and launch a billion-dollar company. And perhaps you want to do them all at once.

Where do you begin? How do you move yourself or your team from the razzle-dazzle thrill of thinking big to the actual task of getting the big job done? How do you move from the sublime to the practical?

You'll be tempted to explain, to make a case, to persuade your audience about the merits of your Delusional Ambition, to "bring them along" or "enlist" them for the journey, as the organizational theorists would say. This desire to explain is the natural instinct of good people. Offering information and proof points and "reasons to believe" is a generous act indeed.

But it's also the disastrous mistake made by The Reasonables. All that explaining—on the heels of a great ambition—sticks your audience in place, keeps them thinking, mulling, and, even worse, questioning and arguing. At this stage, weighing pros and cons is all con.

Now is the time to obsesses about Action. What do you want your audience *to do*—not think, not feel, *just do*. Do you want them to work the weekend, finish their homework by 7 p.m., eat a yogurt, call now, visit a website, vote at the public library on the way home from the office, wash their hands, share a hashtag? The Muse is crystal clear about the very next step that needs to be taken, the thing to be done.

Let's call this the **Inspir-Action**—the inspiring action that is the first step toward achieving your Delusional Ambition. It's small thinking with big effects. In fact, the *specificity* of your Inspir-Action is a complement to the *sublimity* of your Delusional Ambition. It makes the haze clear. It makes the ridiculous conceivable.

And it begins to build converts to your cause without the need to resort to pesky arguments. Behavioral psychologists have identified the counterintuitive insight that it's easier to change behavior than it is to change thinking; in fact, when our behavior changes, our thinking follows—not vice versa. Let me write that again, because it's easy to miss how radical a notion it is:

When our behavior changes, our thinking follows.

That's a hard pill for The Reasonables to swallow. They want to believe we "think through" our actions *before* we take them. But the Muse knows better. The Muse knows the best way to move people is to...*get them moving.*

Sol's Dictum

"The human body can do anything for thirty seconds."

—SOL BRANDYS, Coach and Trainer

Sol is my trainer, the man who has taken me, an exercise-averse business executive, and turned me into—if not a gym rat—certainly, a gym mouse. He has helped me find the joy in exertion, the pleasure that comes the moment you push out of that last push-up your body can possibly handle, arms shaking, alarmed that your face will be smashed on the wooden floor. Sol once coached me through a regimen on a rowing machine so intense that I puked in a bucket. It was one of the proudest moments of my life—because pride always follows the almost-fall.

Lifting groceries, lifting kids, lifting spirits. Thank you, Sol.

The human body can do anything for thirty seconds.

And Sol would know. His parents met during World War II in the shadows of a concentration camp. His thinking about exercise and diet is informed, in part, by the lessons in endurance he was taught by his family's awful experience.

Though I'm certain I lack the fortitude to survive what his parents did, I chant Sol's dictum at those moments I'm crossing my threshold from can-do to can't-ever-do. Maybe it's exercise. Maybe it's the patience demanded by parenting. Maybe it's writing this book. *Thirty seconds. Thirty seconds. Just thirty seconds.* It's a ridiculously precise rule to follow.

At some point, it ends. Of course, it does. But that point is much farther away than you ever imagined. It's thirty seconds and thirty seconds and thirty seconds and so many more thirty seconds away. So much closer to your Delusional Ambition.

Simon Says

In the late 1980s, Jeremiah Sullivan, a professor at the University of Washington, bucked the conventional wisdom of management theory with his belief that a leader's *words* could have a greater impact on an organization than that leader's goals or strategies. It's amazing to think that was a radical proposition but, in a world ruled by Reasonables, of course, strategy and tactics would get credit for the good stuff. Professor Sullivan wanted to identify the kind of language a great leader employs to motivate a team. His framework—Motivational Language Theory (MLT)—proposes three *types* of language that work and, as with Aristotle's "Three Modes of Persuasion," it's a mix of touchy-feely and damn concrete:

1. **Meaning-Making Language.** This is language that links a team member's job to a higher purpose. This is classic Simon Sinek *Start With Why* language, and as discussed in the previous chapter, I believe much of this meaning-making language becomes inspiring when the ambitions are stretched to grand and delusional levels.

2. **Empathetic Language.** This is language that establishes a bond between a leader and her team. It builds trust and faith. Not surprisingly, it's the kind of emotional language that many managers find most difficult to employ, often dismissing it as

touchy-feely and inappropriate in the workplace. When we get to the Fifth Skill of Inspiration: Love, For Real, we'll offer some tips and techniques for helping you express the kind of empathy that actually gets results.

But it's the third type of language Professor Sullivan identified that I'd like us to consider now:

3. **Direction-Giving Language**, or in academic jargon, perlocutionary language, meaning communication that has "action as its aim." This is language that tells you what to do, outlines next steps, establishes expectations, timelines, and criteria for success. These are commands and imperatives, the kind occasionally barked by teachers, parents, and traffic signs.

According to Jacqueline and Milton Mayfield, two professors at the University of Texas who have tested Professor Sullivan's theories in the crucible of actual corporations, this direction-giving language "works" by providing crystal clarity about expectations set for a team, thus *reducing uncertainty and the anxiety* that often accompanies it. "In a sense," the Mayfields say, "direction-giving language offers us the psychological safety of knowing what is expected and what to expect in return."[1] *A psychological safety net.*

I learned about the Mayfields from Dan McGinn who is an editor at *Harvard Business Review* and the author of a book called *Psyched Up: How the Science of Mental Preparation Can Help You Succeed*, which, as the name clearly implies, is a book with lessons for getting yourself stoked before a big performance. It's a smart, fun, and useful read, but my favorite chapter is one that examines the pep talks coaches give their teams before big games. McGinn takes us inside the locker rooms to the moments when coaches summon their inner Muses and, by dint of words, bring the very best out of their teams. These are the moments when coaches turn teams into champions. And, as you can imagine, they do it with rousing, poetic exhortations: "Clear Eyes. Full

Hearts. Can't Lose," says the fictional, irresistible Coach Taylor from Dillon, Texas.

Or so we believe that's how these pre-game sermons work.

The truth, as McGinn uncovers it, is that these pep talks are entirely more pedestrian. When he studies the real-life speeches of an acclaimed coach like Knute Rockne (whose famous "Win One for the Gipper" speech might, in fact, be apocryphal) or the fictional exhortations of Coach Norman Dale in *Hoosiers*, played with ferocious intensity by Gene Hackman, McGinn finds very little poetry, very little lyrical language that sets spirits soaring. Instead, he finds *MLT's* "direction-giving language"—coaches being very precise about the tactics they expect their teams to employ: *"Pass four times before shooting.... Neutralize that shooting guard.... Box out that star rebounder on every play....* Yes they appeal to the players' emotions," McGinn writes, "But they also focus on the game plan and *the specifics of precisely what the team needs to do* to win the game."[2]

McGinn goes on to explain that this information-giving language is often more effective than the emotion-rousing variety—*especially when a team is playing an unknown opponent. That's* when a speech that is filled with specific and actionable instructions proves its value: when you're facing something unknown, unclear, or maybe, as our friend Burke would have it, something sublime. Apparently, the power of these action-oriented directions diminishes as a player knows her opponent better; in those cases, the "meaning-making" language of ambition or purpose can stand on its own. Roger Federer, for example, doesn't need an instruction manual of tactics when he faces his frequent opponent, Rafael Nadal; no, he just needs to be reminded he's competing to be the greatest player of all time.

But when you're staring down the road of a Delusional Ambition, scared and confused and overwhelmed and uncertain—all good, virtuous, emotion-arousing feelings, mind you—then, at that moment, vivid and concrete Inspir-Action becomes your guiding light.

The Delusional Ambition might be to win the national title, but the Inspir-Action is to box out the star rebounder. The Delusional Ambition might be to reverse climate change, but the Inspir-Action is to get your neighbor to the polling place on Election Day. The Delusional Ambition might be to clean your arteries of cholesterol, but the Inspir-Action is to eat butter-free popcorn at the movie on Friday night. The Delusional Ambition might be to topple the patriarchy, but the Inspir-Action is to post #metoo on your social channels if you have been a victim of sexual predation. *Both* expressions—the grand and the gritty, the delusional and the precise, the spirit-rousing and the body-moving—conspire to inspire.

MODERN MUSE: A BUCKET OF ICE
No Questions Asked

You might remember the summer of 2014. It was a bleak time. Police in St. Louis shot Michael Brown, an unarmed black man, igniting an explosion of angry and violent protests across The United States. ISIS reared its ugly head, establishing their caliphate across The Middle East. Russia invaded Crimea. Ebola struck the world. And Robin Williams died.

Yet amidst this sad and scary chaos, a strange and heartening phenomenon was born. More than seventeen million people filmed themselves as ice water was dumped over their heads, often by their own hands. Almost *half a billion* people viewed these videos on Facebook, watching their friends and family and celebrities like Oprah, Bill Gates, LeBron James, and even President George W. Bush and the Pillsbury Doughboy pour freezing water on themselves.

We have Pete Frates to thank for the Ice Bucket Challenge.

Pete was an all-star school athlete and for a short time, a professional baseball player in Europe. In 2012, he was panicked to feel his body struggling to accomplish the most mundane tasks, like buttoning his shirt. Pete had been a home-run hitter, after all. This wasn't normal. After some frantic Googling, Pete saw a doctor. who after some tests, broke the terrible news to Pete and his family: Pete had amyotrophic lateral sclerosis (ALS), often called Lou Gehrig's disease after the famous Yankee who suffered from it.

On that day, Pete hatched a Delusional Ambition. He told his doctor he'd raise a billion dollars, a billion dollars to crack a cure for ALS. His family was incredulous.

But Pete meant what he said. Inspired by the ridiculous things he saw folks doing on YouTube, he devised a plan that was perfect for the social media era: he would challenge his friends to donate money for ALS research *or* dump a bucket of ice water on their head. Donate or douse.

On the heels of his Delusional Ambition, he cracked a plan to start making it happen.

Slowly, the Ice Bucket Challenge spread, thanks, in part, to the connections Pete had with professional athletes. But the Challenge really took off—"went viral"—when one of those athletes, professional golfer Chris Kennedy, challenged his cousin, Jeanette Senerchia, on national television: donate or douse, he said. Jeanette did both, in honor of her husband who was also afflicted with ALS. Soon enough, social media was littered with millions of people challenging each other, pouring water on their heads, and donating money to the ALS Association. The campaign raised more than $200 million worldwide (and even years later, donations are up 25 percent) and some of that money was used for medical research that discovered a gene linked to the disease.[3] It's not quite the billion dollars Pete had imagined, not yet at least, but it's a great leap toward his worthy goal.

And, although some critics charge (fairly) that most of the folks watching these videos had no clue what ALS was or why they should care about it, a quantitative breakdown of Google search results demonstrates that the effort did *significantly* raise awareness of the disease. In fact, searches for information about ALS increased 200 percent during the heyday of the challenge, even besting searches for Justin Bieber one month.[4] That said, it's true that more than 95 percent of folks who participated did not search out more information on the disease.

Think about that: millions of people dumped freezing cold water on their heads without knowing why they were doing it. They did it because they were told to. Some did it because so many other people were doing it. To others, it looked fun. And a small percentage did it for ALS. But they all did it because they were given a blueprint for doing it, crystal-clear directions to follow if you wanted to be part of the phenomenon. They just didn't do it for ALS.

This was passion and, in some cases, an awful lot of passion minus some reason.

The Ice Bucket Challenge was a triumph of action. People *did*—and in so doing, they took a leap toward solving the genetic riddle of a terrible puzzle. Is it okay they didn't really "understand" the disease? Is it okay that that didn't really want to be bothered learning and investigating? Well, if you're Pete or Jeanette, no, it doesn't matter one bit. What matters is what people *did*.

Bodies Beat Beliefs: Skin in the Game

But Inspir-Actions don't just create foot soldiers in the march toward a goal; they create converts. And they do so because action affects attitude; in fact, it's a curious truth of human nature that we often adjust our "beliefs" to fit our behavior, not vice versa.

Take sex.

Reverend Ed Young is a sex-pushing evangelical minister. As the pastor of a Dallas-based megachurch, he encouraged his (married) congregants to have sex every day—no matter what—for seven days straight and then, eventually, forty days. He figured the best way to repair tired and frayed marriages was to focus on the *behavior* of spouses, not their feelings. He called it his "sexperiment."[5]

Reverend Young was right. After weeks of daily sex, couples reported an increased intimacy in their relationships, a recharging of their marital vows.

It's a tactic not limited to love. It works in war as well. Take the torture of boot camp: the very act of waking up each morning to have your ass kicked by a drill sergeant increases the levels of patriotism amongst army recruits.

So, too, with diets: change your eating habits, and your beliefs about food will follow. Give up ice cream and cookies and, sure enough, soon enough, your craving for ice cream and cookies will diminish.

This is all true because our brains are more stubborn than our bodies. Our brains are too hard to change, to move. It takes the slow roll of evolution, in fact. Changing behavior, however, is a relative breeze.

Starbucks has turned this insight about the power of action to transform beliefs into *the* engine for their business. The *ritual* of ordering a coffee at a Starbucks—*I'll have a grande half-caff latte with two pumps of caramel, please!*—is one of the very things that *creates* the premium value of the brand. If we want people to believe that our coffee is worth four dollars a cup, they said, let's start by changing their behavior, herding them into an experience that dramatizes the special-ness of our cups of joe. A "large" coffee might be worth a couple of dollars, but a "venti"—oh no, just saying that word makes the very same coffee seem worth even more. Starbucks is obsessed about what you say, what you do—because they know that behavior drives belief.

Directions Make the Difference

The power of action—of direction-giving language—was also employed by the Obama campaign's much-vaunted get-out-the-vote operation in 2008. It was an effort that helped propel him to victory, and one that made wonderful use of Inspir-Actions. It was an approach they fine-tuned in 2012, as the campaign team prepared for a heated re-election campaign. They assembled a clandestine team of psychologists, including heavyweight behavioral psychologists like Robert Cialdini and Richard Thaler, to help them fine-tune their pitch to voters.[6]

One of their most powerful tools was an innovative approach to canvassing—both door-to-door and by telephone. Traditionally, a candidate's representatives would approach a potential voter, pitch their candidate, and then ask how that voter intended to vote. They'd mark your answer on the spreadsheet on their clipboard—and then the campaign would use that information to determine which "messages" you should receive in the future. With a preponderance of personal data available to marketers, the savviest of these operations would be able to fine-tune that messaging for maximum effect. Knowing your job and your model of car and where your family last vacationed would—*could*—help them figure out exactly the right way to pitch their candidate to you.

The Obama Campaign made smart use of all this personal data, but they also implemented another strategy. Based on the insight that *potential* voters were much more likely to be actual voters if they answered three straightforward questions—*when* would they vote; *where* would they vote; *how* would they get there—the Obama canvassers wouldn't leave a house or end a phone call until a voter talked them through their intended voting routine: *After I drop the kids at school but before I go to Starbucks, I'll pop by the fire house to cast my vote.* That Action—making a plan—made all the difference. According to a report from Harvard's Kennedy School, this Inspir-Action "boosted turnout by 4.1 percentage points." It was "twice as effective" as the standard approach.[7]

And so, in tandem with the lofty rhetoric and Delusional Ambition of the Obama Campaign, was at least one simple Inspir-Action: make a plan to vote. Don't just get moved; get moving.

Golden Rules

Dump water on your head. Double-cover the point guard. Have sex today. Take a full thirty seconds to order your complicated coffee. Picture your route to the polling place. Post *#metoo*.

All of these examples of Inspir-Actions ask a person to behave in a certain way in a certain moment. They work because they give people something to do, not something to ponder and debate. And some of these examples—like having sex and drinking coffee—can grow into habits and rituals that last a lifetime.

But sometimes our aim stretches beyond a particular moment. We don't just want to inspire you to vote for our candidate; we want to inspire you to join our cause. We don't just want you to win this basketball game; we want you to grow into an adult with grit and determination. We don't just want you to buy a cupcake from the sustainable bakery we opened; we want you to help us save the planet. We don't just want you to put down the drinks "one day at a time;" we want you to quit drinking, get a job, heal your family, and enjoy a long, full, healthy life.

Sometimes—oftentimes—we don't just want to "move" an audience in the moment; we want to shift their very existence.

When our ambitions are that sweeping, we need to give our audience something more lasting than short-term directions; we need to give them a Golden Rule—a guideline for what to do in any—in every—situation.

The greatest Golden Rules require very little thinking to execute; they pitch themselves to the heart in your head. Consider the best-known one: *"Do unto others as you would have them do unto you."* It's a maxim that all of the world's major religions promote, and it's meant to prompt a way of behaving that's intuitive and easy. At heart, it's all heart: *how would I* feel *if she did that to me? How would I* feel *if I were treated that way?* It's an *emotional* calculation you're asked to make, one that starts with an act of great creativity: first, imagine the situation were reversed; get yourself inside the other person's skin; and then, check in with your feelings: if they're not quite kosher, refrain from doing whatever you were about to do.

The Golden Rule is an act of imagination and empathy, not reason or logic.

I think Sol's dictum—the idea that we can do anything for thirty seconds—is a Golden Rule. It's an evergreen instruction to keep going that can be invoked in myriad situations when we just don't want to. Straining to finish a workout? Think about thirty seconds. Straining to live by the Golden Rule with your obnoxious coworker? Start with thirty seconds.

In fact, most "inspirational quotes"—the homespun wisdom we find on refrigerator magnets and bumper stickers—are Golden Rules: *Dance like nobody's watching... Make your own luck... You miss 100 percent of the shots you don't take...* These are Golden Rules that extol some very specific virtues: being less self-conscious; working hard; and taking risks, respectively. The problem with these examples, however, is that they're well-worn clichés and, as we'll see in the next two chapters, clichés lack the stopping-power that inspiration demands. They become background noise, easy to ignore. The *best* Golden Rules do exactly what these Hallmark platitudes strive to do—they wrap up a virtue in a memorable instruction.

Three Techniques for Finding Your Inspir-Action

Having identified your Delusional Ambition, it's now time to find your Inspir-Action—the specific step you're asking your team, your audience (or yourself) to take towards achieving your goal. The trick is to follow the advice Strunk & White gave in their famous primer on good writing: make it vivid and concrete. "Eat better food" won't cut it; "eat only vegetables" probably will. "Close more deals this quarter" falls short—but "double your sales calls" doesn't. Muses have mastered the ability to flit from the grand to the tactical in the flutter of a sentence.

Now, it's important to remember that the Inspir-Action is probably not the actual thing you want to accomplish itself. If it's genuinely a wild ambition you're after, it's hard to imagine any singular action will achieve it. The road to starting your own company, for example, involves working up your own courage to do so, perhaps quitting your job, securing funding, designing a business plan, and bringing along the support you'll need from your family and friends. At least.

Here are three techniques that will help you identify the Inspir-Action that will *set you in motion toward* your desired goal:

Technique 1: One Small Step...

Find the absolute smallest thing that might be done toward achieving your goal. And I mean the smallest. Then the next. Then the next. Breaking down a chain of behavior into its smallest component parts make it instantly less daunting.

Gym trainers have mastered the technique of "first-stepping" their clients to a better, healthier body. They break down a long-term goal—lose twenty pounds, run a marathon—into component steps. Leaders seeking to inspire should do the same: start with your Delusional Ambition and map the steps back to the here-and-now reality. You'll have your blueprint.

And it might be that achieving your Delusional Ambition will take several steps or involve a variety of concurrent actions. Saving the planet, for example, might involve a series of Inspir-Actions, from recycling to educating children about the effects of energy waste to buying an electric car to donating to an organization influencing public policy about climate change. That's great. Capture them all. For most of us, there's nothing more arousing than checking off all the items on a long to-do list.

Technique 2: Create Assassins (and Other Amazing Jobs)

Everybody appreciates being given a special job to do. It's flattering and motivating. So look at your audience and start assigning them the variety of roles you'll need to accomplish your goal—and make sure they each sound important or, at least, enjoyable.

Teachers are brilliant at doing this. Good ones have mastered the art of getting unruly kids to behave, and the best of them don't do so with threats and punishment, but with the curious act of adding to the kid's burden: they give the kid a "special" job to do. *Billy, I need you to be the General of Sticks*—and, before you know it, Billy is picking up and organizing all the ice cream pop sticks that the class has been using to learn multiplication. And of course he is: he's the general of sticks!

One of my sons wasn't too happy when his soccer coach relegated him to defense—and center back, at that, the position that needs to "stay back" and protect the goal while the rest of the team gets to move upfield and score some points. My son felt bored, even a little punished by his place on the field. I was even worried he'd quit the team—until a chat with a teammate's father who, coincidentally, also played center back when he was younger. This dad explained to my son that he had the coolest position on the field: he was "the team assassin." That's right: it was his job to "take out" anybody that slipped by the mid-field. Suddenly, my son was interested. An assassin? He gets to be an assassin! He gets to be Jason Bourne on a soccer field!

And this isn't just a technique that works on kids who might not know any better. We all want to feel like we're contributing to a project in a special way. Look at your team: who do you want to be the "conscience" and who can be the "closer" and who can be the "architect" and who can be the "joy squad?" Look at your team and give them sexy, fun, cool, important roles—the kind of roles that imply very clear action to be taken. You'll see them throw on the mantle of those positions and get busy.

Technique 3: Write Your Golden Rules

Am I asking you to compose a Golden Rule, like Confucius and Buddha and Jesus and Mohammed? Of course, I am. All along, I've been telling you you're a Muse.

Remember our Three Types of Inspiration. The first was Inspiration by Virtue—the kind of inspiration we feel when we're moved by the way a person lives her life. Perhaps we're inspired by the way somebody faces a particular moment, perhaps a tragic moment like cancer or divorce; or maybe we're inspired by the way a person seems to wake up and face every single day with a spirit that we envy: our mother who works harder than anybody we know; that friend who always follows her heart; heck, the Dalai Lama who does absolutely everything with gentle kindness.

Behind these people, we can likely find a Golden Rule by which they live. They might not ever articulate it. It might be instinctual, second nature, but it's there: *What Would Mom Do? What Would Helen Do? What Would Forrest Gump Do? What Would Bono Do?* These are Golden Rules that help us direct behavior—our own and others—across a range of situations and circumstances. They become rules for *living*.

In fact, if you look at any life and apply a little creativity, you'd likely be able to identify some sort of "code" by which it is lived. That person always says "yes." That one listens like his life depended upon it. And she never takes bullshit from anybody. Muses give the gift of these Golden Rules to their audiences. They pick the rules that will help achieve their Delusional Ambitions—and they give them to an audience for whom they become the ever-present, never-thinking prompts to *do.*

So, a simple trick, fill in the blank: What Would ____ Do? Try to find the person who exemplifies the trait or approach that you desperately want your audience to adopt. Do you want a team exude joy? *What Would Ellen Do?* Or do you want them to win by dint of sheer hard work? *What Would Serena Do?* Do you want them to show more love? *What Would a Puppy Do?*

In addition, you should imagine your ideal future, the moment at which your Delusional Ambition becomes an awesome reality. What will be *different* about your audience then? Will they be collaborating, working together as a smooth-humming team? Will you be twenty pounds lighter and full of vigor? Think about what will be different and then a compose a Golden Rule that asks for that behavior to begin today... *Trust your teammate... Eat like you're at the beach...*

And remember what you must never do: at all costs, avoid arguing. Remember my friend Dan Goldstein's grandmother's maxim: "Arguments convince nobody." It's a rule by which Muses abide. If a coach is detailing why a defensive strategy makes more sense than an offensive play, he has already lost the battle of motivating the team. If Al Gore is debating whether a 15 percent or 20 percent reduction in carbon emissions makes for sounder public policy, the cause of reversing climate change becomes a lost cause. If you're negotiating, you're not inspiring.

DELUSIONAL AMBITIONS!

INSPIR-ACTIONS!

"HOLY SHIT!"

"ALRIGHT, WE GOT THIS!"

I WILL LEAD THE MOST INNOVATIVE COMPANY IN THE WORLD.

PUT TOGETHER A BUSINESS PLAN.

LET'S BE THE MOST INTERESTING THING IN THE WHOLE BAR.

MAKE SOME INTERESTING COMMERICIALS.

I WILL ABOLISH SLAVERY.

ANNOUNCE THE PLAN.

WE'LL BE A "LIFE CULT" THAT ERADICATES POVERTY IN AFRICA.

ASK "WHAT WOULD GANDHI DO?"

I'LL COMPLETE ANOTHER MARATHON 25% FASTER.

READ AN ARTICLE ABOUT MARATHON STRATEGY.

HELP MY KID FULFILL HER DREAM TO BE PRESIDENT.

ALWAYS TAKE HER SERIOUSLY WHEN SHE SPEAKS.

AIM FOR ACTION WORKSHEET

MY DELUSIONAL AMBITION: _____

FIND THE FIRST STEP

_____ ↖

HOW?

_____ ↖

HOW?

_____ ↖

HOW?

_____ ↖

HOW?

_____

CREATE "ASSASSINS"

WHAT JOBS CAN I ASSIGN?... _____

_____

GOLDEN RULES

ALWAYS: _____ *NEVER:* _____

WHAT WOULD: _____ *DO:* _____

CHAPTER 8

The Third Skill of Inspiration: Show Up To Stir Up

(How Breaking the Rules with "WTF Moments" Creates an Awesome Atmosphere)

The Muse breaks the rules, but not for the hell of it.

No, The Muse breaks the rules to create a sense of new and unimagined possibilities for an audience. Once the expected course of events is gone, anything, no matter how delusional, just might happen.

We've all walked into places that feel pregnant with the possibility of magic—strange, sacred places, like old churches on a rainy day, an ancient forest where the path seems to end in a grove of majestic trees, or the moment the lights go down in a theatre before a film introduces us to a whole new world. These spaces are awesome, sublime. They move us. They might even disorientate us.

Muses can create that sense of magic, of power. In fact, they must. Conference rooms and offices and factory floors and locker rooms aren't generally, by their nature, all that moving.

How you enter a space. How you look. How you sound. Where you sit. When you speak. These are some of the tools we all have to use to take an ordinary space, an ordinary moment, and charge it with the kind of awesome power that makes people stop and feel the birth of something new and extraordinary.

A Lying, Inspiring Entrance

In the early 1970s, when Paramount Pictures decided they wanted to make Roald Dahl's beloved book, *Charlie and the Chocolate Factory*, into a film, Mel Stuart, the director, knew he wanted Gene Wilder to play the part of the eccentric chocolatier. Nobody else would do. Wilder would eventually agree with one condition: he wanted to script his opening scene; he wanted to write the very first moment he'd appear in the film.[1]

Fine, agreed Stuart. It seemed an easy price to pay to get the man he wanted.

You probably remember the scene, the first time you laid your eyes on Mr. Willy Wonka. The children with their golden tickets, their parents and guardians, reporters and TV cameras, and hordes of curious townspeople are all gathered outside the wrought iron gate of the chocolate factory, its imposing Victorian façade soaring into the sunshine. They're waiting to see the recluse the world hadn't spied for decades. Who was he? What did he look like? What would he do?

And while the world waits outside those wrought iron gates, the bell tower chimes nine times and the factory door slowly swings open. From it emerges a decrepit man with a pronounced limp, hardly able to walk without the support of his cane.

It's a slow and awkward moment, the longest unedited shot in the film. We watch Willy Wonka inch step-by-step down a red carpet covering a precarious cobblestone walkway. As Willy Wonka drags himself toward the crowd, disaster strikes: his cane gets stuck between two cobblestones. The cane is standing more upright than the man himself. But he doesn't see it. My God, Willy Wonka takes the next step, extends his hand to grasp his cane, but his cane isn't there! It's one half-step behind him. The great Willy Wonka, at the moment he steps back onto the public stage, is about to fall flat on his strange face.

Watch that fall.

It might be the greatest fall on film. Wonka's body seems to hinge at his feet, as if there's a stiff rod running through his body, toes-to-top-hat. his head falls, taking his body with it, in a straight plane, about to smash on the cobblestones.

Drama.

Disaster.

But, of course, not at all.

For, at the very last split second, Wonka tucks his head under his body, rolls into a somersault, and springs upright again. The crowd erupts in wide grins and rousing applause. In a split second, the man has confounded and delighted them. He's gone from old to young. This is the great Willy Wonka—an embodied fountain of youth.

Years later, Gene Wilder was asked about his demand to script this moment. Why that? What were you thinking? Wilder explained that that moment would be the very first time his co-actors—the children especially—would lay their eyes on his character. He wouldn't meet them before shooting began. He wouldn't introduce himself backstage. No, that moment was the very time they—and the rest of the world—would lay their eyes on Willy Wonka. And, as Gene Wilder said, "From that time on, no one will know if I'm lying or telling the truth."[2]

No one will know if I'm lying or telling the truth.

That's an entrance, a disorientating entrance, an entrance that would get the most authentic performances from his co-stars. From that moment on, their surprise would be real surprise; their laughs, real laughs; their fear, real worry. Willy Wonka showed up in a way that made his colleagues better. Like Dr. Michael Joyner's audacious prediction created a team of superhero marathoners, Gene Wilder's disorientating entrance created a cast of first-rate actors. He was a Muse.

Pitch Imperfect

For those of you who only know about advertising from *Mad Men* and *Bewitched*, you might not realize just how arduous a process it is for an agency to "pitch" a client. Before they show up for the final meeting with their best ideas, they have to go through a gauntlet of other steps in the process: filling out reams of paperwork describing their capabilities; holding a "chemistry" session where the prospective client can get to know the team; strategy sessions; first round and second rounds; feedback in phone calls; budget meetings; and then, at last, a final presentation. Winning an account is a long, grueling process for an agency.

And I imagine that's the case with many other businesses as well. It takes work—meetings and meetings—to get work.

In one of my jobs, I was tasked with finding a new ad agency for our company, a process that involved my team and I meeting with more than thirty ad agencies to find the best fit. Most of these agencies were terrific, led and staffed by people who had helped other clients achieve great success. And, because they were marketers, they knew how critical their "positionings" were. They identified their "secret sauce"—their beliefs or processes that made them different and better than the rest of the competition.

This agency believed in data and technology. *That* agency believed in making a brand "famous." *Another* agency believed it was critical to "disrupt" the conventions of a company's category. *This* agency was passionate about social media. *That* one had a process that was collaborative. *That* other one did not.

It was a smorgasbord of delicious and different options.

Or so it should have been.

Despite the very real differences in what each agency *believed,* they were identical in how they *behaved.* Just about every single one of these agencies "showed up" to our meetings in exactly the same way:

1. They brought seven to ten people, because they wanted us to meet the "day-to-day" team as well as the leadership.
2. They all sat around one side of the conference room table and introduced themselves, one by one.
3. They each shared a beautifully designed PowerPoint presentation explaining their history, the location of their offices, their capabilities, and their other clients.
4. They discussed their "secret sauce" positioning that made them unique.
5. They'd then "prove" the power of that positioning by sharing a couple of case studies, work they did for other clients with glowing results, naturally.
6. Then they'd all say a version of the same curious thing, "It would be presumptuous of us to have an opinion about your business at this early stage, but we have done a little bit of research and thinking and would love to share our preliminary thoughts."
7. They would then leave no time for discussion, even though every one of them had begun by saying they didn't want to do a "one-sided" presentation.

I exaggerate—but only very, very slightly.

I was genuinely shocked by how similar each and every ad agency showed up. And I know I shouldn't have been. I had done the very same thing dozens of times when I worked at agencies myself! But being on the other side—being the audience—made me realize how brain-deadening dull these creative marketers could be.

And here's the tragedy of it all: their genuine, compelling differences didn't really matter when they each showed up in a way that felt exactly the same. *What* they were saying was irrelevant because of *how* they were saying it.

And I've realized in my work since then that this phenomenon is not unique to the world of ad agencies. So many businesses that need to "pitch" new clients end up aping the very same conventions: law firms, accountants, salespeople, even Hollywood agents—all showing up in the very same way. And, when they do, they sacrifice their most valuable possession: their own narrative.

The human brain has a crafty capacity to deal with things that look and feel and sound exactly the same. When faced with "commodities," our brains are momentarily stumped, but quickly look for little differences, nuances that we then grow into great differences. We exaggerate. We caricature. We take the small things and make them the deciding things.

And so, in our pitch, for example, my team quickly began referring to the "Techy" agency and the "Save The World" agency and the "Douchebag" agency and (my favorite) "The *Scooby-Doo* Kids" agency. All of these caricatures were, as caricatures often are, both true and false. They were based on a kernel of evidence distorted into a stereotype. And it happened because the agencies themselves sacrificed their opportunity to control their own narrative. Would you do that? Would you leave your chances of winning *anything* up to the odd stereotypes hatched in the mind of your audience?

No, of course not. You'd assert control.

One agency I met did stand out from the pack: Wieden+Kennedy, the agency that's helped Nike and Coke and Old Spice and countless other brands succeed on the back of powerful communications. Most people in the industry will tell you Wieden+Kennedy is the greatest ad agency of all time—and yet they themselves wouldn't. They didn't.

When I first met them, the crew from Wieden+Kennedy had what seemed like a gutsy approach to sharing their talent. They showed us the last ad a client did *before* coming to Wieden+Kennedy—and then the first ad Wieden+Kennedy did for them. To us—to most human beings—the Wieden+Kennedy work was far superior. What an approach! This was a slam dunk, self-evident argument in favor of the agency's awesome talent.

Or, at least, it should have been.

Instead, the team from Wieden+Kennedy proceeded to tell our team how *flawed* so much of their own work was. They saw mistakes where we saw brilliance. They explained to us that it took time— sometimes even a couple of years—to get to the *really* good stuff. They had to learn a brand, build trust with a client, experiment and fail and try again.

That's when I went from admiring them to trusting them. They were hired.

Where every other agency told us how good they were, Wieden+Kennedy told us how hard they were—on themselves and their clients. They were vulnerable and human—and it was utterly captivating. Sure, a track record of amazing work and results helped their case, but here was a team that "showed up" in a radically refreshing way, full of trust-building authenticity.

Willy Wonka shows up and lies. Wieden+Kennedy shows up and tells the brutal truth. But both of them show up and create "WTF Moments." And in so doing, they provide a powerful lesson: you can't inspire with business as usual.

Now, Back to Lincoln

In Chapter 6, we discussed Lincoln's Delusional Ambition. Instead of aiming for some sort of war-ending compromise, he set his sights on the greatest cause he could imagine: the perfection of the country.

Great—but then, he needed to *communicate* his ambition in a way that would actually get the country moving.

Gettysburg didn't have a grand stage or lighting rigs, but even on that blood-stained battlefield, Abraham Lincoln was able to find a way to alter the atmosphere. We all know the famous first phrase of the Gettysburg Address: "Four score and seven years ago...." And most school children learn that those words are based on an old-fashioned way of counting. A score is a twenty-year stretch, and so a little quick math deduces that Lincoln was saying "eighty-seven years ago...."

But why—*why*—didn't he just say, "Eighty-seven years ago"?

Most of us assume that, in the 1860s, common language was full of "scores" and such phrases. Perhaps we think folks marked their age by saying such-and-such a date was their two score and three-year birthday.

We'd be very mistaken. That's not the way people spoke in the 1860s. In fact, it's not the way they had spoken for centuries. No, Lincoln was purposefully employing a classical rhetorical device to signal the import of the moment. He was alluding to a famous few verses from the Bible's book of Psalms (in fact, a rather bleak bit saying we each have only seventy years on this Earth), a reference his biblically-learned audience would certainly know. Lincoln purposefully began with such a highfalutin phrase to indicate this would be a highfalutin moment. "What?" we'd ask. "Huh?" we'd wonder. "What the heck is happening here?"

And that's precisely the point: a moment of disorientation.

And it wasn't just Lincoln's language that tilted the spaces he inhabited. It was his look as well. Historians describe him as a scruffy man. In her book, *Forged in Crisis*, Nancy Koehn shares a description of Lincoln showing up for one of his famous debates with Senator Stephen Douglas from a source who was there:

[Lincoln] wore a somewhat battered 'stove-pipe hat'... [His] ungainly body was clad in a rusty black frock-coat with sleeves that should have been longer.... His black trouser, too, permitted

a very full view of his large feet.... I had seen, in Washington and in the West, several public men of rough appearance, but none whose looks seemed quite so uncouth, not to say grotesque, as Lincoln's.[3]

Wow, Lincoln was gross. Essentially, he showed up to the debate looking homeless. But intentionally or not, that appearance was part of Lincoln's power to move an audience. The "ordinary rules" had been broken. The brave man who did so could maybe—just maybe—do anything.

Another war-time leader, General George Patton, also used his appearance to break the frame for his audience. It was a little-known rule in the official army code of conduct that generals were actually exempt from wearing the uniforms authorized for other soldiers. They could technically wear what they wanted, though most, of course, followed tradition. Not Patton. He very consciously adopted a flamboyant style: his trademark helmet emblazoned with his four general's stars, but also jodhpurs and a short unconventional "Ike" jacket he had privately tailored. He'd cap off his look by strapping ivory-handled revolvers to his side. When Patton showed up to address the troops, the troops knew it. They could see that here was a different kind of leader.

And then, when Patton opened his mouth, the soldiers really knew they had somebody extraordinary on their hands. He was vile and foul-mouthed, filling his speeches with obscenities. And Patton knew exactly what he was doing. "You can't run an army without profanity," he asserted, "And it has to be eloquent profanity. An army without profanity couldn't fight its way out of a piss-soaked paper bag."[4] Look at how he begins his most famous and inspiring speech, his address to the Third Army on the eve of the D-Day Invasion. Remember, these are young, frightened soldiers, many of them just boys who all know the ridiculously ambitious landing and cliff-scaling mission before them. Patton starts with no hint of kindness:

Be seated. Men, all this stuff you hear about America not wanting to fight, wanting to stay out of the war, is a lot of bullshit.

Americans love to fight. All real Americans love the sting and clash of battle. When you were kids, you all admired the champion marble shooter, the fastest runner, the big-league ball players and the toughest boxers. Americans love a winner and will not tolerate a loser. Americans play to win all the time.5

All that bluster while wearing pinkish riding breeches. WTF indeed.

You might remember I started this book with a profanity-tinged confession: *I fucking hate Bono*. My editor—and my wife—weren't so sure about that decision. It might be rude and off-putting to civil readers—and if it was, I apologize and thank you for sticking with me this far nonetheless. I wrote that sentence primarily because it was true, but also because I was trying to be a little Patton, to use vulgarity in a context where it might be a bit eyebrow-raising. It's a tactic that works. Try it. Drop an f-bomb when you shouldn't. Or, like Lincoln, reach back to an ancient bit of odd rhetoric. Either way, use your language to disrupt the routine.

Let's Make Picassos

And here's the wonderful news. All of this "showing up and stirring up" doesn't just grab the attention of your audience; it's not just some sort of presentation gimmick. Oh, no, disorientating your audience can ultimately make them better. It can open them up to new possibilities. It can inspire them to boldness themselves.

Takeshi Okada teaches at the University of Tokyo and in 2016, he and his colleagues asked an epic question: can we *become* creative? Our bias, of course, is that creativity, like smarts and beauty, is a gift from the gods. Some people have it; others don't. We all know folks who swear they're "not creative"—and, in some industries, like marketing, we've even institutionalized the prejudice: *You are the "creative" department. You are the "strategy" department...*It's a sad sort of psychological apartheid.

Of course, we want to believe that "anybody can be creative" and, sure enough, scores of psychological studies show that even the most buttoned-up of The Reasonables, with the right encouragement, can have flights of fancy imagination.

But Professor Okada was flirting with a more profound question: can we grow *great* artists? Can we nurture somebody into becoming a Picasso or a Shonda Rhimes? What would we have to do to inspire somebody to create amazing, original art?

Like most academic experiments, this one started with undergraduate students who needed some extra cash. The scientists gathered groups of them, all with one thing in common: none of them could draw particularly well; there wasn't an artist amongst them. But, soon enough, they would be asked to become artists. Each of the students would be asked to give their very best effort to creating an *original* drawing.[6]

But first, they'd be poked and prodded—in a clinical scientific way, of course.

Professor Okada gave the students an array of ordinary, everyday objects like drinking glasses, flower vases, and oranges and he told them that each day, for the next three days, he would like them to draw that object. If you picked a teapot, for example, you'd be drawing a teapot each day for the next three days. Simple enough.

But some of the students would be in for a surprise. On the second day, Professor Okada gave *half* of the students an additional responsibility. He gave them a work of art that he wanted them to copy—but critically, it was a modern, abstract work of art. Think of a painting by Jackson Pollock or a Van Gogh, for example. Before going back to drawing their plain old teapot, these students would have to attempt to imitate the funky creativity of a groundbreaking artist.

They tried.

And, on day three, when all of the students returned to drawing their plain old teapots, a clear and fascinating difference emerged: those students who had copied the abstract painting the day before drew pictures that a panel of professional artists rated as "better"—both creatively *and* technically—than the pictures drawn by the students who never had to copy the Van Goghs and Pollocks.

In other words, a quick dip in the pool of funky, abstract art helped "regular students" make much better art than they otherwise ever could.

Professor Okada and his team redid the experiment changing a multitude of variables. What happens if we ask students to copy a work of art that is realistic, not abstract? What happens when we simply ask students to strive for creativity and originality? What happens if we ask students to just "think about" modern art?

Wildly, as it turns out, just *looking at* modern abstract art was just as powerful a driver of creating better art as actually copying that abstract art had been. Let me be clear about that: *looking* at funky art made these people more creative.

But that wasn't the case with "realistic" art. Not at all, in fact. And, after much more work, Professor Okada came to his conclusion, "Exposure to styles of artwork considered unfamiliar facilitated creativity in drawing while styles considered familiar did not do so."[7]

And if you think that summary is a leap from Professor Okada's evidence, listen to his neurological explanation for the results. He writes that, as students interacted with the abstract art, their "cognitive restraints became relaxed, and new perspectives were formed."[8]

This is mirror neurons with colored pencils!

Their cognitive restraints became relaxed. Their System 2 prison guard took a hike. A bit of reason was removed from the situation—and in its place was born a burst of originality and courage.

Listen up, people: when we break conventions and become a force of originality, we inspire our audience to break conventions and become a force of originality.

In the face of what's bold and surprising, we become bold and surprising. In the face of what's familiar and ordinary, we remain familiar and ordinary.

MODERN MUSE: CINDY FUCKING GALLOP
Lincoln in Leather

Cindy Gallop bills herself as "the Michael Bay of business," because she "likes to blow shit up." But not for the hell of it. Cindy Gallop actually wants *to build* something: an economy—a world!—that unleashes the full force and awesome power of diversity. After a career running one of the very greatest ad agencies of all time, Cindy is now an entrepreneur and an activist. She speaks to tens of thousands of people each year—from massive crowds at global conferences to CEOs in oak-paneled offices—and to every audience she brings her message, her conviction based upon decades of red-hot success *and* red-hot frustration: diversity fuels success. We shouldn't just make room at the tables of power for women and people of color and those who have aged past their supposed prime because it's the "right" thing to do; no, we should do it because it's the *smart* thing to do. Women and mothers and minorities of all kinds will make our work better because their perspectives will make our work richer.

And, while it seems like such an easy message to endorse, Cindy won't settle for polite head nods from corporate chieftains who promise to cobble together a feeble diversity plan. Day in and day out, in dozens of tweets, posts, and speeches, Cindy names names. She shares her outrage with her millions of followers at those leaders and companies who, either stupidly or insidiously, keep women and people of color on the lowest rungs of the corporate ladder. In fact, one prominent creative director even developed an emoji of Cindy stampeding on a horse: *You've Been Galloped* is the fate of the very worst sexists and bigots and, God forbid, those executives who are or protect sexual predators.

As Cindy told me, leaving her role as CEO of an agency was a moment of "liberation." No longer did she have to tow some corporate line, even a corporate line in which she believed. Now, Cindy says, she speaks as "me. I can say whatever the hell I want. I can talk about my ideas."[9]

And when she does, the world trembles a little bit—some tremble in fear, but many others tremble with excitement, the kind of excitement that comes from feeling more giant, from feeling inspired.

You can easily watch Cindy in action. Find her speeches on YouTube and you'll get a quick sense of her insight, her wit, her passion—and the ability of those virtues to fire up a crowd. But what you *won't* see are the dozens of people in the audience—many of whom are women or black or gay—who cry because they feel understood and then tighten their fists because they feel angry and then stand up and march out of that conference room with the ferocious determination to make their unique imprint on the world, even if it means burning down some of the barriers in the way.

Cindy is a Muse.

And, like the greatest Muses, her power is born of a grand idea and fueled by passion. It's built on a bedrock of authentic values.

But while you watch her speak, you can't help but notice something else: Cindy is no preacher; she embodies the point she's making. She, being fiercely herself, wearing whatever the hell she wants, which is usually some drop-dead gorgeous designer outfit, stalks the stage like Serena Williams stalks a tennis court, dropping f-bombs with dramatic flair. She says her goal is to get people "to do" things—and so she embraces "the shock of the new to surprise an audience."[10] Not for the hell of it but because it works.

Cindy never says that "diversity raises the bar"—oh, no, that's a radical idea smothered by the polite language of a board room. Cindy says "diversity raises the *fucking* bar." That's a radical idea decked out in the language of inspiration.

That "fucking" matters.

You might even say that "fucking" matters to Cindy's audiences as much as "Four score and seven years ago" mattered to the assembled mourners at Gettysburg. Cindy, like Lincoln, shows up to stir up, purposefully using language to make a point: the old rules will now be broken.

Techniques to Show Up To Stir Up

Unlike some of the other skills of inspiration—like delusionalizing your ambition or identifying your Inspir-Action—this third skill is obviously highly dependent upon the situation in which you find yourself. Different rules apply in different places. It could be a giant arena, a corporate conference room, an office, a stage, a kitchen table, or a long car ride. And depending upon your setting, you'll adapt different tactics for sure.

Nonetheless, there are three stages to *Showing Up To Stir Up* that will apply no matter where you are, be it giving an inaugural address to an eager country or a dose of quick inspiration to a kid on his way to class.

Step 1 is Disorientate. That's right, going back to the very first time the Muses showed up to Hesiod wandering with his sheep, the very first act of any Muse must be to show up in a way that disorientates—that breaks the rules of "ordinary" expectations and signals something strange is about to occur. Now, obviously, mythological goddesses and rock bands and presidential candidates have powerful tools at their disposal to control a given environment. They can *literally* set up stages. But any environment can be a place where a Muse can disorientate. It can be a very subtle act. If a CEO decides to abandon her usual chair at the head of a boardroom's table, sitting instead alongside her colleagues, she's disorientating. If a coach asks a player to come into his office, shut the door, and take a seat, that's disorientating. Those are instructions that "break the frame" of a typical locker-room interaction. It might be a teacher who sits in an empty desk staring in the same direction as his students. I once worked with a presenter who would stand before an audience and pause—an awkwardly long pause, like forty seconds—before speaking. That's disorientating. It's confounding.

And all of this applies equally to the moments in which you're seeking to inspire yourself. Don't build a habit; change a routine.

Like trainers tell us we need to alter our workout routine because our muscles "get used to" the same exercises and stop growing, so, too, do we need to alter our "emotional routine"—and changing our atmosphere is a strategy for changing our feelings. Declutter. Or clutter. Drive a different way to your destination. Listen to music you've never heard before. Change your breakfast. Speak in rhymes. Do anything that shakes up your status quo.

So, if you're seeking to inspire in a given situation, ask yourself which tools you have to disorientate your audience. How can you show up in a way that breaks the rules of expectations and signals something new? Consider:

Where you position yourself. What's expected? Sitting at a table? Behind a desk? Standing in front of a laptop to project PowerPoint? Whatever it is, defy it. Make it a walking meeting. Sit on the desk. Present from the back of the room. If you study the images from Barack Obama's first presidential campaign, you'll see that he was generally positioned in one of two places: either completely alone on a grand stage (a hero) or immersed in crowds of supporters (man of the people). Where you wouldn't find him is in the position of most politicians running for office: on a stage with a dozen or so hardcore supporters and local politicians. That's the convention Obama broke.

What you wear. One of the most irritating trends in men's fashion has been the custom of guys wearing "outrageous" socks under otherwise conservative clothes. That's supposedly where they show their personality: with peeks of polka dots beneath a hem. It's pathetic. Use the tool of your appearance to serve your interest in inspiring. Look different. Dress *against* the conventions of a situation.

How you begin. You can only start speaking once. Don't waste that moment. Like my colleague with the unnaturally long pauses, use your position to control your audience. Let them wait. Or take a page from great storytellers and start in media res—in the middle of the action. Get into it, make it exciting, and if the audience is initially confused, great. They'll figure it out—and when they do, they'll be proud and dizzy and ripe to hear you.

Profanity. Yes, it's a handy tool for "breaking the rules"—and if you're uncomfortable with it, you should probably use it. But profanity, remember, doesn't have to be vulgar. It's language that is irreverent. So you don't have to drop an f-bomb, but you might want to poke some sacred cows. Is a board room lined with oil painting of previous chairmen, all white and dull? Insult them. Has your kid never heard you express your disdain for a neighbor or a relative? Go for it. These "profane" acts have a great power to disorientate—and even better, expose an authenticity that is critical for moving people.

Tone of voice. We are conditioned to speak in an affect that is reasonable, not emotional. We are trained in a cadence that is matter-of-fact. You'll need to alter that if you want to inspire, to find a time of voice that reflects the feelings you want to instill: anger, determination, love, urgency, and so on.

Step 2: Elevate. The Muse captures attention. She does not blend in. Obviously, a speech on a stage provides a classic opportunity to assert a high-ground position but, in many of the instances in which we need to inspire, that convention isn't available. Instead, the Muse must find other ways to assert authority. Central to this endeavor is the theme we've been exploring throughout the book: never argue. The Muse is an oracle, not a debater. When we argue, we "bring ourselves down" to a level where we can be wrong. That's a dangerous place to be. To avoid that strategic sandpit, the Muse can employ a few techniques:

Disarm. Admit that your perspective is not one based on facts and data alone, but in feeling and conviction. As soon as you do so, it'll be difficult for people to engage you "rationally" without looking like logic bullies. *"Because I feel so..."* is an echo of a parent saying *"Because I said so..."*—and while perhaps it's as equally frustrating, it also elevates the speaker to a realm beyond reason. Only an authority can get away with such a declaration. Try it the next time you're in a business meeting, for example. Somebody will inevitably say, "But your feelings aren't a reason for us to do this or that." And, in that moment, that person will look small and petty while you start to soar.

Personalize. Personalize everything. The Muse wants to bring others along, but doing so requires establishing a first-person authority. And so, the Muse speaks in the first person—"I" and "me" and, most importantly, "we." When you say "we," you do two magical things: first, you assume the authority to speak for the group you're addressing. You've become its spokesperson and leader, and second, you've created a space in your idea for the other person to inhabit. It's as

if you've set a place for them at the table. Traditionally, instructions are written in the second person—*You must do this. You should do that.* But the genius of Nike's tagline, for example, exposes the power of the first-person perspective. *Just Do It* could be understood as the second person perspective, the brand talking at you: *you* just do this... But the real power of those words happens when it's understood in the first person: *I* should do this. Let *us* just do this...In those moments, the voice shifts from the brand talking to you to the voice in your head inspiring you. The Muse speaks for the group, not to the group.

Step 3: Fill the Air with Feeling. This, as you know by now, is everything. This is where we express our passions in a way that triggers the mirror neurons of our audience. We express our anger or hope or conviction or fear—and we do so in a way that changes the environment.

MODERN MUSE: FERRAN ADRIÀ
You've Never Had These Carrots

Ferran Adrià is one of the world's most acclaimed chefs. He owned elBulli on Spain's hilly Catalonian coast which, for several years, was rated the number one restaurant in the world by the critics at Michelin. It was near impossible to get a reservation, but for the lucky few who did, elBulli was much more than a great meal; it was a spectacle.

Adrià is the godfather of molecular gastronomy, a term he despises, but a style of cooking he pioneered. Practitioners of this modernist approach to cooking use the tricks of chemistry to alter the way we experience food. You've likely heard of foams—sauces pumped with air until they become so light they disappear in your mouth leaving only the purest taste of what had been foamed. But there's more: fish can become cotton candy; ravioli bursts in your mouth—but only when a certain note from a certain song is hit; balloons pop and turn into taffy.

I admit, I'm a fan of these food fireworks—so different from the simple, well-cooked peasant food of my mom's kitchen. This isn't dinner; it's theatre. It's head-spinning stuff—but it's not just showing off. There's a point to it all.

I was lucky enough to attend an event with Ferran Adrià at the New York Public Library a few years back. It was an august gathering of the good and the great in the culinary world—there was Lidia Bastianich, there were the top food critics, and there was me, ready to mop up Adrià's magic the way other guys might fawn for LeBron James. Adria talked—and talked for what felt like a long time. His English wasn't very good, so much of what he said had to be repeated through a translator. He talked about his favorite topics: creativity, science, the laws of food and eating, why he insists on calling his kitchen a laboratory. But honestly, it all felt very esoteric until the question-and-answer period when some punter worked up the courage to ask Adrià a very simple question, the one on the minds of most people who encounter his alchemical culinary creations: "Why? Why all the hoopla, Ferran? Can't you just take a few high-quality ingredients and cook them beautifully? Why be so strange?"

Adrià no doubt had his answer ready, and relied upon the translator less than before. He said something like: "Thank you for that question, sir. I start from a belief, the belief that every single carrot in the world is different. Every carrot tastes different, even if only in small and subtle ways. It must. It's grown in a different bit of soil, watered with different drops of rain and water and fed a different angle of sunlight. No two carrots are exactly the same. But if I give you a carrot that looks like the carrot you had yesterday and looks like the carrot you had the day before and like all the carrots you had as a young boy, you will never stop and say, 'Holy shit, I have never had this carrot.' You will not feel the difference. When you eat that carrot for the very first time, you should taste it as if you're tasting it for the very first time."

That's Ferran Adrià's genius, I believe. He transforms the ordinary, the yesterday, the has-been *thing* into the most fresh and wonderful *thing* you can imagine. And he does it by breaking the rules. For Ferran Adrià, disorientation is a strategy, a strategy to blow minds wide open.

Use this chart to outline the "rules" of a given situation—perhaps the ones "spoken" but, more likely, the ones always unconsciously followed. Write them, figure out how to break them, and then come up with your plan—your one way—to show up to stir up.

SHOW-UP TO STIR-UP WORKSHEET

	RULES	RULES BROKEN
LANGUAGE	_____	_____
APPEARANCE	_____	_____
LOCATION	_____	_____
CUSTOM	_____	_____
	_____	_____
	_____	_____

MY SHOW-UP TO
STIR-UP PLAN:

CHAPTER 9

The Fourth Skill of Inspiration: Talk Like Music

(How a Lyrical Language Makes People Move)

"Maybe the difference between speech and music isn't all that great. We infer a lot from the tone of someone's voice, so imagine that aspect of speech pushed a little further. The weird cadences of a Valley girl, for example, might be viewed as a species of singing. The malls of Sherman Oaks are a setting for a kind of massed choir."

—DAVID BYRNE, *How Music Works*

"Nothing to fear but fear itself."
"Clear eyes. Full hearts. Can't lose."
"Four score and seven years ago"
"Nevertheless, she persisted"
"Groove is in the heart."
"Just do it."

These are *lyrics*. Some happen to be in songs.

We've established, firmly enough, that music moves people, but if David Byrne, the former front man for Talking Heads, is right—and I think he is!—the line between talk and music is a fine and fuzzy one. There's a point at which our speech can be *like* music. It can be lyrical.

We can, in fact, *Talk Like Music.*

And yes, in part, that does require an exercise of art: composing lyrics. Part of Talking Like Music is fiddling with your language until common phrases become unforgettable earworms.

But, as we learned from mondegreens, words themselves are hardly the be-all and end-all of music. *Feeling*—affect—is what matters most. Talking Like Music, we'll see, has very little to do with carrying a tune in perfect pitch.

"Music is a higher revelation than all wisdom and philosophy."

—LUDWIG VAN BEETHOVEN

Well, of course Beethoven would say such a thing. But in his day, such a thing was pretty darn radical. Beethoven lived during what musicologists call the Romantic Period, a moment in music history that challenged the clear-cut style of the previous period, the Enlightenment, sometimes called the Age of Reason. The Enlightenment was a period of western history when philosophers and scientists were sweeping aside the superstitions of the "dark" ages and championing a rational approach to the world, a belief that human intelligence and the scientific method could answer the ageless riddles of the universe. The sun isn't a god. The earth isn't flat. People are not born to be slaves. It was an exciting time of discovery, a spark of freedom that ignited the American Revolution and, eventually, the Industrial Revolution. Arguably, we still live in the light of this movement, believing that clear thinking and crisp logic point us toward truth. Reason has triumphed over ignorance—and we are better for its victory.

But Beethoven wasn't so sure. He wasn't a particularly devout man. There's no evidence, for example, that he ever attended church services. But he certainly believed in a power "higher" than human reason alone: call it God, or, heck, call it music.

Music possesses us. It works hard on us all. Songs shift our moods, whether we're hormonal teenagers locked in our bedrooms looking for our "true" selves or grownups stuck in a crummy commute tapping our toes when the right tune comes on. Music literally moves us.

Wesley Morris, a music critic for the *New York Times*, described the dramatic phenomenon in a tribute to Aretha Franklin in which he the power of her most famous song to pull our puppet strings:

> *Ms. Franklin died on Thursday, at 76, which means "Respect" is going to be an even more prominent part of your life than usual. The next time you hear it, notice what you do with your hands. They're going to point—at a person, a car or a carrot. They'll rest on your hips. Your neck might roll. Your waist will do a thing. You'll snarl. Odds are high that you'll feel better than great. You're guaranteed to feel indestructible.*[1]

Try it. Go ahead, give "Respect" a listen—and see if you can keep your hands on you lap. Or listen to "Happy" or "Lose Yourself" or "Fight Song" or "In Da Club" or any other tune that has reliably swelled your energy. Listen—observe your body move and your feelings heighten. You will feel indestructible.

But we know this. The pressing question is *how* does music move us—and how can we steal some of that intoxicating power as we become world-shaking Muses?

Zach Wallmark is a jazz musician who happens to be a psychologist. In fact, he's the professor who runs "The MuSci Lab" at Southern Methodist University, where he and his team dig deep into the human brain trying to excavate the mysteries of music.

He also talks like music. Listen to how he explained to me what happens when we hear a song we love:

> *You become overcome or ravished. It's a state of radical vulnerability. You lay yourself out. You hand over central control to an alien entity, a force—and to the human beings creating it....*
> *Music is something dangerous because it has such control over our emotions.*[2]

You hand over central control to an alien entity. Wow. Sign me up.

As I try to catch my breath, Professor Wallmark then gets usefully academic. He clarifies that music works both "bottom-up" and "top-down." By "bottom-up," he means it works biologically. Our brain stem responds to particular sounds that trigger our limbic system, the reptilian part of our nervous system that controls our moods. He explains, for example, that climaxes in songs—be it "The Hallelujah Chorus" or "A Day in The Life" by the Beatles—are often marked by certain sonic constants. They're loud, for sure, but they also tend to "occupy more pitch space." They have "more dissonance and rougher timbre." And, just as I'm about to be lost in a whirl of words I don't understand, Professor Wallmark hits me with the zinger: "Just like a human scream." These climaxes are "sounds of danger," he says, "They're the musical equivalent of seeing a bear."[3]

Wait a second, when I'm driving faster than I should be, singscreaming along to the Clash, my body feels terror, the exact same kind of terror it would feel if a grizzly bear were towering over me?

Yes, biologically, it does.

But the brilliance of the moment is that, right as our body panics, our brain *simultaneously* recognizes that the threat—the bear—isn't real. Like a rollercoaster. The terror (Burke!) is both true and completely fictional. Music is its own safe word.

And that's just climaxes. Music is composed of sounds that can conjure the entire rainbow of human feelings. It can make you feel like your heart has been ripped from your chest—and you'll enjoy it, because you'll know that she hasn't *really* left you for your best friend.

Or maybe she actually has.

Because, as Professor Wallmark teaches me, music also works "top-down;" in other words, it works on our conscious nervous system, our thoughts and memories, the things we can process somewhat rationally. We know, for example, exactly how a "Little Red Corvette" looks. Bottom-up, that song is all sex, but top-down—well, come to think of it, top-down, it's all about sex as well.

So many songs tell stories. Those work top-down. There are characters who do things—and just like characters in movies, we identify with some of them and, when we do, we feel their emotions, their highs and lows, like they're our own.

But lyrics can do so much more than tell a story. They can do so in a way that arouses emotions from the complexity of associations and experiences we each have.

I ask Professor Wallmark to help me understand my all-time favorite Beatles song. It's the one about the old guy who might be called "Flat Top." He has eyeballs made of candy—and for some reason, we need to be told that his feet are at the bottom of his legs, beneath his ankles and knees. Most importantly, *here he comes*—and he's "groovin'" at a snail's pace.

What the hell is "Come Together" *about*?

I tell Professor Wallmark that I "understand" the song was an homage to Timothy Leary and the pioneers of the psychedelic drug movement. It's a trippy hymn to tripping—and the lyrics are "supposed to be" nonsensical.

But why—I really want to know why, when I hear that song—and I hate hippie drug culture—do I feel so groovy myself? There's no story at all. Why do I sing those words and feel so happy?

Professor Wallmark skips to another late Beatles song, the one about a girl named Lucy and a sky lit up by diamonds. Those lyrics—like the ones in my song, the eyeballs made of candy and the fingers like a monkey and the gum on the shoe of a walrus—well, those lyrics, Professor Wallmark says "call upon a pre-established well of associations," in this case, including associations with a sweet and carefree childhood. These lyrics are the language of *Alice In Wonderland*, of children's fantasy mixed with the Dali-like language of psychedelic surrealism. It's a language that makes me feel innocent and free.

"Come Together" is schizophrenic. Bottom-up, it's all march and swagger and a little bit filthy. Top-down, it's all little children chasing rabbits in fields of flowers. Together, it feels like kick-ass sweetness. That's not even a thing, but it feels *fucking* brilliant.

Like Lincoln beginning the Gettysburg Address with that bizarre, old-fashioned elocution. When he says, "Four score and seven years ago..."—a phrase nobody alive would've used to mean eighty-seven years—it's all top-down associations. He's calling upon a "pre-established well of associations." He wants that moment to feel biblical, to feel holy.

Lincoln and Lennon. They talked like music, even—especially—when they were talking nonsense.

Talk Like Music Top-Down: Talk Lyrical

"You campaign in poetry. You govern in prose."

—MARIO CUOMO

It's not a surprising belief from one of the greatest orators of his political generation, who nonetheless couldn't muster the fortitude to run for president. New York Governor Mario Cuomo, like many a politician, understood that campaigning—moving people to vote for you—was an exercise in art, not engineering. And he knew his preference was the former.

Perhaps no politician of our lifetime has demonstrated the truthfulness of Cuomo's axiom more than President Barack Obama. No-Drama Obama famously ran his administration with technocratic precision but campaigned with soaring oratory. Al Gore promised to lower carbon emissions by 25 percent. He lost. Barack Obama promised to reverse the rise of the oceans. He won. And, of course, he didn't win because of that statement, but he did exhibit an uncanny ability to use words to mobilize masses. Listen to his announcement speech from Springfield, Illinois:

And if you will join me in this improbable quest, if you feel destiny calling, and see as I see, a future of endless possibility stretching before us; if you sense, as I sense, that the time is now to shake off our slumber, and slough off our fear, and make good on the debt we owe past and future generations, then I'm ready to take up the cause, and march with you, and work with you. Together, starting today, let us finish the work that needs to be done, and usher in a new birth of freedom on this Earth.[4]

Quest and destiny. See as I see and sense as I sense. Shaking off slumber and sloughing off our fear. *Slough?* But, yes, slough it off and march toward a new birth of freedom on this Earth (Lincoln, natch). This is poetry, language with rhythm, words that are carefully chosen and ordered to evoke emotion, words that are curated to transport an audience from the here and now to the there and better.

And, very importantly, these are uncommon, unusual words, not the sort of language with which we talk to each other day in and day out.

Poetry—lyrical language—often trades in strange phrases, finding unfamiliar words and drawing fresh associations. It's an ancient language. Like music, its hallmark is meter, beat, and the wordplay that travels on those waves: rhymes, near-rhymes, alliteration, assonance. Poetry is where meaning meets sound and, together, they conspire to illicit powerful feelings.

So lyrics works differently than mere speech does. Their intent is not simply to communicate information, but to evoke emotion. And they do so, in some ways, by short-circuiting our logical, rational brains. Lyrics rarely dress like an argument or unfold like a conversation. Instead, they arrive with an oddness that stops our rational wheels turning. That's why Obama prefers "shaking off slumber" to "just waking up." Its power lies in its unusualness. It's a hook, an earworm, more memorable and repeatable than common language.

Obama very purposefully chose to announce his candidacy in the boyhood hometown of President Abraham Lincoln, a leader he invoked throughout his speech. We already discussed the odd lyricism of the first few lines of the Gettysburg Address, but almost every sentence in that very short speech uses some sort of poetic device, not just highfalutin language but simple words beautifully strung together (Listen to the alliteration and the internal rhymes: "The world will little note, nor long remember..."), ending with a classical poetic device, an epizeuxis, an artful repetition of a word or a phrase three times for special emphasis: "of the people, by the people, for the people." *That* we enshrine in our collective memory; had he simply said "the people's government" we'd have forgotten it all.

So how do we become lyricists, artists, poets, crafters of words that inspire, when most of us often feel incapable of stringing together a few coherent sentences?

Well, the hard truth is that if you want to move people with your words, you need to become a word artist. You need to cultivate the facility to twist words into new, nuanced stimuli.

Which isn't as hard or daunting as it seems.

When I was part of the advertising team helping Arby's, the fast-food restaurant chain famous for its roast beef sandwiches, turn around its flagging business, we developed a simple slogan: "Arby's. We Have the Meat." It was simple declaration of what the place sold, delivered with some meat-like conviction. Our creative director thought, sighed, and then added one letter: "Arby's. We Have the Meat*s*." It wasn't just an act of pluralizing the menu's offerings; it was an act of distorting the language. The meats? What's "The Meats"? Sounds like a medical condition or a punk-rock band, and it still tells me Arby's has got much more than roast beef. They have chicken and brisket and ocean meat, even. But there's something odd, something unusual about "The Meats." It's irrational. It's food and it's a mood all at the same time. It's a delicious state of mind.

With the addition of that one simple *s*, our creative director made that slogan Talk Like Music, and the campaign gave Arby's the comeback they needed, rocketing their business with the best sales increases in the entire category.

So how do we all become the sort of people who add an s and make all the difference?

Work.

I can't recommend a better way of doing so than consuming a steady diet of art—whatever art you enjoy, be it high or low or old poems or new movies. Art (a terribly pretentious word, for sure) helps us access the very feelings we will need to access in others. Start with what you know, what feels good to you. It doesn't have to be abstract painting or old-fashioned novels. You can lose yourself in a weekend of *Scandal*.

But then work your way through the great word art that's at our disposal, available almost everywhere, from a bookstore to the internet. Commit to reading a poem a day, a novel a month. Throw out your business books and modern advice tomes (like this one). Remember the great speeches you've heard, and then go read the transcripts. And as you read, read slowly; don't read to consume information but linger on the words, how the authors string them together, the rhythms they create, the feelings they evoke.

And writing.

As you delve into words that Talk Like Music, you'll need to try your hand at writing words that Talk Like Music. And the key here is to be playful, experimental, to get a hundred things that sound stupid or wrong or imperfect until you find the one thing that doesn't.

Look again at the Delusional Ambition you wrote on page 196. Is there a way of rephrasing it to make it more lyrical, stranger, more unusual? Doing so might be the first step toward making that goal a reality.

There are certainly a host of "literary devices" that can be used to Muse up your language. Alliteration allows audiences to enjoy your words as if they're being carried by a calming current. But for our purposes, the most promising devices might be metaphors and similes—the ones that compare what you're discussing to something else that's more vivid and descriptive... I want to win *like Ali*... I want my restaurant to feel *like my grandmother's kitchen*... I want you to believe in yourself *like you believe in gravity*...

Start there.

And then, look at your answers to the Passion Prompts on page 107. They should be filled with the raw material of great lyrics. How did you explain your Ambition to a child? Is it filled with late-Beatles-like words, short and round and sweet? How did you describe what the world will be like when your Ambition is achieved? Go on: what will be the soundtrack of that future, wonderful world? How will people feel—and how does that make you feel?

And remember Professor Okada and his experiment to stoke creativity. Take a stab and write something—your ambition, your Inspir-Action, your first or last words to your audience—and then put it aside and read something funky and odd. Find some Shakespeare or an amazing contemporary Japanese poet. Find some stimulus in the Appendix, "30 Days of Muse Snacks." Soak them up—and then come back to your words. Before you know it, you'll be Talking Like Music.

Talk Like Music Bottom-Up: Talk Feeling

You might think being a word artist is difficult but, if I'm being honest, the hardest Talk Like Music muscle to master is this one: talk emotional. And the difficult part isn't actually doing it, but wanting to do it.

Behind every good song is the same resounding ambition: *let me tell you how I feel*. That's what the musician sets out to do: to share feelings; to transmit emotions—emotions that are often too tricky or particular to put into regular words. These unique feelings need beats and tempos and tones and lyrics—all to convey a what a musician is feeling to the rest of the world.

A song is a confession.

Remember Zach Wallmark's explanation of the sounds of music; sonically, they replicate human sounds: screams, coos, grunts, sighs, cries, laughs. These are the very real noises you'll have to infuse into your speaking—you have a host of instruments to help you: your tone of voice, your body language, your facial expressions, your very breath—all of these elements conspire to communicate emotion. And all of these elements are controllable by you.

So then, be emotional. Go on, do it.

Easier said than done, huh?

I'd like to propose my very favorite exercise in the entire book: Muse Karaoke. It can even be a party game.

Muse Karaoke

Step 1. I want you to make a list of different bands or musicians you know—and the only goal is to make sure the styles are diverse. Write about five of them. Maybe you'll include Bruce Springsteen and Beethoven and Metallica and Kenny Rogers and Taylor Swift. Like that.

Step 2. Write down what you want to achieve. Make a few sentences or a whole paragraph. It could be a combination of words from pages 107 and 144: *I want to quit my job as an accountant and open a bakery that makes the world's best cookies... I want this team I'm coaching to try their hardest and win the championship... I want to discipline myself to stop eating crap, get in shape, and run a marathon...* That kind of stuff.

Step 3. Now, working your way through your list of musicians—one by one—figure out how that musician would retell the story of what you want to achieve. Take, for example, the "quit your job and sell cookies" ambition...

Bruce: I'm a hard-working man grinding it out for the boss. But it's killing me. My job is strangling my soul. I remember my mom's kitchen and the smell of her cookies and how it was the one real thing I could count on when it seemed like the world was against me.

Suddenly, your story is an epic struggle about a boy trying to get back to his momma's kitchen. It's a story of longing.

OR

Metallica: *MAKE MY COOKIES! EAT MY COOKIES! MAKE MY COOKIES! EAT MY COOKIES!*

This is now a tale of pure, hedonistic liberation. It's almost maniacal. Quitting your job and selling those cookies is an act of fierce defiance.

OR

Taylor Swift: You've done me wrong, boss, but I won't surrender. I've got cookies in my heart and a plan in my head. You've seen the last of me while I walk out the door—and soon enough, everybody else will follow and we'll have cookies galore.

Here, your story becomes a tale of empowerment—a girl who won't be wronged, trailblazing a path that others will follow. It's a rousing story of heart and determination.

You get the idea. This is an exercise to help you "try on" a few narratives that might have more emotional punch than a very straightforward one. Some will be silly. Some will be serious. Many will be dead wrong—and you'll feel that in your bones. They won't be genuine. They won't be your story. But I promise you this: if you keep playing, keep choosing artists and imagining how they would "record" your story, you'll discover the feelings behind your ambitions and be much better able to identify and express them. You'll be one step closer to Talking Like Music.

Use Muse Karaoke and the exercises that follow to see if you can re-articulate your Delusional Ambition as lyrically as possible, but then, figure out what the affect of those words really is. What's the driving emotion of your Ambition-achieving? Anger, love, conviction, whatever it is, write it down and, as you seek to inspire, remember it. It'll change the way you talk.

TALK LIKE MUSIC WORKSHEET

MY AMBITION DELUSIONALIZED: _____

MAKE IT LYRICAL?

CAN I MAKE IT ODD?

CAN I MAKE IT BEAUTIFUL?

CAN I MAKE IT RHYME?

CAN I USE A METAPHOR: "LIKE _____" ?

HOW WOULD _____ SAY IT?

HOW WOULD _____ SING IT?

MY AMBITION LIKE MUSIC: _____

_____

_____

_____

WHAT'S THE EMOTIONAL STORY? _____

_____

WHAT'S THE FEELING THAT WILL DRIVE OUR ACHIEVEMENT? _____

_____

CHAPTER 10

The Fifth Skill of Inspiration: Love, For Real

(How the Burden of Love Helps People Rise)

"How do I love thee? Let me count the ways.
I love thee to the depth and breadth and height my soul can
reach."

—ELIZABETH BARRETT BROWNING, "Sonnet 43"

It's one of the most famous love poems of all time, inscribed on so many pretty cards (usually in a swirly script) and recited at countless weddings. And yet, personally, the words leave me a bit chilly. I get it, for sure: she loves me, she loves me so much, she loves me this way and that way—and yet I'm not convinced. I don't *feel* it, certainly not the way Ed Sheeran makes his lover feel:

Go listen to "Shape of You" by Ed Sheeran. It is detail-filled, sometimes painfully so. He talks about where they met: a bar, and importantly, not a club, because clubs aren't places to find real-deal relationships. He remembers what they ate on their first date at a Chinese restaurant, which they went to because he's cheap. They had sweet-and-sour chicken. They talked about their families and they kissed in the back seat of a taxi. But what he really loves about this lover is the shape of her body. It's her *body* that's his everything, the *shape* of her body, its curves, the way it pushes and pulls against his, leaving his bedsheets with her particular smell. Go on, sing it. Dance to it. Swivel to it.

It's her. It's them. It's vivid and concrete, as Strunk and White would remind us to be in their guide to good writing.

Browning, though, is all vague me, me, me. I love you this way. I love you that way. We—and perhaps he—never know *why* she loves him or *what* she loves about him. We just know that she does. Which is fine. It's just not particularly dance-able, not particularly moving.

You can't inspire anybody if you don't love that somebody—or at least something *about* that somebody.

The love doesn't need to be erotic, of course. It doesn't need to be the greatest love of all. But it needs to be real, to be genuine. Nobody will move for you unless they're sure you are on their side, looking out for their best interest. You can call this all sorts of things—affection, admiration, awe, or attraction—but, at heart, it's love, the feeling that another person knows you, believes in you, and supports you.

So, if you want to inspire, figure out *what you love* about the people you're inspiring. This is an act that will require a great deal of effort and imagination, because "what you love" can't be generic. Don't just love their "passion;" love the way they cry when they lose, a cry that is hard and embarrassed, but fleeting because the very next morning, those tears are replaced with an "Eye of the Tiger" intensity. Don't just love their strength; love the way they start Mondays and end Fridays—and never flag in between. Don't just love their body; love the shape and smell and sound of their body. Don't just love them because they're your child; love them for all the ways in which they are not like you, how funny or shy or athletic they might be.

This is the "Only-You Awesomeness"—the very particular thing you love about your team (or yourself), the thing that will be their superpower as they strive toward a Delusional Ambition.

And certainly don't dare think this skill of inspiration only applies to our most touchy-feely personal relationships. No, affection is critical for moving our co-workers as well. In fact, displays of personal emotion in an often-sterile corporate environment can be inspiration itself—dramatic expressions of passion that seem unreasonable. They break the code of a culture that wants to keep things professional, which often means cerebral and measured. No, love is a business strategy.

And when you know what you love about your audience, tell them. Tell them with detail and vulnerability. At that moment, at the moment a person hears why they are loved, their thinky-thinky prefrontal cortex is hushed and their heart is touched. You've mainlined emotion into your audience.

My First Love

I attended a very conservative all-boys Catholic high school, with most classes taught by Marianist Brothers, kind and learned monks who taught me so much, who expanded the only world I knew. They taught me about literature and philosophy. They taught me about books and ideas, and how they can be as meaningful and powerful as any tool a mechanic or welder might wield. They were my early Muses.

But these Catholic brothers also happened to toe a rather conservative line. They were anti-abortion and anti-gay-marriage, for sure, but in demeanor as well, they were clean-cut and conformist. For goodness' sake, Bill O'Reilly went to my high school. It was a first-rate factory for conservative thinking.

Brother Stephen was my English teacher. He still has a booming voice and a dramatic flair. I remember him reciting Emily Dickinson's "I Heard A Fly Buzz—When I Died" sprawled on his back atop his desk, miming death itself. He'd act out every character in *The Canterbury Tales*. Who was this amazing, passionate, bizarre man *dramatizing* the flesh-and-blood feelings that often seemed trapped in prisons of black-and-white words?

Brother Stephen became my speech and debate coach, a team I joined after an aborted attempt to be a wrestler (*Too many push-ups! So many push-ups!*). The debaters were my tribe. We weren't popular, but we didn't mind.

I'd go on to be a championship debater, even once besting Ted Cruz before he was a Senator. I owe a lot of my debating success to growing up in a raucous Italian household, one where every family dinner seemed like an argument, shouts and *fuhgedaboutits* flung around with opinions about almost everything. It was great debate practice.

Unfortunately, it was that very same ethnic upbringing that presented me with my greatest hurdle to speaking and debating success: a terrible *Lawng Eye-lan* accent. I thought "aye" was the way everybody began a sentence.

Brother Stephen saw promise in me, but he also knew I wouldn't win very much with the way that I spoke. He was determined to rid me of my grating Long Island accent that, fairly or not, would limit my ability to excel as a competitive public speaker. Every day after school for months, I'd work with Brother Stephen in his classroom, learning how to abbreviate my long vowels and articulate my strong first consonants. He was a teacher and a coach, for sure, but also a father figure and, I think, a friend as well.

One afternoon in Brother Stephen's classroom, for a reason about which I'm still not sure, he suggested I read a book that would change me: *A Portrait of the Artist as a Young Man* by James Joyce. He told me he thought I'd enjoy it.

I devoured it. No words on a page have ever moved me as much.

The story of Stephen Dedalus is the story of a boy growing up in Ireland at the start of the twentieth century. The book narrates his life, from the time he was a toddler to the time he sets into the world as a fierce young adult. It's a very specific story. Stephen is sent to a strict Irish boarding school. His father loses his job, and the family starts to fall from their middle-class perch. Stephen is tormented by the conflict between his blossoming sensual desires and the regulations of his country's strict Catholicism. And, against all of this personal drama, a political story plays out: Charles Stewart Parnell, an Irish Nationalist virulently opposed to British Rule, dies, sending some of Stephen's family (and much of the country) into a tailspin of grief.

But *A Portrait of the Artist* is also the story of a very typical teenager, one who feels out of place, uncertain, and insecure. He's full of dreams and full of fear. He loves, hates, loves, hates his parents. It's a straight line from James Joyce to John Hughes—stories of misfit teens who dream of someplace better, someplace that deeply understands their very one-of-a-kind souls.

And it's got a great ending.

A Portrait of the Artist is ultimately a story of rebellion, the story of a young man throwing off the yolk of his land's ancient religion and an angry politics and an oppressive father. Stephen wants "to birth himself"—to *birth himself*—into the artist he believes his soul had been destined to be. "I will express myself as I am," he says, sounding like every teenager with an attitude and a diary. Stephen aches "to discover the mode of life or of art whereby (his) spirit could express itself in unfettered freedom."[1] But Stephen knows that kind of freedom comes with a cost, the cost of losing the very ties and institutions that he has known his whole life:

I will tell you what I will do and what I will not do. I will not serve that in which I no longer believe, whether it calls itself my home, my fatherland, or my church: and I will try to express myself in some mode of life or art as freely as I can and as wholly as I can, using for my defense the only arms I allow myself to use—silence, exile, and cunning.[2]

Boom. The novel ends with Stephen leaving his family and his homeland. He's looking "to live, to err, to fall, to triumph, to recreate life out of life."[3] It's an ancient, mythic story: a new birth that demanded death; a creation that needed a destruction; the birth of an artist that needed to slay his past.

This then is the book Brother Stephen gave me. This book about a boy birthing himself into an artist. It was a gift and a blueprint.

As I read *A Portrait of the Artist*, I was aware of the great irony that this book about rebelling *against* Catholicism and faith and family was given to me *by* a Catholic monk at a school that preached the power and virtues of all those things. Brother Stephen gifted me one of the greatest rebel stories of all time. I think he was letting me know that doubt and anger and maybe even heresy itself are all a beautiful part of finding your own way in this world. Maybe he was telling me that he also, at times, felt exactly those things.

Brother Stephen helped me understand that my feelings of being out of place—poor, different in voice and values, embarrassed and ashamed—these were the very same feelings of the very great men who came before me. Brother Stephen made sure I felt understood and known.

The gift of that book was a gift of love, a precise gift of love for the very real fourteen-year-old me.

Of course, this story reminds us all of John Keating, the tweed-coated teacher in the film *Dead Poet's Society*, beautifully and inspiringly played by Robin Williams. Like many a beloved teacher, he was a rule-breaker, a non-conformist. Ripping up textbooks, he stoked the individuality and passions of his students. He stood so powerfully apart from the institution to which he belonged. He was not one of them, not one of the musty, sclerotic school teachers insisting upon a rigid conformity to tradition. He was not a Reasonable teacher.

Perhaps what made John Keating such a hero, such a Muse to his students was his ability to see and support what was unique about each one of them. He saw them as individuals. He saw Neil, for example, as an artist, an actor, where Neil's parents only saw him as a doctor. Keating loved Neil for what Neil was. Keating's motto, of course, was *Carpe Diem*—seize the day!—but it might as well have been *Carpe Ipsum*—seize yourself, be yourself, because you are wonderful, you are worthy of love.

"Tonight, We Make Love"

By the Duomo, the famous opera house in Milan, U2 performed in 2005. It was typical, grandiose U2 fare, but I was struck by how Bono introduced himself to the crowd. He appeared on the stage, and predicted, commanded, "Tonight, we make love." And he wasn't talking about some airy-fairy feelings of kindness. No, you can tell, by the lilt of his voice and the swivel of his hips, he's talking about *making* love. He's promising an erotic experience. "It's okay to flirt," he says.

I'm certainly not suggesting that, to inspire, you must be sexual, but more often than not, you will be sexy—because you're expressing feelings, passions, powerful sensations that conspire to seduce your audience. It's almost prerequisite of successful leadership, as one recent study has demonstrated that more "attractive" candidates are more *likely* to win elections (natch, JFK; ehh, Trump).

And think back as well to the night Clio stormed the forest where Hesiod was wandering. That was some sexy stuff. He thought they were nymphs, the most beautiful and desirable mythological creatures around (well, maybe mermaids).

So then, how do you seduce? There are all sorts of stupid, misogynistic tactics floating about involving playing hard to get and being a jerk, but I don't think they ultimately work in matters of romance or inspiration. I prefer my sweet mother's home-spun wisdom: there's nothing more attractive than confidence.

"Carpe Ipsum— seize yourself, be yourself!"

I already confessed that, before debates, I'd squirrel myself away in a bathroom and chant myself into believing that I was "the JFK of debating!"—and it was a habit that was hard to break. Throughout my career, before a big pitch or presentation, I'd lock myself in a bathroom and chant, "You're the Bono of advertising! You're the Bono of advertising!" It was a way of psychologically slipping on my leather pants, feeling a sense of my own power, and getting ready to strut right into the conference room. Try what works for you but do what it takes to pump yourself into a sexy place before you step onto your Muse Stage.

By the way, the antique advice to nervous public speakers that they should imagine their audience naked is the opposite of an inspiring approach. The idea, of course, is that an audience seems less threating if they seem naked. Make them seem silly in your mind, the logic goes. It de-charges the relationship between a speaker and her audience—which is the very last thing a Muse wants to do.

No, don't imagine your audience being naked and ridiculous; imagine them as beautiful and powerful, perhaps wearing armor, weapons polished, ready to take a hill.

The air, remember, must be filled with feeling, not fear. You are not a nervous oaf who needs to belittle her audience to feel their equal; no, you and they are warriors.

Heroes Need Love

But not all love is leather pants and the scent of sex.

Remember the idea that inspiring, in part, is about making a person into a hero: about seeing what's so special about them and then helping *them* feel that same sense of power in themselves. It's the shift from *extrinsic* motivations (doing things because you have to) to *intrinsic* motivations (doing things because you want to), to making *our* desires *their* desires. And, as psychologists have discovered, this transition is facilitated when "liking, warmth, and interest" are expressed, when a person feels the affection or love of another person or, as the psychologists said, "secured relatedness."[4] This is one reason why students flourish more when their teachers are "warm and caring"—and that's straight out of a very technical science journal!

So loving your audience isn't just about oxytocin-producing seduction; no, it's ultimately about the deep feelings of being supported and nurtured.

You've often heard the phrase, "I wouldn't ask you to do anything I wouldn't do myself." It's often uttered by bosses who are trying to motivate their teams, to demonstrate the reasonable-ness of their request by noting that they did whatever it is they're now asking you to do. It's a statement that's supposed to create empathy while, at the same time, create a sense of reward. The hidden promise of this statement is: if you do what I'm asking, then perhaps, one day, you can become just like me.

I think it's a stupid cliché.

I ask people to do things all the time that I haven't and wouldn't do myself—and I do so for one simple reason: I believe they're better at it than I am. I would ask an assistant manager to handle the budget for a project because I believe he's got a better sense of costs and expenses than I do. I'd ask my team's striker to practice his free kicks all weekend because I believe he's more likely to score goals than I ever was. And I'd ask my kid to clean his room, mow the lawn, and walk the dog because he's my kid, dammit.

The strongest way of showing somebody that we "support" them is to charge them with a task that is difficult.

Chapter 6 established that most inspiring missions are the most challenging, the most delusional. But it's not just because they short-circuit our prefrontal cortexes and arouse our emotions; no, it's because these kinds of audacious missions contain a secret message for an audience: you can.

And the more difficult the mission, the more profound that expression of confidence becomes. George W. Bush talked about the "tyranny of low expectations," but I'd like to introduce the "liberation of delusional ambitions"—the soaring that happens when a person feels the kind of love that stirs their self-conviction.

I hope you're starting to get a sense that the **Six Skills of Inspiration** work together harmoniously: Getting Delusional is a terrifying proposition, but when you identify an Inspir-Action and express your love for your audience, the overwhelming Ambition seems much less so.

So then, how do you do it? How do you express love for an audience—be it your kid who you can read like a book or an audience of complete strangers—in a way that drives them to do the wildest things?

1. **Only You.** We all like to believe that we are singular souls, one-of-a-kind—and I happen to believe that we each actually are. The Muse sees what's unique in an audience—and more importantly, how that uniqueness can achieve the ambition at hand. You see it in many a hero's journey: the peculiarity becomes the power: Hermione's bookishness. Ron's blind bravery. Harry's need for friends. These personality traits become the weapons that save the wizarding world. And so, the Muse has a little connect-the-dots strategizing to do: what is it, specifically, about this team, this person, this audience that makes them so uniquely qualified to crush the Delusional Ambition before them? What will make my son, for example, a great student: his

curiosity? His stamina? His desire to please his teachers? His sheer steely mind? His kindness? If I'm to inspire him, I need to answer that question. And then I need to tell him what it is about *only him* that'll help him soar.

2. *This* **Thing.** My favorite Malcolm Gladwell podcast is one he did comparing country music to rock-and-roll.[5] As no fan of country music myself, I was hoping he'd come down on the side of seeing the raw power in loud guitars. Alas, he didn't. Gladwell makes the case (not just reasonably, but emotionally) that country music is far superior because it more usually exhibits one singular characteristic: specificity. Country music tells stories with real-life details: I drank a bottle of Jack Daniels at the wooden kitchen table when you left me on Tuesday in my own black pick-up truck... Yes, country music trades in the kind of fine-point details that most realistic paintings and photographs employ, whereas rock-and-roll tends to be more impressionistic: I wanna hold your hand, the singer says, but that's about it... Love needs details, and so the Muse needs to be as specific as possible about what it is she loves in her audience.

3. **Yes, You Can.** Alcoholics Anonymous is a hard culture. It demands raw honesty, the kind that makes members feel brutally judged. There's a fatalism to it—you are and always will be an alcoholic; you are one drink away from destroying your life; don't even think about tomorrow. And yet it's been an effective program for millions in recovery. Part of the secret to support groups like AA lies in Skill 2 (Aim for Action) but much of it lies in the faith that a person can be successful. Recovery is, at the very same time, impossible and possible—and the deciding factor is the only the decision of the addict himself. AA "works" because every sober member at every meeting is a refutation of the addict's chant: I am doomed. "No," say the Muses, "you got this." You are loved...It's a simple and critical element of inspiration: tell your audience you believe they can succeed.

Technique: Time Travel

One of my favorite techniques for making people feel loved, feel special, is by placing them in the epic arc of history. Remember the night Bono inspired me? Like many a storyteller, Bono provides a long, long arc to the narrative of his moment. "A long time ago," says the fairytale writer. Bono likewise located this moment—the moment of performing a rock-and-roll song in a sports arena—in a story that stretched to earliest reaches of the civil rights movement: Selma; suffrage; the jailing and liberation of Nelson Mandela; heck, he might as well have thrown in Pharaoh's enslavement of the Israelites as he unfurled every flag of every African nation. For Bono—and then for all of us—his steps are lockstep with the march of human history itself. He pulled the same trick on his tour for the band's William Blake-tinged album *Songs of Innocence* when he drew a decided link from "The Troubles" of the 1930s to the ISIS attacks of 2016 across Europe's cities. For Bono, now is a pivotal point between what was and what could be.

This epic sweep, of course, is one of the many aspects of his art that feels religious. World religions cherish their traditions, the prayers, and the customs that connect them to the ancients and point the way to the eternal afterlife. Each Sunday, the minister puts the moment of that service in the grandest context possible: the deity's primordial design of a universe that might offer each of us the promise of forever. The moment is quick, but the stakes are eternal.

Great inspirers couch their inspiration in grand historical context. They're not exploring space but fulfilling our human destiny. They're not winning a football game but redeeming the reputation of an entire nation. Their struggle is not a battle in a war; it's a clash to protect civilization itself.

One simple tool for helping The Muse locate his ambition in the grand arc of history is *prologuing*. A prologue, of course, is an explanation of what happened before the current events that helps put those current events in perspective. Like 23andMe and Ancestry.com, the

Muse can help an audience find their ancestors, not their literal blood-line, but the folks who came before them, who laid down their toil and treasure in the cause those in the present are now continuing. This can be very specific, as Lincoln did when he invoked the soldiers who died at Gettysburg, or a CEO does when he tells the story of an august corporation's founder. But prologuing can also be more abstract, placing an audience in the company of a "type" of people who came before. When Willy Wonka reminds Veruca "We are the music-makers and we are the dreamers of dreams," he is placing them—Veruca and himself—in an ancient category of people: dreamers!—the very same tribe Steve Jobs extolled upon his return to Apple. Make people feel part of an eternal cause, an ancient crew, and you'll make them feel like the goal before them is more ambitious and delusional.

Another time-traveling technique is the temporal opposite of prologuing: *future-tensing* creates a vision of what might be that is motivating, either because it's so darn desirable (*Can't wait to get there!*) or terrifying (*Must avoid at all costs!*). Athletes, for example, inspire themselves by "visioning" what is to come. Serena Williams as a little girl imagined herself holding the Wimbledon Cup. And, of course, Jesus, like many a religious leader, painted a vivid picture of the rewards at the end of the rainbow, a picture that so many believers have interpreted as everything wonderful on fluffy white clouds. That works for some of them—and for the other believers, perhaps it's opposite—the flaming sulfurous pits of hell—that kicks them into better behavior. The future could be heaven or it could be hell—but either way, it arouses emotions.

As Patton said before shipping out the troops to storm Normandy, "Twenty years from now when you are sitting by the fireplace with your grandson on your knee and he asks you what you did in the great World War II, you won't have to cough, shift him to the other knee and say, 'Well, your Granddaddy shoveled shit in Louisiana.'"[6]

That was Patton's way of showing some love.

Now it's time to find your own...

LOVE, FOR REAL WORKSHEET

OUR SUPERPOWER _____

_____

WHAT MAKES ME (OR THIS TEAM) DIFFERENT
FROM EVERYBODY ELSE? _____

_____

_____

_____

"ONLY-YOU AWESOMENESS" _____

_____

_____

_____

CHAPTER 11

The Sixth Skill of Inspiration: Be True You

(How Radical Authenticity Makes People Move)

Modern Muse: The World's Most Inspiring Recipe

On March 23, 2017, the *New York Times* published a short, odd recipe:[1]

1 bunch of radishes, washed, but left whole
4 tablespoons of excellent and cool unsalted butter
1 tablespoon of coarse kosher salt

The "preparation" called for the cook to divide those ingredients evenly on small dishes. And then serve them.

Three ingredients. Put on plates. Preposterous.

And inspiring.

You certainly could make this dish at home, and with high-quality ingredients, it's a sophisticated hit for dinner parties. In fact, it's food that follows the Third Skill of Inspiration; it "Shows Up to Stir Up" by subverting our expectations that "special" food must be complex. This food is *exquisitely* understated. It disarms.

For more than eighteen years, Gabrielle Hamilton has been serving these radishes at Prune, her restaurant in Manhattan's East Village. And before you think Prune is some sort of raw-food hippie-hut, know that Gabrielle Hamilton has won four James Beard Awards. Prune is both a perfect neighborhood joint and a restaurant to which foodies flock for Michelin-star-winning cuisine.

So what's with the radishes?

As Hamilton writes in an essay accompanying her recipe, the "dish" delights with some dramatic contrast—fiery pepper and sweet, cool butter; crunch and cream. But I think what Hamilton loves most about this food is its utter nakedness. "With only three ingredients, there's nowhere to hide," she writes.

Nowhere to hide. The radishes must be perfectly radishy. The butter must be perfectly buttery. And the salt must be perfectly salty. Substitutions won't do—and Hamilton has tried many of them but, after each experiment, she comes back to the same place: the essence of this amazing dish is the essence of its three ingredients, being themselves, only being themselves, on a plate.

Nowhere to hide. That kind of authenticity is an inspiring ingredient, in both radishes and people.

Ridiculous Radish Power

Alright, Michael, I've stuck with you this far but now we're getting ridiculous. A plate of radishes? What the heck does this restaurant even charge for such absurdity? Please, take me back to the Spanish place that turns carrots into foam.

Bear with me, patient reader, while I tell you a story starring those near-naked radishes:

For one of my wife's special birthdays, I gathered some friends and booked us a table at Prune. But just hours before the meal, I did something terribly annoying: I called the restaurant and asked if we could "add a few friends." The manager explained it was a small space and a crowded night and, although they had a table for our large group, it was still a few spaces too small for our increased number.

I pleaded, and perhaps against her better judgment, the manager relented with the fair warning that it would be a "tight" fit that night.

When my wife and I arrived, we were led by the hostess through the bustling dining room, past a bar behind which a giant old vintage mirror hung. It was a glimmering scene, summertime New York with an elegant French twist—but it was a scene we exited as we descended a curving stairwell that led us to the basement where we found our friends, tight indeed, sardined into a nook in the corner. Down here, it was a steaming hot summer night, and the portable air conditioner rolled into the space did little to cool us down. Down here, it was entirely too bright, too loud, too hot, too cramped.

And down here, though I could hardly imagine it at that moment, I would have one of the greatest nights of my life.

I had planned a menu with the manager, but nothing about how the meal unfolded felt planned. Drinks arrived—cold martinis, filled too high to not spill on the table. And the food our server brought down the tight, turning staircase was elemental, the kind of food you'd imagine is just laid about in the country kitchen of a French grandmother: plates of those raw radishes with that cool butter; a bowl of sardines and mackerel doused in golden-green olive oil; a platter of swordfish sautéed in butter and dressed with herbs. If I recall correctly—the martinis were coming insistently—dessert was berries, just a bowl of berries.

Over this drink and food, we did the best thing good, grown-up friends do: we connected, as friends who left their kids at home and settled into our most relaxed selves. In that middle-aged moment, we took stock of who we had become and who we could still become. We were feeling dizzy, disarmed, dreamy, and loved. It was perfect.

And I'm sure this magic moment didn't happen in spite of the circumstances at Prune; no, we weren't "making the most" of an imperfect situation; the situation was making the most of us. It was a confounding, topsy-turvy evening: what should have been comfortable was cramped; what should have been cool was hot; what should have been hot was just room temperature; what should have been fine, fancy food was completely simple; what should have been an elegant night out amongst the big city's glittering great was a night shared with sweaty friends in a basement by a bathroom.

In all that shifting of expectations, the fancy versions of us, the versions who had put on their hippest clothes for a swanky night on the town, disappeared. Left in their places were friends as real and unadorned as the radishes on those plates.

Now, about those radishes? Did those radishes *really* inspire this moment? Weren't we just a group good, old friends connecting over booze and a meal in a restaurant's basement?

Well, imagine if, down those stairs, the servers brought a different kind of meal, the fancy kind, perhaps a dish composed with such architectural delicacy that the slightest wobble would've spilled the tower of food the chef had so perfectly-built on the plate. *That* food at *that* moment would've sucked all the good vibes from our evening. It would've mismatched the moment. It wouldn't have *fit* and, even worse, the difference between the fancy aspirations of that food and the unfancy reality of our situation would've been frustrating. We'd have been grumpy.

But those radishes—and the fish and the berries—met the moment. They were a symbol telling us, "Hey, relax, chill out, be you." Was it conscious? Probably not. Was it palpable? Definitely.

The authenticity of the place, the people, and the food—the disarming realness of it all—opened us up, wider than the space we often occupied while working so hard to dress ourselves up for our clients, colleagues, and even occasionally, our kids. This was a permission slip to be looser and bigger and better.

Fireworks are amazing, but they're at their most beautiful as they fall toward the ground. It's both the heavens and the earth that move us.

Here's what really blows my mind: I don't believe any bit of that experience at Prune was accidental. In fact, in many ways, it was exactly what Gabrielle Hamilton had intended.

Almost two decades earlier, Gabrielle Hamilton toured this very space in a beaten-up neighborhood of New York City. As she describes it in *Blood, Bones & Butter*, her beautiful, page-turning memoir, it was a decrepit room, with faulty electric wires and dangerous neighbors. It was certainly not a place primed for restaurant success. Nonetheless, Hamilton shook hands with the realtor, promised to consider it, and then went home. The next moment is worth quoting at length. It's worth memorizing:

> *But once back in my apartment, I felt very nearly combustible with something I could not tap down with any blanket of reason or logic I threw in front of it.... I opened the windows to the new spring weather and cranked the stereo with songs I fantasized would bust out of the speakers at my new restaurant. To try and disrupt this electric hum of "rightness" that was taking hold in my gut and now spreading through my being, I recited, at length, my lack of restaurant experience. I punctuated every thought*

with that famous statistic that 80 percent of new businesses go under in the first year.... In spite of my efforts to be rational, the birds and sunshine were in concert outside, as if egging me on, and while I told myself that I couldn't possibly open a restaurant in New York City, the most critical and sophisticated place on earth where I would be eaten alive by some restaurant reviewer... I nonetheless merrily pulled out my salad bowls and wooden cutting boards and wondered if it would be a health code violation to use them in my restaurant.... As I reminded myself of my total lack of credentials, not to mention my total lack of one thin dime...I simultaneously fantasized.... I sprawled on the couch in my bare feet, staring into the middle distance, and wondered how I might serve walnuts from the Perigord and a small perfect tangerine so that the restaurant patrons could also sit at their table after the meal and squeeze the citrus peel into the candle flame to make fragrant blue and yellow sparks as I had done on my mother's lap as a child.[2]

"Something I could not tap down with any blanket of reason or logic.... In spite of my efforts to be rational." Music cranking. Pulling out cutting boards. Imagining the ideal scene. As Hamilton told me, she felt an actual "physical tremble." She knew opening this restaurant was "absolutely the right thing to do."

As you know by now, reader, this is the fierce working of the Muse, smashing the machine of your reason, seducing you into forgetting the laws of blinkered reality, and then shoving you on a course to live your dream.

Of course Gabrielle Hamilton signed the lease.

But then what? Now she had to design, plan, build, staff, and open a restaurant. As she explained it to me, she was "negatively inspired." She knew what she didn't want to do, which was to open some ridiculous, pretentious Manhattan restaurant.

She remembered Margarita.

Years earlier, Gabrielle Hamilton was a wreck. In the mid-1990s, she was poor, lost, professionally drifting, and purposeless. As she admits, she was contemplating "the long permanent sleep" of death. Instead, she escaped to Europe, arriving in Amsterdam as a nineteen-year-old with only $1200 to her name for "the coldest winter Europe had seen in fifty years." Eventually, she made her way to Greece, where she was literally starving. "I'd eaten nothing but a raw onion, a sack of salted pumpkin seeds, and a glass of warm dry vermouth in the previous five days" she remembers.[3] A raw onion and pumpkin seeds. For five days!

She was in Greece, lost like Hesiod was lost and, like him, about to meet a Muse. This one ran a restaurant "far beyond the stretch of tourist traps" along the beach.

There was an old wooden gate and a few old tables in the garden of a farmhouse. The cooking was done on an old four-burner stove. There weren't any choices. There wasn't even a menu. Just a yia yia, Margarita, who served a platter of grilled fish and fresh tomatoes, seasoned with nothing but the freshest olive oil and some salt from the nearby Mediterranean Sea. This food was arrestingly, beautifully simple.

Like those radishes would be.

Years later, when Hamilton leapt into launching her own restaurant, she was inspired by her memory of Margarita's anti-fancy authenticity. At Prune, "There would be no foam and no 'conceptual' or 'intellectual' food; just the salty, sweet, starchy, brothy, crispy things that one craves when one is actually hungry."[4]

As a marketing strategist, I believe this is a perfect brief. It's "vivid and concrete." It's got a great enemy. And, most importantly, it's dripping with authenticity, the last virtue of a great Muse.

As we'll see in this chapter, after all the ambition-making and action-stoking and atmosphere-crafting—after all the razzle-dazzle—authenticity is the energy that makes a Muse most powerful.

Bono's leather pants *and* Gabrielle Hamilton's radishes. You'll need them both.

The True You Always Wins

Marketers are always trying to measure their marketing. What's working? What's not? How do we know? And beyond the blunt metric of straight-up sales—*Did more people buy our thing after they saw our stuff?*—there's a thicket of contradictory opinions about what really matters.

When I worked at one ad agency, my team wanted to develop a tool to help us understand the alchemy behind great marketing. Of course, we wanted our tool to be a lure for nervous clients, but we genuinely wanted to understand what separated successful brands from the rest. What made a brand like Five Guys, for example, catch fire in a category of competitors that were struggling to stay relevant? What made BMW and Apple so valuable? What were Hyundai and Dell missing?

We worked backwards. We looked at brands that were empirically successful based on sales, stock performance, and market share and then, with some pretty sophisticated data wizardry, we identified the attributes they had in common. It was a list of almost ten characteristics, including "trustworthy," "innovative," and "fits my life."

We realized that these characteristics could be divided into two—just two—themes: one was about energy. A brand that was "energetic," "full of momentum," "making a mark," and "getting attention" was more likely to succeed than one that was sleepy. We called this theme Dynamism.

The other theme was about trust. Brands that "did what they promised," "were used by others," and "stood the test of time" would endure beyond flash-in-the-pan breakout brands. We called this theme Authenticity.

And over more than fifty thousand surveys in dozens of different categories, our math held up. Brands that exhibited both Dynamism and Authenticity dominated their marketplace. The "true you"—with a bit of spunk in your step—always wins. We made a map that proved it:

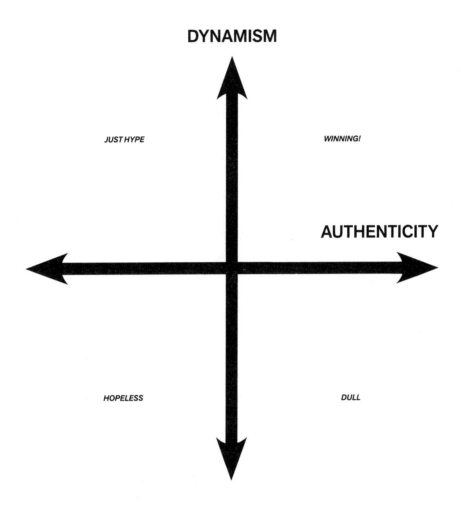

This index became a valuable tool, helping our agency win business but, more importantly, over time, helping us develop marketing that would actually move our clients into that coveted upper-right quadrant. As it turns out, making a brand dynamic is relatively easy. Do marketing—and make it good and attention-getting. Make it funny and emotional. Use celebrities. Be on the Super Bowl. Stoke controversy. Activate mirror neurons! All that, we could do.

Authenticity, however, was a trickier play. We realized that it was almost impossible for marketing to move the perceptions of a brand's Authenticity. Doing that demanded the slow grind of time and evidence, usually the kind of evidence that would be found in products and experiences themselves, not ads and Tweets.

And, of course, this makes perfect, intuitive sense. Quick shifts in authenticity are inherently inauthentic. Authenticity is earned over eons and sacrificed in a blink. It's why we're wary of leaders who seem to "reinvent" themselves. A brand can do it, like Domino's did, but it generally requires a wholesale, concrete change in the actual thing being sold.

People don't have the luxury of quickly reinventing themselves. It's almost sinful.

How to Be Yourself. Quickly.

In her book *Presence*, psychologist (and another TED Superstar) Amy Cuddy says that when you meet a person, especially in a professional context, you instantly size them up with two questions: 1) Are they competent? and 2) Are they trustworthy? Only when you sense that they are both competent and trustworthy do you follow them. But interestingly, according to Professor Cuddy's research, trust is the far more important attribute—and not just generic trust, but the kind of trust that's rooted in real "warmth and likability."[5]

That insight gives us a way of understanding authenticity. It's not just "being yourself" but being yourself in a way that's "warm and likable" that attracts people, that moves them closer to you. That's the difference between a curmudgeon and a crank: the former is charming—the latter is just a jerk.

But the challenge of Professor Cuddy's insight is that our audiences judge our "trustworthiness" instantly and almost unconsciously. This presents a puzzle: authenticity is earned over time, but it needs to be communicated in an instant. How do we show up authentically *in a moment*? How do we *quickly* communicate the kind of authenticity that's usually earned over long stretches of the calendar?

We're told from the time we can hear to "Be yourself!"—presumably, you've got the "yourself" part of the equation handled. You know who you are. You know your values and your perspective and your loves and hates and sense of humor.

It's the "be" part of that simple command that's tricky.

There are two techniques that will help you show up authentically, and both of them require a bit of self-analysis:

1. **Share Your Singularity.** What makes you unique and different?
2. **Share Your Shadow.** What makes you flawed and imperfect?

The first—Share Your Singularity—is the easier one to understand. What makes you so very you? The answer likely lies in your Delusional Ambition, especially if it's been sauced up with your personal passion and expressed with the lyricism and emotion of music. Do you want to cheer the world with cupcakes? Do you want to be the Steve Jobs of healthcare? Do you want to be the slingshot that finds the vulnerability of your company's greatest Goliath? These are expressions of singular souls, and I hope that every exercise throughout this book will help you become one as you become a Muse.

That said, it's useful to articulate, especially to yourself, what makes you unique. It's probably not one attribute, but an idiosyncratic combination of traits and experiences. Are you the funniest scientist you know? Are you a Wall Street tiger with the heart of a puppy? Are you a CEO mom? There's a worksheet at the end of the book to help you experiment with a variety of ways to describe your singularity. Play with it. Find one that feels right—and own it as a badge of your honor.

That's the easy part. Sharing Your Shadow is much harder.

Shadow Power

"Glory be to God for dappled things [...]
All things counter, original, spare, strange;
Whatever is fickle, freckled (who knows how?)
With swift, slow, sweet, sour; adazzle, dim [...]"

—GERARD MANLEY HOPKINS, "Pied Beauty"

We make the mistake of believing that a Muse needs to be "better" than the people she wants to inspire, needs to be an esteemed voice of authority.

But that belief belies so many of the examples throughout this book. These are flawed Muses: grenades of ego, sometimes incapable of kind human relationships and occasionally deeply morally deficient. They have vices. They have tempers. Look at Kennedy or Steve Jobs or Serena Williams. Heck, look at Bono. I fucking hated Bono because he's so genuinely hate-able: moralizing, pretentious, a bit ridiculous.

But, he is *so fucking* Bono.

And that's the point: superiority doesn't inspire. In fact, it often repels. It's our flaws and imperfections that make us "warm and likable." Our ego and temper and worry and shame and ambition and lust—all the aspects of our personality that we try to hide from the public's judgment—are exactly the traits that contribute to our magnetism.

The psychologist Carl Jung calls these broken parts of our personality our "shadows"—and he believed, like Peter Pan did, that without these shadows, we're only half-people. And how inspiring can a half-person be?

I remember once roaming the aisles of Chartres Cathedral on an overcast weekday. It's an old French church that seems to be stretching toward the sky, with columns and buttresses that pull the space upward, thrusting toward the heavens. On this particular day, the sun struggled to find its way through the clouds and through the beautiful stained-glass windows, leaving the sanctuary cloaked in shadows. You couldn't quite see. You couldn't see where a column ended. You couldn't see what statue was tucked in a corner. You couldn't quite see the eyes and the faces of the few worshippers kneeling in the pews.

And this is where I had the most awesome religious experience of my life, a Bono-level episode of inspiration. Growing up Catholic, I was familiar with the term "the mystery of faith," but only here and now in this sacred castle did I feel the mystery of faith. I've never been more convinced that there is a God, a spirit worthy of our adoration and deserving of our obedience. I spent that afternoon and days to follow wondering how I might serve this God, whether I could devote my life to a monastic existence of work and prayer, preferably in the French countryside.

I was inspired. And I really don't believe I would've felt that way if the sun had been shining through the stained-glass windows.

Shadows, Jung schooled, don't erase light, but complement it. Shadows are where light and dark meet, where sacredness lives.

And yet, all around us, people are desperate to put their "best feet forward," to show what makes them good and great and virtuous and strong. The result is a world in which everything feels like fake two dimensions.

Look at politics or, once again, at marketing. It's a world of smiles and perfect families, a *The Truman Show*-like reality in which everything is perfect to the point of being unappealing.

Occasionally, all too rarely, there's a refreshing rip in the pretty picture. Love them or not, Obama and Trump have been expert at sharing their shadows—one too cool when the world wanted heat and one too hot as the world wants cool. Part-robot, part-devil—and in those shadows lies the power to be a Muse. Bill Clinton's approval ratings actually increased after he confessed to his affair with Monica

Lewinsky—not because people approved of his behavior, but because he was "owning" his horndog shadow. And think about some of the heroes from this Golden Age of television: Tony Soprano, Walter White, Don Draper. We're *on the side* of these anti-heroes, in part *because* they're so transparent about their sins.

In fact, it's only when we share our shortcomings and imperfections that people lean in and begin to trust us.

Very few brands have learned this lesson. Dominos, as I mentioned earlier, revived their struggling fortunes only after admitting their pizza was pretty darn terrible and committing to making it better. That admission of inferiority bought them a second look from the marketplace that no "new and improved" slogan alone could have.

Today's consumers don't trust the artificial, two-dimensional images that used to work in ads. Sadly, many brand managers haven't figured this out. They're selling fairy tales in a reality TV world. They haven't learned that imperfections can actually be a source of great appeal. It's not that people are drawn to products' shortcomings; it's that they've grown suspicious of things that seem too pure. To be strong, brands need authenticity, and that can be found in a brand's shadows, or its darker attributes—what market researchers call "negative equity" and brand managers try their hardest to hide.[6]

Years ago, I was lucky to work on Ragú pasta sauce. For years, Ragú was in a pitched battle with Prego over which sauce was thicker. We ended that fight by accepting Ragú's shadow. Our brand wasn't as rich and chunky as Prego, but that could be an advantage. Chunky sauce may be good for grownups, but it's not for the typical ten-year-old. Instead of trying to convince the world that Ragú was hearty, we celebrated what it truly was: a kid's delight. The strategy reversed a decade-long sales decline.

Perhaps my favorite example of "shadow branding" is the London police force's dramatic recruitment campaign from 2000. The effort eschewed the traditional trappings of recruitment advertising. It didn't promise an exciting career, valuable skills, or the respect of schoolchildren. Rather, it showed how difficult the job was. One ad featured Simon

Weston, a badly scarred Falklands veteran whose artillery boat had been bombed. The war hero wept, asking viewers to imagine "going 'round to someone's house to tell a man that his wife and child have been killed in a car crash." Another commercial asked viewers to envision how horrible it would be to have to respond to a call about a baby who had died in his sleep—to collect the child's teddy bear in a plastic evidence bag as the inconsolable mother watched. These ads depicted police work as distressing, and yet they attracted recruits. To gauge the effectiveness of the campaign, the ads directed prospective applicants to a dedicated phone number and website. More than a hundred thousand inquiries flooded the recruitment office, and from that eager pool, the police force selected six thousand new officers—a 50 percent increase over the previous year, according to the British Home Office.

Part of the appeal was that the ads issued one big professional dare: are you brave enough to be a police officer? But something deeper was at work. A survey conducted by TNS Gallup found that people who had seen the ads were twice as likely to "respect the police" as those who hadn't. The difficult part of policing—its dark and scary shadow—made the London police brand more authentic and, thus, more appealing.

The lesson here? Perfect purity is perfectly dull. We're hardly ever attracted to slick virtue; we love people with all their faults and flaws and contradictions. We love them because of all their faults and flaws and contradictions.

And so, find and share your shadow.

Step 1: Finding Your Shadow

You likely already know your flaws and shortcomings. These are things that embarrass you, that gnaw at you, the things that always rear their head and make trouble. You've likely heard them when you argue with your partner or in job performance reviews or in the quiet recesses of your mind when you worry that you're just not "something" enough to succeed.

I'll give it a go:

I've got a raging ego. I feel the need to prove that I'm the smartest person in any room—and if you doubt that, I'll argue and debate you into submission and shame. (I know, I know, it's ridiculously ironic given all I've been writing.) It's a terrible characteristic. It's caused me to lose friends, alienate colleagues, and fall far short of my potential. Heck, what is this book but a display of ego? I can dress it up in the generosity of wanting to "teach" and "help"—and I do, I do—but that's hiding from the truth: I think *I* know something special. Every advice-giving author does.

This ego is also the "shadow" of another trait, one that's more sad than terrible: insecurity. I joke that it's rooted in my being adopted (the step after being unwanted!) but, for whatever reason, I worry that I won't be loved as fully and deeply as I want to be. So I demand attention! I bully my way to respect!

Oh, I'm such a cliché!

And luckily, you are as well.

Oh yes, there are nuances and textures and shades to your shadow but, for the most part, there's a common cast of culprits. What's yours? Are you selfish or greedy? Are you lazy? Are you not as honest as you should be? Do you procrastinate? Do you gossip?

And where was this shadow born? Are you terrified you're not good enough Are you ashamed of something you've done? Have you fallen in love with the wrong person?

Use the worksheet at the end of the book to identify your shadow—and then love it, embrace it. *Which is not to say that you shouldn't work on improving it*—but only that you should recognize that your shadow is an integral part of who you are and, as such, is worthy of your love and respect. You can love the lazy part of you that would always rather curl up on the sofa in sweatpants *and* work hard on shifting yourself into high-gear.

But, once you know your shadow, once you can give it a name and start a relationship with it, you can share it. You can share it in a way that makes you a more powerful Muse.

Step 2: *Sharing Your Shadow*

Here's the good news: hiding your shadow is harder than sharing it. The True You has a way of spilling out in your communications whether you'd like it to happen or not.

I've been struck in researching this book by how many inspiring movies star Robin Williams. *Good Will Hunting, Awakenings, Dead Poet's Society, Hook, Patch Adams, The Fisher King*—these are movies that leave people feeling more alive and ambitious. And it can't be an accident. A friend who's a professional comedian offered a theory: when you look at Robin Williams, the first thing you see is the pain in his eyes. Even when he's shouting and manic and exhorting us to *carpe diem*, there's a pain, a sadness in his eyes, perhaps the sadness that ultimately led him to take his own life. I think it's that sadness that makes Robin Williams a Muse, that separates him from any old huckster trying to bring out the best in us. Whatever he does, you see something true, something authentic.

For Coach Taylor in *Friday Night Lights*, perhaps it's regret, sadness that he couldn't save Jason Street or make it as a college-grade coach. Maybe it's guilt for LeBron James and shame for Barack Obama. Maybe Martin Luther King was angry. And do you think maybe Donald Trump feels so terribly alone?

These aren't just armchair psychoanalyses, but attempts to give a name to the very real characteristics that move these particular people through their world. All of these people can likely articulate their Delusional Ambitions—but we *feel* their secret shadows as they spill out in strange and unconscious ways, in their eyes their tone, their choices. We feel their authenticity—and it moves us.

So you can certainly do what I did earlier: name and share your shadow. Tell your kid who is terrified of failing that you are terrified of failing—and then help him crack a Delusional Ambition and an Inspir-Action. Lower your voice, Talk Like Music, and tell him you love him so much you want to show him the impossible parts of the world before him. But make sure he knows your fear.

Remember that team who has to work yet another weekend on a stupid project for the client that stinks? By all means, reframe the job: it's not about winning this pitch, but helping this narrow-minded client realize their own opportunity to change the world. Make sure your team feels your love as you baby-step them through the plan for the next few days and time-travel them to the moment when they company no longer needs to pitch such stupid clients. But make sure they also feel your shadows. They already know about your ego, so maybe share your fear that, as you get older, you'll become irrelevant in an industry that thrives on the cool of youth.

And yourself? As you commute yet again to the job you hate with dreams of your own business—your cupcake shop or your baseball coaching consultancy—so vivid and real that you hardly need imagination to picture them, what should you do? Yes, stretch your ambition to its most delusional level. Find your Golden Rule. Be the Cher of Cupcakes, for goodness sake—but also tell yourself that it's exactly your persnickety, annoying, uptight, borderline-OCD that will make you a success. Make your shadow your secret weapon.

One last tip that comes from a tennis story, which might be true or not. "Pistol Pete" Sampras is no Roger Federer, but he's one of the greatest players of all time, having won fifteen Grand Slam championships. He was known for his weapon: a serve that was strong and strategic. But apparently, early in his career, it's a serve that would fail him at the end of matches. After crushing an opponent, when closing out the encounter, he'd stumble. His serve would fall apart. He'd double-fault.

I'm told a coach gave him advice: when you toss the ball for those final few serves, release your grasp on your racquet. Hold it lightly, with just your thumb and your forefinger. Loosen up. In fact, change your very successful grip so that it's impossible for you to tighten up and fail. Loosen up.

I'd like to believe that every time Pete Sampras served to win a match at Wimbledon, he did so while holding his racquet as delicately as he would hold a teacup.

When you're not trying—when you're just being—you win.

Loosen your grip. You'll be moving stones in no time.

Modern Muse: Hamilton!

All the Skills

Even if you haven't seen *Hamilton*, the Broadway sensation created by Lin-Manuel Miranda that went on to become the most-awarded (and perhaps most-loved) theatrical performance in American History, you've felt its power. Friends, family, and strangers all over Facebook have been rapturous in their reviews: life-changing, some say. "The best art I have ever seen in my life," Michelle Obama famously anointed it. It would be hard, in fact, to think of a character who has been more of a Muse in our modern history than Miranda's version of this founding father.

So even if you haven't seen the show, don't hesitate to listen to the soundtrack; it's every word that gets sung and spoken on stage. And what surprises me the most about this version of *Hamilton* is how many of those words are insults. He's called a bastard and a Scotsman (which is meant to sting), condemned as impatient and arrogant and untrustworthy, criticized for talking too much and dismissing the perspectives of others, and for being entirely too young, too scrappy, and too hungry for his—and our fledgling country's—own good.

And that's just in the first ten minutes of the show!

The insults continue, mostly lodged by the man the play establishes as his rival, the cautious, plotting, tongue-holding Aaron Burr. It's a classic dramatic showdown: young, impetuous genius versus old, cautious yeoman. Mozart versus Salieri. JFK versus Nixon. The Muse versus The Reasonable.

In fact, I think Hamilton is the embodiment of a Muse. He practices our Six Skills brilliantly—filling the air with feeling while frying the reasonable objections of a dying world order and its sclerotic defenders:

1. Ambition: Get Delusional.

Hamilton has big plans for America—not just creating a new country free from the tyranny of Britain, but birthing the greatest nation the world has ever known. He's playing for delusional stakes: history itself, showing that self-government, the birthright of free people, all people, can actually work.

Hamilton's also, of course, delusional about his own role in that history-making. Or is he? He believes himself to be the engine of the revolution and the architect of the new country's government. He writes at a furious pace because he genuinely believes his words are the words that will make all the difference between failure and success. He is just like his awesome country.

2. Action: Aim For Action.

Hamilton is a man of verbs. Even his words are given an active stance: he's writing, writing, always writing. But he's always very clear on the next step that needs to be taken: declare independence; secure funding; get the French on board; assume the debts of the states; get rid of Jefferson; get rid of Burr. He's a whirlwind of doing who also makes it clear to his audience just what they need to do. It's interesting that he left the "why" to Jefferson in the Declaration of Independence. Hamilton knew the Constitution—the blueprint for how the government would operate—was his own domain.

3. Atmosphere: Show Up To Stir Up.

Every actor who assumes the role does so with their own style but, in the original performance, Lin-Manuel Miranda makes his first appearance on stage as Hamilton in a beguiling, subtle manner. Right after the chorus tells the triumphant story of his escape from a life of squalor, a childhood that was plagued by parental deaths and a cousin's suicide, how his brilliant mind—his tenacity—brought him to the mainland, we in the audience are baited. We are pumped to meet this guy. He's the star, after all. But when Aaron Burr asks for his name, Miranda's Hamilton strikes an almost-quiet tone: He says his name. The music even lulls a little. He says his name again. It's just a flash, only one second until he becomes all brash bravado telling the world that they better wait and see all the awesome things he'll accomplish—but in that one almost-quiet moment is a powerful disorientation. The man we expected to arrive as a star comes as a shimmer.

Oh, and, of course, he's not a white man at all. No, these founding fathers are Latino and black and, in so being, a radical stir-up of the history books.

4. Attitude: Talk Like Music.

Well, this is everything, especially in a musical, isn't it? But take one of the show's most famous lyrics, Hamilton's insistence in song "My Shot" that he won't waste the awesome opportunity history has delivered to him, he won't throw it away...There's nothing particularly odd or lyrical about that simple sentence. It's the kind any of us could write, would say, as an expression of determination. And yet that quotidian line has assumed a supernatural power because of the fierce determination with which it is said. It is the delivery—the affect—that makes all the difference. In those words, through those words, you feel Hamilton's insistence that he will be the hero the moment has demanded.

5. Affection: Love, For Real.

Perhaps this is the skill that Hamilton needs to practice more than the others. He is, after all, aching ego incarnate. Sure, he expresses some genuine love for his wife, her sister, and his young co-revolutionary, John Laurens, with whom some historians detect a sexual relationship. And he has a deep and genuine love for his son, Philip. But, for the most part, Hamilton is an "I" Muse, not a "We" Muse. His inspiration works by example more than exhortation.

That said, there's an awful lot of "love tough" in his demands for his countrymen. He makes it clear that forming this new nation will demand a tax of blood and treasure—and it's a tax they ought to pay, proudly and defiantly. He does love America—and shows that love by burdening the new citizens with the weight of history itself.

6. Authenticity: Be True You

Hamilton "owns" his shadows. Most of the insults recorded above come from Hamilton himself. He's so fully-aware of his own unpolished nature, and how that up-start attitude might be a problem in a delicate world. When Burr tells him again and again to shut his mouth, listen more, show greater caution, we all know it's futile direction. Hamilton is Hamilton—and will be Hamilton. And perhaps it's that uncompromising embrace of his own authenticity—as complex and messy as it is—that makes Hamilton not just a hero for our time, but for any time.

Seriously, go listen to the soundtrack—right after you finish the next few pages.

When all is said and dreamed and done and debated, there are two things that will make you a Muse. Your Delusional Ambition and yourself. Take this worksheet seriously. Think, sleep, walk, exercise, shower, ask people who love you and people who don't—but figure out what makes you undeniably you. Because you will win.

BE TRUE YOU WORKSHEET

MY / OUR SINGULARITY. _____

_____

MY SUPERPOWER. THE THING THAT
MAKES ME TICK AND THRIVE. _____

_____

_____

_____

MY / OUR SHADOW. _____

_____

MY SHORTCOMING, MY SHAME. THE THING I WORRY GETS
IN THE WAY—BUT JUST MIGHT BE MY SECRET SUPERFUEL. _____

_____

_____

_____

30 Days of Muse Snacks

Here's a list of "Muse Snacks" to last you a month—acts of creativity that will help you become fluent in the language of feelings. Some you know, and some you don't, but hopefully, each will short-circuit your prefrontal cortex just enough to help you feel something fresh and powerful. I've restricted the list to works that should be easy to track down. Many will take just a few minutes to experience, though I've included a few longer pieces—like movies and even a couple books—that are worth the extra time if you can find it. And, finally, a confession: while these offerings are culled from a survey I conducted of thousands of people on social media, many are simply personal favorites of mine. It's hard to quantify what's "more" or "less" inspiring—so I've relied on the heart in my own head (which I've realized is a frightening mix of pretentious and adolescent, like a cross between *NPR* and John Hughes). I hope some of these suggestions work for you:

Alexander McQueen's Fashion Runway Shows. Many to choose from by this provocative and skilled designer, including "No. 13" in which a model in a formal white dress is spray-painted by robots. Freaky beautiful.

Grace VanderWaal (and her ukulele) auditioning for "America's Got Talent" on June 7, 2016. Fragile has never sounded so strong.

Maria Mitchell's Journals and Letters. Read the words of this amazing nineteenth century astronomer and advocate for more women in science. My favorite quote: "When we are chafed and fretted by small cares, a look at the stars will show us the littleness of our own interests." Also: Watch *Hidden Figures,* a story of the African-American women scientists working at NASA who put John Glenn into orbit.

Nanette by **Hannah Gadsby.** Starts as stand-up comedy and ends with your mouth wide open and your heart hanging out of your chest.

The White Darkness by **David Grann,** a book (and an article in the *New Yorker*) telling the harrowing tale of an expedition across Antarctica.

Opening Credits, *Orange is the New Black.* Watch the close-up faces of real prison inmates as Regina Spektor sings a song about what "animals" we wrongly think they are. Also, check-out the **opening sequence to** *The Affair* for more haunting TV beauty.

"When I Grow Up," Super Bowl ad from Monster.com in 1999. A twisted way to remind us what matters at work.

Eminem, Saturday Night Live, November 18, 2017. At his best.

Haikus by Matsuo Basho. The (traditional) Japanese master of the art form. Spend time reading and rereading—chanting out loud—his three-line gems.

Brandi Carlile, "The Mother." If you're not a parent, this might make you want to spawn. If you are a parent, this will make you better. Then listen to **"So Big/So Small"** from *Dear Evan Hansen* and prepare to have your gut ripped and your heart expanded by a mother's perfect/ imperfect love.

Batkid, San Francisco. Check out the Make-A-Wish Foundation's chronicle of how a city made a kid's dream come true. Video is on their website.

Mark Rothko. If you can see one of his paintings in person at a local museum, go and stare, just stare, until the layers reveal themselves. I thought he was the worst—until I *felt* it.

Sojourner Truth, "Ain't I A Woman" Speech. I'm embarrassed to admit I wasn't familiar with this one growing up, but it's worth a read. An entrancing cadence to some very big thoughts.

Science Fair, a documentary about the smartest kids from some unlikely places doing extraordinary things.

Project Runway, Season 4. This is reality TV in which the contestants have actual talent—and this season was one of the best. Freak flags flying and draping.

Maya Angelou, "On the Pulse of Morning." She wrote this for Bill Clinton's inauguration—and you should watch her read it. Then watch **Robert Frost read "The Gift Outright"** at JFK's swearing-in. In these moments, politics and poetry make spirit-lifting bedfellows.

Apollos Hester. Find the interview with this high school football player who is one sweaty, awesome Muse. And then see if you can't stop smiling.

Vampire Weekend, *Vampire Weekend.* Pick any song on this debut album. Listen to it and read the lyrics. Hardly ever had nerdiness been so cool.

Dan Barry's Essays. Start with "A Teenage Soldier's Goodbyes on the Road to Over There" then continue with anything this *New York Times* columnist has written. Stories that take you into the deepest parts of the people we pass every day.

"The 20 Photographs of The Week," *The Guardian.* Every week this newspaper collects some of the most dramatic images you can imagine.

Kanye West, "Jesus Walks," the video. He might have gone crazy, but this is a masterpiece.

George Saunders, "Victory Lap," a harrowing short story that helps you see the world—and the choices we might make—from fresh and odd perspectives.

Serena Williams Highlights. Find them on YouTube—and, as Professor Iacoboni recommends—watch them with the sound turned off.

Professor Perlman's Monologue in *Call Me by Your Name.* Watch the clip (or read it in the book by André Aciman in a section called "Ghost Spots"). A father's tender love and wisdom for his son's broken heart. And then listen to **"Still Fighting It" by Ben Folds**, a gut-wrenching moment of a dad telling his son what life really asks of us.

"If You Let Me Play," Nike Commercial. So many are great, but this is my favorite, a mash-up of girls and data that make a wallop of an argument for equal rights. Also check out **"I Feel Pretty,"** with Maria Sharapova for another reminder of what women can do when they are allowed to play.

Kehinde Wiley's Portraits. Famous for his official portrait of Barack Obama, Wiley's paintings show the heroic aspects of his subjects, who are usually African-American, with explosions of vivid color.

Motionpoems. An organization founded by poet Todd Boss that pairs contemporary poets with filmmakers, because apparently, the YouTube generation likes its poetry filmed. Dip into the website and explore.

David Foster Wallace's Commencement Address at Kenyon College. Smart never felt so deep.

U2, "The Miracle (of Joey Ramone)." Perhaps my favorite from the band. A song about the moment an artist became an artist, thanks to an artist.

Romantic Poets on Autumn: John Keats' "To Autumn" and Percy Bysshe Shelley's "Ode to the West Wind." Two old poems extolling the un-spring-like awesomeness of the season.

Mini-Muse

This has been a book of some pretty grand pronouncements: *reason is the sworn enemy of inspiration! Make your ambitions as delusional as you can dream! Twist your language and share your brazen feelings! Find your shame-filled shadows and share them with the world!*

It's exhausting stuff.

And although I'm far from licensed to commit self-help, I do genuinely believe the techniques and tips throughout this book will help you move the world and achieve your dreams. I *know* they'll help you be a more passionate, fascinating, and authentic human being, and that unleashed version of you is only a good thing for you, for us, and for the universe.

But maybe you don't yet buy what I've proposed. Maybe you're not quite enthusiastic about being delusional and stirring up and breaking rules and Talking Like Music. That's okay. That's even understandable. What I'd like to suggest, however, if you're not ready to go full-hog Muse, is to start practicing the **Six Skills of Inspiration** *a little bit*:

1. **Get Delusional.** Ask yourself how your goals can become *a little bit* more grand and ambitious. How can you nudge your dreams *just beyond* your level of comfortable reason? You don't have to commit to saving the galaxy, but maybe you can leave your mark on it.

2. **Aim For Action.** This should be an easy one. You might not yet be ready to craft a Golden Rule, but try to be as specific as possible as to what you want people to do—and in so doing, resist your instinct to explain and argue, live—and let people live—in the thrill of doing not thinking, for *a little bit.*

3. **Show Up To Stir Up.** Figure out how break the rules of your situation *a little bit,* without freaking folks. Maybe you won't drop f-bombs in the board room, but you can use your pauses and your clothes and your body language to signal something fresh and new.

4. **Talk Like Music.** No need to break out the fountain pen and compose verses, but try to consider the words you use to express your goals *a little bit* more than you might ordinarily do. How can your language become more playful and memorable? And while you're at it, dial-up that attitude *a little bit* more. Let the world see and feel your feelings.

5. **Love, For Real.** Gushy-mushy declarations of love aren't necessary, but *a little bit* of affection goes a long way. Figure out what's so darn special about the people you want to move and let them know, with *a little bit* of very sincere eye-to-eye contact.

6. **Be True You.** And while you certainly don't need to rip yourself open and bare your soul to any audience you encounter *a little bit* of vulnerable storytelling will have remarkable effects. Open up, share, and in so doing, you'll create an empathetic bond that quickly becomes a slingshot to accomplishing great things.

My point is simple: the skills we've reviewed in this book can all be practiced, step by step, day in and day out—and as you do so, you'll grow yourself into the Muse you were meant to be. The only requirement is that you commit to express your feelings, to expressing yourself emotionally. *That's* the good, powerful, magic stuff.

Finally: I truly, genuinely believe you can do extraordinary things. I believe this because I think I might know you. You're eye-rolling, perhaps, calling bullshit on this claim. How could I possibly know you? Well, I've spent years writing this book, picturing my readers, imagining you, imagining how each word you read will sound in your mind, what might be interesting or clever or run the risk of being stupid or corny. I've spent years thinking about you, and if you're anything like the thoughtful, ambitious, generous, funny, passionate person I dreamed you would be, the person who has devoted precious time to an odd book like this, I know you can do extraordinary things. They might be quiet and personal. What you do might change only your life. Or maybe your extraordinary things will be grand and public. What you do might kick your own ass or tilt your team or build your company or move the world. But do extraordinary things, I have no doubt you can, because I have no doubt you can take the passion on your insides and get them to your outsides. And make no mistake, all the lessons and tips and tricks and techniques you'll find in this book boil down to that one simple truth: if you can share your feelings, you can inspire. Your passion will be your leather pants.

Endnotes

Introduction: On Hero-Making

1 A few magazine articles tell story of this song:
  Richard Buskin, "Classic Tracks: David Bowie's 'Heroes,'" *Sound On Sound*, October 2004, https://www.soundonsound.com/techniques/classic-tracks-david-bowie-heroes.
  Krishnadev Calamur, "'Heroes' at the Wall," *The Atlantic*, January 11, 2016, https://www.theatlantic.com/notes/2016/01/bowie-berlin-1987/423564/.
  Andy Greene, "Flashback: David Bowie Sings 'Heroes' at the Berlin Wall," *Rolling Stone*, June 9, 2016, https://www.rollingstone.com/music/music-news/flashback-david-bowie-sings-heroes-at-the-berlin-wall-90149/.
  Will Hermes, "David Bowie's 'Heroes:' How Berlin Shaped Eclectic 1977 Masterpiece," *Rolling Stone*, October 14, 2016, https://www.rollingstone.com/music/music-features/david-bowies-heroes-how-berlin-shaped-eclectic-1977-masterpiece-120315/.
2 From an interview with Bill Demain quoted in Calamur, "Heroes."
3 Throughout the book, you'll see I've engaged in linguistic gymnastics to avoid quoting the songs I discuss, since the cost of quoting songs in a book is truly prohibitive. Luckily, lyrics to all of them are just an internet search away.
4 Plato, *The Republic and Other Works*, trans. Benjamin Jowett (Anchor; 1st Anchor Books Edition, 1960) Book IV. Plato's worry about the potential insidious effects of music contradicts a quote that's popularly mis-attributed to him: "Music gives soul to the universe, wings to the mind, flight to the imagination, and charm and gaiety to life and to everything." Plato never wrote such a thing, despite what you'll find on Pinterest.
5 Hermes, "'Heroes': How Berlin Shaped."

Chapter 1: Mysterious Ways

1 David Foster Wallace, "Roger Federer As Religious Experience," *New York Times*, August 20, 2006, https://www.nytimes.com/2006/08/20/sports/playmagazine/20federer.html.
2 This show was a stop on the band's Vertigo Tour. There's plenty of footage online, including versions of this introduction to "Where The Streets Have No

Name," but for the best effect, you should watch the band's concert film, *Vertigo 2005: Live From Chicago* (Island/Interscope, 2005).

3 Bono, interviewed by Joe Coscarelli, "U2, Preaching Defiance, Heads Back To Paris," *New York Times*, December 2, 2015, https://www.nytimes.com/2015/12/06/arts/music/u2-preaching-defiance-heads-back-to-paris.html. This interview was conducted days before U2 would return to Paris for a show they were supposed to perform weeks earlier. The band canceled the original performance which had been scheduled for November 14, 2015, the day after terrorists stormed Paris and killed 130 people. In this interview, Bono calls ISIS a "death cult."

4 For a thorough review of Bono's charitable efforts, see Ellen McGirt, "Bono: I Will Follow," *Fortune*, March 24, 2016, http://fortune.com/bono-u2-one/.

5 That George W. Bush quote is from a documentary that examines U2's contribution to fighting the HIV epidemic in Africa, "VICE Special Report: Countdown To Zero," *VICE*, 2015.

6 From the video, "The Making of 'A Beautiful Day'" (extended version) released on U2.com in 2000.

7 Elizabeth Gilbert, *Big Magic: Creative Living Beyond Fear* (New York: Penguin, 2016), 34.

8 Throughout the book, I'll generally refer to a Muse as a person—a person seeking to inspire oneself or an audience. But all of the skills presented can be applied to any "entity" that needs to communicate, like a brand or a political movement or a team or a performance. Essentially, these skills of inspiration help anybody or anything that seeks to move others.

9 Viktor Shklovsky, "Art As Technique," 1917, https://warwick.ac.uk/fac/arts/english/currentstudents/undergraduate/modules/fulllist/first/en122/lecturelist-2015-16-2/shklovsky.pdf. Shklovsy, a thinker in the Russian Formalist School, wrote extensively about this notion, but the idea that art's power lies in its ability makes the ordinary unfamiliar dates way back. See Samuel Taylor Coleridge writing about William Wordsworth: "To combine the child's sense of wonder and novelty with the appearances which every day for perhaps forty years had rendered familiar...this is the character and privilege of genius." Samuel Taylor Coleridge, *Biographia Literaria* (Penguin, 1817). Page 49.

Chapter 2: There's a Heart in Your Head

1 Both my mother's and father's families immigrated to New York from Calabria, Italy in the early 1900s. My maternal grandfather started a vegetable stand in Greenwich Village, and my two uncles fought in World War II, in the Pacific theatre.

2 Later in life, Sartre clarified what he meant when his character in *No Exit* uttered this line. He was trying to make the subtle point that we judge ourselves through other people's perceptions of ourselves. Nonetheless, the phrase has become a useful shorthand for the universally-accepted idea that other people are often a hassle.

3 Aristotle, *Rhetoric*, trans. Hugh Lawson-Tancred (New York: Penguin, 1992), Book II.
4 The last dozen years have brought so many books that make the case that our brains hardly every reason in a logical way. The ones I've found most valuable (and enjoyable) include:
   Dan Ariely, *Predictably Irrational: The Hidden Forces That Shape Our Decisions* (New York: Harper Collins, 2009).
   Jonah Berger, *Invisible Influence: The Hidden Forces That Shape Behavior* (New York: Simon & Schuster, 2016).
   Robert Cialdini, *Pre-suasion: A Revolutionary Way to Influence & Persuade* (New York: Simon & Schuster, 2016).
   Antonio Damasio, *Descartes' Error: Emotion, Reason, and The Human Brain* (New York: Penguin, 2005).
   Malcolm Gladwell, *Blink: The Power of Thinking Without Thinking* (New York: Hachette, 2007).
   Chip Heath and Dan Heath, *Switch: How To Change Things When Change Is Hard* (New York: Crown, 2010).
   Jonah Lehrer, *Imagine: How Creativity Works* (New York: Houghton Mifflin, 2012.
   Daniel Pink, *Drive: The Surprising Truth About What Motivates Us* (New York: Riverhead, 2009).
   Cass Sunstein and Richard Thaler, *Nudge: Improving Decisions About Health, Wealth, and Happiness* (New York: Penguin, 2009).
   And the big kahuna of them all: Daniel Kahneman, *Thinking, Fast and Slow* (New York: Farrar, Strauss, and Giroux, 2013).
5 From a talk at Harvard Business School as quoted in Colleen Walsh, "Layers of Choice," *Harvard Gazette*, February 5, 2014, https://news.harvard.edu/gazette/story/2014/02/layers-of-choice/
6 Heath and Heath, *Switch*.
7 In *Descartes' Error*, Damasio takes the rationalist critique of emotions head-on and makes the point that *too little* emotion leads to bad decisions, "Keep a cool head, hold emotions at bay! Do not let your passions interfere with your judgment…. The sage will advise us, we should experience emotion and feeling in only judicious amounts. We should be reasonable…. I will not denty that uncontrolled or misdirected emotion can be a major source of irrational behavior…. Nonetheless, what the traditional account leaves out is [this]… Reduction in emotion may constitute an equally important source of irrational behavior," 52–53.
8 Yes, I know Hillary Clinton did arouse great enthusiasm amongst a sizable population excited by her and the prospect of the first female president, but Donald Trump was the more powerful agitating force throughout the campaign.
9 Dan Balz, "The Midterm Elections Shape Up as a Battle over Intensity. Are Democrats Ready?" *The Washington Post*, June 30, 2018, https://www.washingtonpost.com/politics/the-midterm-elections-shape-up-as-a-battle-over-intensity-are-democrats-ready/2018/06/30/701da98c-7bd1-11e8-aeee-4d04c8ac6158_story.html?utm_term=.1cb1848c6011.

10 Vance Packard, *The Hidden Persuaders* (New York: Ig Publishing, 2007).

11 Robert Heath, "The Low-Involvement Processing Theory," *ADMAP Magazine*, March 1999, https://www.warc.com/content/article/ The_lowinvolvement_processing_theory/9095.

12 Les Binet and Peter Field, *Marketing in The Era of Accountability* (London: World Advertising Research Center, 2007). Binet and Field updated their findings in a 2013 report, "The Long and Short of It: Balancing Short and Long-Term Marketing Strategies," *IPA*, 2013. While their work demonstrates that "rational" communications can make a mark on some short-term metrics, they conclude that real, enduring value is built emotionally over time.

13 Les Binet quoted by Emma Hall , "IPA: Effective Ads Work On The Heart, Not The Head," *AdAge,* July 16, 2007, https://adage.com/article/print-edition/ ipa-effective-ads-work-heart-head/119202/.

14 Binet and Field, *Accountability.*

Chapter 3: The Inspiration Advantage

1 *King James Bible*, Genesis 2:7, emphasis added.

2 Eric Garton and Michael Mankins, "Engaging Your Employees Is Good, but Don't Stop There," *Harvard Business Review*, December 9, 2015, https://hbr. org/2015/12/engaging-your-employees-is-good-but-dont-stop-there. For the survey, Bain & Company partnered with the Economist Intelligence Group.

3 Teresa Lesiuk, "The Effect of Music Listening on Work Performance," *Psychology of Music* 33, no. 2 (April 2005), and for an overview of other research: Jonathan Fader, "How Music Can Help You Get Ahead, the Right Way," *Psychology Today*, March 13, 2015, https://www.psychologytoday.com/us/blog/ the-new-you/201503/how-music-can-help-you-get-ahead-the-right-way.

4 Dr. Costas Karageorghis, quoted in Fader, "How Music."

5 Justine Musk, "I Was A Starter Wife: Inside America's Messiest Divorce," *Marie Claire*, September, 2010, https://www.marieclaire.com/sex-love/a5380/ millionaire-starter-wife/.

6 Quoted in Richard Feloni, "Former SpaceX Employee Explains What It's Like to Work for Elon Musk," *Business Insider*, June 24, 2014, https://www.businessinsider.com/what-its-like-to-work-for-elon-musk-2014-6.

7 Federer as quoted by David Foster Wallace, "Roger Federer As Religious Experience," *New York Times*, August 20, 2006, https://www.nytimes. com/2006/08/20/sports/playmagazine/20federer.html and Annie Dillard from a brilliant essay she wrote, "Write Till You Drop," *New York Times*, May 28, 1989, https://archive.nytimes.com/www.nytimes.com/books/99/03/28/specials/dillard-drop.html?oref=login.

8 The story is told by Ed Caesar, *Two Hours: The Quest To Run The Impossible Marathon* (New York: Simon & Schuster, 2016), and abridged by him in "The Epic Untold Story of Nike's (Almost) Perfect Marathon," *Wired*, June 29, 2017, https://www.wired.com/story/nike-breaking2-marathon-eliud-kipchoge/. This specific quote comes in an article from the doctor himself: Michael J. Joyner, "What It Will Take To Run A Sub-Two-Hour Marathon,"

Sports Illustrated, May 26, 2016, https://www.si.com/edge/2016/05/26/
michael-joyner-prediction-science-reality-running-sub-two-hour-marathon.
9 Caesar, "Epic Untold."
10 Joseph Campbell with Bill Moyers, *The Power of Myth* (New York: Anchor, 1991),
123.
11 Campbell, *The Hero With a Thousand Faces* (San Francisco: New World Library,
2008).
12 Dave Paulson, "Story Behind the Song: 'Eye of the Tiger,'" *Tennessean*, February
14, 2015, https://www.tennessean.com/story/entertainment/music/story-behind
-the-song/2015/02/14/eye-toger-jim-peterik-rocky-sylvester-stallone/23316471/.

Chapter 4: Beware the Muses

1 David Mitchell, "Kate Bush and Me: David Mitchell on Being a Lifelong Fan of
the Pop Poet," *The Guardian*, December 7, 2018, https://www.theguardian.com/
books/2018/dec/07/david-mitchell-kate-bush-lyric-poetry.
2 Author's interview with Mark Fitzloff, November 2018, Minneapolis and
Portland.
3 Hesiod, *Theogony and Works and Days*, trans. M. L. West (Oxford: Oxford University Press, 2009).
4 Hesiod, *Theogony*, 3.
5 Federer as quoted by David Foster Wallace, "Roger Federer As Religious
Experience," *New York Times*, August 20, 2006, https://www.nytimes.com
/2006/08/20/sports/playmagazine/20federer.html.
6 Wallace, "Roger Federer."
7 Jim Stengel, *Grow: How Ideals Power Growth and Profit at The World's Greatest
Companies* (New York: Crown Business, 2011).

Chapter 5: Science!

1 There's a series of videos online from GoCognitive of Dr. Rizzolatti discussing
his discovery and a great overview of it and its implications from Lea Winerman,
"The Mind's Mirror," *Monitor on Psychology* 23, no. 9 (October 2005), https://
www.apa.org/monitor/oct05/mirror.aspx. To access the videos referenced, please
visit: https://www.youtube.com/watch?v=yKPTuCoop8c. If you'd like to read the
original scientific study, however, Dr. Rizzolatti and his colleagues published
their first paper of findings in 1992: G. di Pellegrino et al., "Understanding Motor
Events: A Neuropsychological Study," *Experimental Brain Research* 91, no. 1
(October 1992): 176-80.
2 Video from GoCognitive, 2011 and 2012.
3 Video from GoCognitive, 2011 and 2012.
4 Vilayanur Ramachandran, "The Neurons That Shaped Civilization." Filmed
November 2009 in India, TEDIndia video, 7:37, https://www.ted.com/talks/
vs_ramachandran_the_neurons_that_shaped_civilization?language=en.
5 Dr. Marco Iacoboni has published extensively on mirror neurons and their
function in human beings. His book is a bible on the subject: Marco Iacoboni,
Mirroring People: The New Science of How We Connect With Others (New York:
Picador, 2008).

6 Author's interview with Iacoboni, October 2018, Minneapolis and Los Angeles. And for a great explanation of mirror neurons and sports, check out Le Anne Schreiber, "This Is Your Brain on Sports," *Grantland*, November 4, 2011, http://grantland.com/features/this-your-brain-sports/.

7 Iacoboni et al., "Grasping the Intentions of Others with One's Own Mirror Neuron System," *PLOS*, February 22, 2005, https://journals.plos.org/plosbiology/article?id=10.1371/journal.pbio.0030079.

8 Interview with Iacoboni.

Chapter 6: First Skill: Get Delusional

1 Chloe Schildhause, "An Oral History on the Evolution of the Upright Citizens Brigade and It's Influence on Improv," *Uproxx*, February 2015, https://uproxx.com/movies/ucb-oral-history/.

2 *Oxford Living Dictionary*, s.v. "delusion (*n*.)," accessed February 21, 2019, https://en.oxforddictionaries.com/definition/delusion.

3 Edmund Burke, *A Philosophical Enquiry into the Sublime and Beautiful* (New York: Penguin, 1998), Part II, Book II.

4 Burke, *Philosophical Enquiry*.

5 "Steve Jobs Introduces 'Think Different.'" Filmed September 1997, posted November 28, 2016, Youtube video, 15:52, https://www.youtube.com/watch?v=FDD5G2_6hdA.

6 Jim Stengel, *Grow: How Ideals Power Growth and Profit at The World's Greatest Companies* (New York: Crown Business, 2011).

7 David Weinberger, "The Folly of Accountabalism," *Harvard Business Review*, February 2007. https://hbr.org/2007/02/the-hbr-list-breakthrough-ideas-for-2007.

8 K. Mulvihill et al., "Athletes' Self-Regulatory Responses to Unattainable Athletic Goals: Effects of Need-Supportive vs. Need-Thwarting Coaching and Athletes' Motivation," *International Journal of Sports Psychology* 49, no. 3 (2018): https://www.cabdirect.org/cabdirect/abstract/20183243361.

9 Mulvihill et al, "Athletes'."

10 Mulvihill et al, "Athletes'."

11 Mulvihill et al, "Athletes'."

12 John F. Kennedy, "We Choose To Go To The Moon." Filmed September 12, 1962, posted August 27, 2008, Youtube video, 17:48, https://www.youtube.com/watch?v=ouRbkBAOGEw.

13 Nancy Koehn, *Forged in Crisis: The Making of Five Courageous Leaders* (New York: Scribner, 2018), 157–67.

14 Koehn, *Forged*, 167.

15 William Shakespeare, *Henry V* (New York: Signet, 1998) act IV, scene iii.

Chapter 7: Aim For Action

1 You can find the facts of this story here, including a link to Jim Carrey recounting the tale to Oprah: Alex Santoso, "Jim Carrey Once Wrote Himself a $10

Million Check," *Neatorama*, October 7, 2012, https://www.neatorama.com/origin/2012/10/07/Jim-Carrey-Once-Wrote-Himself-a-10-Million-Check/.

2 Jacqueline Mayfield and Milton Mayfield, *Motivating Language Theory: Effective Leader Talk in the Workplace* (New York: Palgrave Macmillan, 2018), 15.

3 Daniel McGinn, *Psyched Up: How the Science of Mental Preparation Can Help You Succeed* (New York: Penguin, 2017), 91.

4 James Surowiecki, "What Happened to the Ice Bucket Challenge," *New Yorker*, July 25, 2016, https://www.newyorker.com/magazine/2016/07/25/als-and-the-ice-bucket-challenge, and Katie Rogers, "The Ice Bucket Challenge Helped Scientists Discover a New Gene Tied to A.L.S.," *New York Times*, July 27, 2016, https://www.nytimes.com/2016/07/28/health/the-ice-bucket-challenge-helped-scientists-discover-a-new-gene-tied-to-als.html.

5 George Weiner, "ALS Strikes Out Justin Bieber (in Search Volume): Measuring #IceBucketChallengeAwareness, *HuffPost*, August 28, 2014, https://www.huffingtonpost.com/george-weiner/measuring-icebucketchallenge-awareness_b_5723642.html.

6 Gretel C. Kovach, "Pastor's Advice for Better Marriage: More Sex," *New York Times*, November 23, 2008, https://www.nytimes.com/2008/11/24/us/24sex.html, and Ed Young, *Sexperiment: 7 Days To Lasting Intimacy With Your Spouse* (New York: Faithwords, 2017).

7 For a comprehensive overview of behavioral psychology in the 2008 campaign, see: Sasha Issenberg, *The Victory Lab: The Secret Science of Winning Campaigns* (New York: Crown, 2012); and this article has a good description of the techniques Obama's campaign employed in 2012: Benedict Carey, "Academic 'Dream Team' Helped Obama's Effort," *New York Times*, November 13, 2012, https://www.nytimes.com/2012/11/13/health/dream-team-of-behavioral-scientists-advised-obama-campaign.html.

8 The academic study: David W. Nickerson and Todd Rogers, "Do You Have a Voting Plan?: Implementation Intentions, Voter Turnout, and Organic Plan Making," *Psychological Science* 21, no. 194 (January 8, 2010). And a great summary: Dan Ariely and Supira Syal, "How Science Can help Get Out the Vote," *Scientific American*, September 1, 2016, https://www.scientificamerican.com/article/how-science-can-help-get-out-the-vote/.

Chapter 8: Show Up To Stir Up

1 Julia Brucculieri, "Gene Wilder Agreed To Play Willy Wonka Under This One Condition," *Huffington Post*, August 29, 2016, https://www.huffingtonpost.com/entry/gene-wilder-agreed-to-play-willy-wonka-under-this-one-condition_us_57c-498d0e4b09cd22d920723.

2 Brucculieri, "Gene Wilder."

3 Nancy Koehn, *Forged in Crisis: The Making of Five Courageous Leaders* (New York: Scribner, 2018).

4 Ron Roberts. "Dropping Bombs: On Patton, Profanity, and Character," *Modern War Institute*, February 9, 2018, https://mwi.usma.edu/dropping-bombs-patton-profanity-character/.

5 The George C. Scott rendition of this speech from *Patton* (1970) earned him an Oscar for best actor, but it's totally sanitized. Read the original: George Patton, "Speech to the Third Army," June 5, 1944, http://www.pattonhq.com/speech.html.

6 Takeshi Okada and Kentaro Ishibashi, "Imitation, Inspiration, and Creation: Cognitive Process of Creative Drawing by Copying Others' Artworks," *Cognitive Science* 41, no. 7 (November 7, 2016), https://onlinelibrary.wiley.com/doi/full/10.1111/cogs.12442. And summarized: Thomas Ward, "Can Conformity Be Creative?" *Psychology Today*, March 22, 2017, https://www.psychologytoday.com/us/blog/creativity-you/201703/can-conformity-be-creative.

7 Okada and Ishibashi, "Imitation."

8 Okada and Ishibashi, "Imitation."

9 Author's interview with Cindy Gallop, December 2018, Minneapolis and New York.

10 Author's interview with Gallop.

Chapter 9: Fourth Skill: Talk Like Music

1 Wesley Morris, "Aretha Franklin Had Power. Did We Truly Respect It?" *New York Times*, August 16, 2018, https://www.nytimes.com/2018/08/16/arts/music/respect-aretha-franklin-death.html.

2 Author's interview with Professor Zach Wallmark, November 2018, Minneapolis and Dallas.

3 Author's interview with Wallmark.

4 Watch it: "Barack Obama's Presidential Announcement." Filmed February 10, 2007, in Springfield, IL, posted December 10, 2007, Youtube video, 22:03, https://www.youtube.com/watch?v=gdJ7Ad15WCA, or read the transcript: http://www.washingtonpost.com/wp-dyn/content/article/2007/02/10/AR2007021000879.html.

Chapter 10: Love, For Real

1 James Joyce, *A Portrait of The Artist as a Young Man* (New York: Penguin, 2003).

2 Joyce, *Portrait.*

3 Joyce, *Portrait.*

4 K. Mulvihill et al., "Athletes' Self-Regulatory Responses to Unattainable Athletic Goals: Effects of Need-Supportive vs. Need-Thwarting Coaching and Athletes' Motivation," *International Journal of Sports Psychology* 49, no. 3 (2018): https://www.cabdirect.org/cabdirect/abstract/20183243361.

5 Malcolm Gladwell, "The King of Tears," July 2017, in *Revisionist History*, podcast audio, 42:00, http://revisionisthistory.com/episodes/16-the-king-of-tears.

6 George Patton, "Speech to the Third Army," June 5, 1944, http://www.pattonhq.com/speech.html.

Chapter 11: Be True You

1 Gabrielle Hamilton, "The Wonder of Three Ingredients," *New York Times Magazine*, March 23, 2017, https://www.nytimes.com/2017/03/23/magazine/the-wonder-of-three-ingredients.html.

2 Hamilton, *Blood, Bones, and Butter: The Inadvertent Education of a Reluctant Chef* (New York: Random House, 2012).

3 Hamilton, *Blood.*

4 Hamilton, *Blood.*

5 Amy Cuddy, *Presence: Bringing Your Boldest Self To Your Biggest Challenges* (New York: Little, Brown, 2015).

6 Parts of this and the next few paragraphs originally appeared in *Harvard Business Review* as Michael J. Fanuele, "Embrace the Dark Side," October 2006.

Acknowledgments

I always love reading this section in other books. It's a look into the real life of an author. Who matters? Who made the difference? And yet, now faced with writing my own notes of gratitude, I'm flummoxed as to how anybody else does it. So many people have contributed to my writing this book. I've been blessed with friends, teachers, colleagues, bosses, and clients who have made my thinking sharper and my perspective wider. I'd like to especially thank those who have reminded me, as my mom used to say, that "Life isn't a debate!" They are the folks who have tended to my feelings and, by their example, reminded me to tend to those of others. I will hunt you down and hug you all.

I've had the greatest teachers. Burt Koza, who taught me American History in junior high school, passed away this year. He was my O.G. Muse, the man who kindled my passion for big, fat, uncynical world-shaking ideas. In high school, Brothers Stephen Balletta and George Zehnle helped me see that ideas are only as good as the words that carry them into the world, words that must be clear and could be beautiful. Even better, they showed me I might have some words like that. And at Vassar College, Susan Brisman, Brian Lukacher, Tony Wohl, and Susan Zlotnick were professor-wizards who helped me find some important pieces of myself that I had misplaced in Victorian Britain. Beth Darlington, on a magic carpet with a holy grail and a spirit that stretches as far as you can feel, taught me to love the heart in my head.

I'm also so grateful for Joe Veltre, agent extraordinaire, who took me through the maze of this process with wisdom and class. Joe's belief made this book real, and his counsel made it better. I'm indebted to him, Tori Eskue, and the whole crew at the Gersh Agency.

And massive thanks to Debra Englander, my editor, whose admonition to "Be useful!" is the best brief I could've had. At daunting moments, Debra, you've been both encouraging and practical—true muse virtues.

The team at Post Hill Press, including Heather King, Seane Thomas, John Bogdal, and Holly Pisarchuk has been this first-time writer's dream! Thank you so much for taking a chance on me, but never once making it feel that way.

Jaime Robinson, Lisa Clunie, and the brilliant team at Joan Creative, especially Katie Persichilli, Scott Sanders, and Gonzalo Hergueta, who have made this book look better than I could've dreamed it. Their kindness, insight, talent, and friendship have been inspiring.

A very special thanks to Dr. Marco Iacoboni, Professor Zach Wallmark, Gabrielle Hamilton, Cindy Gallop, and Mark Fitzloff for taking the time to explain complex and magical things to me with kindness and insight.

Cylin Busby Ross, Damon Ross, Katrina Knudson, and Eddie Gamarra aren't just the most amazing friends, but lucky for me, top-notch pros in matters of words, books, and stories. Your reading, guidance, wisdom, and encouragement through every stage of this process has meant the world. Damon and Eddie, brothers, if this book is part me, the good parts are certainly part you.

And Joanna McHugh Fanuele, this book wouldn't exist without your belief in me. You've got a supernatural ability to work, juggle, and time-travel, and to do it all with grace and strength. Without your love, I'd be lost and lesser. With you, I'm me. Thank you for being my ground and my sky.

Boys—Ollie, Leo, and Charlie—you'll read this someday and realize how foul-mouthed your father could occasionally be. I hope you'll also realize that you are Muses, beautiful creatures who possess all the power you need to accomplish whatever you dream. You are empathetic, resilient, and hysterical. You are heroes, already, so watch out, world...

Finally, thank you, lovely libraries, for harboring me while I wrote. The libraries at the University of Minnesota, St. Thomas University, and the Hennepin County public libraries in Linden Hills and Wayzata were my studios, gyms, barracks, cafes, chapels, and mostly quiet spaces. The folks who work at those libraries were my unwitting pit crews. Thank you.

About the Author

Michael Fanuele is one of the world's leading marketing strategists, having helped brands around the world succeed with fresh and surprising insight. He has, in fact, sold tea in China.

Michael has also done politics, stand-up comedy, and written for the *Harvard Business Review*. He is currently the Founder/CEO of Talk Like Music, a consultancy that helps people, places, and brands become more inspiring. Although he has a native New York spirit, Michael's loved a life that has taken him around the world with his wife and three totally awesome young sons. He watches a lot of youth soccer, plays far too little tennis, and loves whiling away a weekend with good friends and daunting recipes.